The Ego Unravelled

How to Live a Positively Joyous Life

Theresa Borg BA (Hons) DHP DCH GQHP

Copyright © 2018 Theresa Borg

All rights reserved.

ISBN: 10 1986845265
ISBN-13: 9781986845267

All rights reserved. No part of this book may be used or reproduced in any manner whatsoever without written permission of the author except for the 'fair use' of brief quotations embodied in critical articles or reviews. For further information contact the author at:

HTTP://WWW.POSITIVELYJOYOUS.COM

The information presented in this book should not be considered or treated as a substitute for professional medical or mental health advice: always consult a medical practitioner. Any use of the strategies and information in this book is at the reader's discretion and risk. The author cannot be held responsible for any loss, claim or damage arising from the use, misuse or suggestions made.
The moral rights of the author have been asserted.

Other books available:
Tour the Core-The Pathway to a Positively Joyous Life 2014
ISBN: 9781517480134

DEDICATION

This book is dedicated to my wonderful son Steven. Thank you so much for your patience and much needed technical help and support, in getting yet another project off the ground.

CONTENTS

	Introduction	Pg 1
	Plato's Cave	Pg 5
1	The Brain is a Computer	Pg 7
	The Band Exercise	Pg 23
2	What is the Ego?	Pg 25
	The Eyes Have It	Pg 37
3	Perception, Projection and the Confusion of Cause and Effect.	Pg 38
	Owning Your Projection	Pg 52
4	The Ego and its Temple	Pg 53
	Mind and Body Effect Exercise	Pg 70
	Physical Discovery Exercise	Pg 71
5	Case Study	Pg 73
6	The Unchangeable Belief	Pg 78
	RISPARRS Exercise	Pg 97
7	Fear as Control	Pg 99
	Good Boy/Girl in Jail Exercise	Pg 117
8	Attack Spirals	Pg 118
	Spot the Attack Exercise	Pg 131
9	Significant Relationships	Pg 132
	Updating the Files Exercise	Pg 150
10	The Gift of Giving	Pg 151
	Seeing the Mechanism in Action Exercise	Pg 166

11	The Ego Loves Sin	Pg 167
	Reclassifying Sin Exercise	Pg 182
12	Forgiveness	Pg 184
	Forgiveness Exercise	Pg 194
13	The Illusion of Time	Pg 195
14	Case Study Revisited	Pg 204
15	Father and Son	Pg 211
16	Whole life living- The Integration of the Ego	Pg 226
17	Unravelling the Dream	Pg 238
	Bibliography	Pg 244
	About the Author	Pg 246

ACKNOWLEDGMENTS

My heartfelt thanks also, to all of the many teachers that have changed my life through so generously sharing their knowledge and life experiences, so that I too may change the lives of others.

Introduction

I think that life is like a game of Monopoly. You can play the game by mindlessly throwing the dice, moving around the board and paying your fines. However, eventually you start to notice that everyone else seems to be doing better than you are in the game and so you start to ask how? The answer that you are likely to be given is simple: when you land on certain properties, buy them, then add houses and hotels and make as much money as you can. The point is that as soon as you begin to really understand the mechanisms of the game, you *can* become a winner.

Information and knowledge are powerful assets. But what really makes the difference? Surprisingly perhaps, it is the fact that you asked for help. Thus, by reading this book you have indeed asked for help in understanding how to win at the game of life.

It is the split mind that produces the Ego and so by understanding its mechanisms, my aim is to help you to play the game more intelligently. In this way, you should not only be able to win more often but also to enjoy the game itself!

In 2007, as I was beginning to emerge from a deep depression, I found a book that unbeknownst to me at the time, would change my life forever. The book was called A Course in Miracles (ACIM).

The book is a study course aimed at teaching the difference between what is real and unreal. It does this by undoing the Ego (fear-based thoughts) and revealing Love and Truth. These are the only things that really exist but remain hidden behind the veil which blocks true vision. The veil which the Ego constructs.

My first time of reading I put the book down and remember thinking *"That was a waste of life; I didn't understand a word of it!"* It is a very challenging book and this appears to be the experience that most people have upon the first read. It was to be another six years before I would ever pick the book up again.

However, I had now become a student of the Course and unbeknownst to me, I was then directed to a myriad of other teaching resources such as personal revelation, books and people that channel advanced teachers who could help me to understand it.

I had no clue until very recently that they were all providing little pieces to complete the puzzle of how to undo the Ego.

Apart from ACIM, the other sources that have inspired and directed my journey have been Bashar (Messenger) as channelled by Darryl Anka and a multitude of teachers of the Law of Attraction (LOA). The most influential teacher of LOA for me has been Abraham, as channelled by Esther Hicks. I have studied these sources so intently and continuously that it is difficult now to differentiate my thoughts from theirs. As I believe that this is *my* Universe and my creation, that hardly seems difficult to believe.

However, for most people it is difficult to believe that they are powerful creators of their own Universe. Within the split mind there are two 'parts' of you. One knows that you are Spirit: timeless and powerful. The other is the fear-based, small self 'I', that is a creation of the Ego. I will show you that it is vitally important to complete the practical exploration of these two 'selves' which are formed by two very different thought systems which often operate at odds with each other. By exploring and understanding the tricks of the Ego you will be able to unravel it and utilise the enlightened free-thinking of the Spirit.

Therefore, it is important to understand that the book will be addressing almost two different levels of reality. One offers the practical tools of coping within the material, physical universe as the small self 'I'. The other level is the greater reality of the Spirit that you truly are and that you must endeavour to become a pure expression of. This level addresses the more ideological ways of thinking and of being in a purely thought-based reality. These will be highlighted by capitalisation of relevant words.

Your Universe: the *You*-nique version of your world is your creation only. You see everything through your own beliefs, values and perceptions and those are never the same as any other human being alive. Heaven on Earth isn't a place; it is a state of mind that arises from behind the darkness where the Ego once was and blocked out the light. Therefore your state of Heaven on Earth - or a positively joyous life - is revealed when you have let go of all of your Ego's fear-based programming.

But let me be clear; when I talk about God and Heaven etc, that I am referring only to the All That Is. I want to make it clear that I separate God from the organised religions that purport to serve in 'His' name. (I know organised religions give a lot of comfort to many people so I am just speaking for myself here.) Religion, for me, is no longer synonymous with God. God for me now is All That Is; not human, but energy. God is the energy of Love. So although we will be looking at your relationship to All That Is via the Spirit, this is mainly a practical guide to undoing the Ego and understanding what is really going on in 'life'. So whilst you are reading this book I would ask you to suspend any old judgements and definitions about the word God for the moment. Be a clean slate. Think of this as 'All That Is', if you have an old programming issue. In this way, the Ego will be unable to thwart your open-mindedness to new ways of thinking.

What I have found is that the more open minded I am, the more joyous and loving that I become. This is a book that will help you to recover the lost joy and understand the greatness of who you are *meant* to be through practical understanding of who you *appear* to be.

This book aims to show you how to do that. But you must be ready to let go of your 'stuff'. A child that has no knowledge of money but has found a coin may not realise that to swap it for the note that he is being offered would make him richer. The Ego will keep reinforcing a perceived gain of safety and security that comes about by staying in your comfort zone. But like the small child, if you can just open your mind and trust the information presented throughout this book, you too will become richer.

And so I aim to weave a beautiful tapestry of how *I* understand the theories of energy vibration and Law of Attraction, as well as psychology, spirituality and mindfulness work together to create what you think of as your only reality.

Again, this is just the way that I have put all the pieces together. They are logical, reasonable and work fantastically well for me and all of those that I teach and heal. There are other ways I am sure. All I can offer is the gift that I have received by putting it all together for you in my own way.

Part of my way is to recognise that every element of our thinking and consequently our experiences are intertwined and thus get tangled up. Therefore, it will be necessary to return to the many recurrent themes of the Ego in each chapter. This is because the Ego has confused and inverted many of them in order to keep you caught up in its web. As the new ways of thinking I am advocating are complex, this return will perform the task of continually reinforcing your understanding. We will be, as they say in Neuro-Linguistic Programming, 'chunking down' into more palatable pieces the huge subject of how you are fundamentally creating your reality and causing your own suffering (or enlightenment) simply by the way that you think and perceive.

What I love about being a Clinical Hypnotherapist, Life Coach and teacher is that not only am I teaching but I am also learning so much from every student and client I engage with. As you give, you receive. Therefore, I will use examples from my own life and work throughout the book to illustrate how these theories play out in real-world situations. I will also strip things down to the basics so that you can understand these fundamentally challenging theories without any of the usual confusing jargon.

To aid your continual revision and growth, I have ended each chapter with a quick summary of the main points. I have also added some simple, practical exercises that can help you to personally integrate some of the theories discussed and actively apply your learning to your own life.

However, if you do not do the exercises remember that it may be because your Ego doesn't want you finding out this information and improving your life from it! To do the exercises or not, is completely your choice but at least question why the Ego would not want you to practice or discover your personal programming.

After all, there are only two things that can really be proven to exist:
1. You are conscious and
2. You have free will at all times.

The most basic facets of being conscious and having free will are total responsibility for everything that you are experiencing, as no-one can enforce anything upon you. If you are the problem however, you also become the solution and this is the most empowering state to be in.

Taking these truths to be the only truths, I will be continually showing you how this power has been slowly eroded by the Ego. More importantly, I will be showing you how to take it firmly back.

In conclusion then, this book will present my attempts to explain the mechanisms of the split mind, and to reveal the whole, positively joyous you. I am not saying that I am an expert in anyway shape or form. I am still a student. Everything is work in progress. I always find that as soon as I think that I have life figured out, my next lesson arrives to remind me that I still have things to work on. That's ok. That's how it should be in some ways as I do not want to stand still.

My first book is called **Tour the Core-The Pathway to a Positively Joyous Life**. I now consider this to be the starter and this book to be the main course. It is not mandatory or even necessary to read that book before this one, but if you do you will have a stronger foundation for the subjects and ideas taught here. The Tour explores the most basic tenets of simple psychology, the Law of Attraction, spirituality and mindfulness. It also has work-sheets that can help you uncover and heal some of the hidden belief programmes that you are holding on to and perhaps 'suffering' from.

So let us begin our journey to a positively joyous life by creating a solid foundation on which to build a strong temple. Understanding first, how your brain and mind work together to create the basic game of life, will set the scene for the introduction of the real problem in our life: The Ego.

Theresa Borg
London, 2018

Plato's Cave

Plato suggested that there were 3 men chained together so tightly that they could not even move their heads. These men had been there all their lives and the cave is all they had ever known. They had only ever seen the back wall of the cave.

Free people on a raised walkway pass behind them and their shadows are cast upon to the back wall of the cave. The 3 men watch these shadows and believe that this is their reality and all there is. They spend their lives trying to guess which shadows will appear next.

Eventually one man frees himself and turns around to see a colourful world of free people outside of the cave. He realises all that they saw and thought they knew as reality was wrong. He tries but cannot convince the others to turn around and be free themselves. They actually threaten to kill him; such is the strength of their fear that they could be wrong.

****

Most people will fight tooth and nail, out of fear, to maintain their cherished view of reality.

But, is it not true that once you have seen the Light you would not choose to remain bound in the darkness?

Theresa Borg

Chapter 1

The Brain is a Computer

"The human brain has 100 billion neurons, each neuron connected to 10 thousand other neurons. Sitting on your shoulders is the most complicated object in the known universe." Michio kaku.

There is a fundamental structure that creates and continually reinforces your experience as a physical being. It creates a self-perpetuating feedback loop that unless innately understood, creates the same life everyday, every year and perhaps even every lifetime. You cannot change the structure but you can change the content.

I call it the Bear and it looks like this: (Read clockwise)

Beliefs

Reinforcement   Emotion

Action

Your thoughts or beliefs lead to an emotional state that then determines your action. The belief is the cause and the emotional response and action are the effects. This then, reinforces your original belief. We shall look more deeply into this structure in chapter 6 -The Unchangeable Belief but until then, it is important to remember that this is how your reality is being created.

You have probably been taught the rule 'seeing is believing'. You may be at an important lunch and knock over a glass and say *"See, I told you I was clumsy"*. In truth, the belief that you are clumsy makes you nervous and causes the hand to slip. Thinking that 'seeing is believing' is how the world works will only make you a victim to external events that appear to be out of your control. However, your empowerment comes from understanding how the systems of the mind and creation truly work. As we can see from the Bear cycle, the actual truth is that 'believing is seeing'. This gives you a powerful way to change your life because what you think and believe is always under your control. Thus throughout the book you will be shown how important it is to be mindful of the choices that you make.

So keeping the Bear in mind, let us begin with the mechanics of how the mind works. It is vitally important to understand before we start, that mind is different to the brain. Mind is akin to software that uses the hardware of the brain to express itself through. The internet for example, which is software, cannot be accessed without some form of hardware.

The computer system and screen on which it can be displayed are the necessary hardware.

The internet is a source of information for the computer. This data is streamed into the computer from another destination and then displayed on the screen. I think of the internet if you like, as the Soul. The Soul is the essence of who you really are and is not in the body. It is the conceiver of your higher thoughts. The brain then, is merely the receiver of those ideas which it then projects out onto the screen of your environment and body. The conscious, split mind perceives the information it sees on the screen and reflects upon it, which then causes an action. This perception will be made by the Ego thought system *or* the Spirit. These two parts make up the split brain which will be explained more in chapter 2. The resulting information gleaned from the action taken is then streamed back to the Soul which causes the next thought or idea to be streamed to the brain. This process is happening millions of times per second.

The thoughts and ideas sent from the Soul once filtered through the mechanisms of the brain can become a flawed, limited or corrupted version of the original. If the quality of your computer hardware is poor or your screen has low resolution, then your experience of the internet can only be poor. However, the quality of the information being streamed from the Soul, like the internet, will always remain pure and unaffected at source.

The brain then, because it is simply hardware, is benign when it comes to having a conscious opinion as such. It only serves to facilitate the mind. Like the operating system of your computer it has no opinion on what is right or wrong or good or bad for you. It simply follows the instructions with which you or somebody else programmes it.

Neuroscientists tell us that the brain builds up nets or webs of associated information and experiences. The brain then matches data about 'reality' coming in from the senses against its pre-stored patterns. These neuronets we will call files. If your understanding of computers is not great, it may be helpful to think about these as paper files that you have stored in filing cabinets around the office of your mind.

There is not a picture of an apple in your head, for example. You build up neuronets or an identikit picture based on what someone taught or programmed you to believe about apples, (red or green, round with a stalk, good for you etc). Your brain then notes these elements and looks for the matching data which opens the file for 'apple'.

Now if you were at school and the teacher threw an apple at your head for being naughty, you may have cried and felt humiliated. Into your file for apple, you would now have the feelings of humiliation and perhaps hatred of teachers, attached and stored in relation to that object. Years later, that experience may be forgotten or you may have disassociated yourself from it. But now you may find yourself unconsciously avoiding apples.

This is because every time you see or think of apples the whole file opens, including the page with humiliation on it.

Because your natural instincts are to avoid pain you will unconsciously avoid apples. You will then rationalise this as *'I just don't like them'* or *'Just the thought of them makes me feel ill!'*

The other thing that it is important to realise about these files is that you just need one word to open the file. However, within every file there is a huge subtext of other ideas and subjects that you may never be conscious of. Who would guess that within a folder about apples, a hidden subtext of humiliation would be lurking?

You will have many things attached together such as work and money, love and hate to name but a few. So there will be many subtitles and attachments to every file, which open automatically but remain 'hidden' because they are sitting under the one main umbrella or label that you use. This is why you are often unaware of why you are behaving in a certain way with particular people or events. We will explore this in more detail in chapter 9 which is about relationships.

In Aldous Huxley's book 'A Brave New World' there is a clear example of how you can become conditioned and learn to associate things together. In this dystopian future, babies are bred for a pre-destined life of work. The babies live in a nursery and are conditioned to enjoy their future-designated roles. One group of babies are given beautiful pictures of nature to look at but are then randomly jolted by an electric shock or a loud noise. The babies over time develop distaste for nature and so are happy to avoid it. This makes them ideal candidates for long periods indoors doing factory work. In addition, Ivan Pavlov used dogs to study 'Classical Conditioning'. He discovered that his dogs were salivating every time his lab assistant entered the room because they had learned to associate *him* with food, whether it was dinner time or not.

Let us return to your apple 'issue'. Eventually you may feel that it is causing you a few problems in your life. You may receive an internal nudge from the Spirit encouraging you to delve into the unconscious to find the old file and its negative attachments. On discovering the root experience and subsequent beliefs from it, you would then be able to overwrite, update or delete the old memory and file. Just like on a computer, any file can be updated or deleted. This is what you are doing if you do any self-development work.

So where do all of our files and programming come from?

Well, as a matter of fact, you are already being programmed in the womb. Whatever a mother is feeling goes straight into the foetus through the placenta. As the brain is already forming and storing vital information that the baby will need to survive once born, the brain records everything. If the parents were in a relationship, of domestic violence for example, the baby will be experiencing the mother's fear and pain, chemically in the womb. Therefore, the root feeling being programmed even from pre-birth would be that the world is a scary and dangerous place. Going forward this would induce a base vibration, or expectation perhaps, of a life of fear and pain.

Once born and up until eighteen months to two years, the baby still has no sense of an independent self and is unable to differentiate themselves from their environment. Therefore, for all intents and purposes this baby *is* its mother, father and everyone else.

In this family the baby would be experiencing the pain of the mother and the anger of the father. It is also being programmed with 'this is how a man behaves'; 'this is how a woman behaves'.

This becomes clearer if we think about a mother bear and her cub. The cub is biologically programmed to believe that everything that the mother teaches it is: correct, essential for survival, and is in its own best interest. The cub 'knows' that if it doesn't unquestioningly copy and follow everything that its mother does it will simply not survive.

Well, you still have the same primal programming deep within you. Until your critical abilities develop, you are programmed to copy everything that your parents do without question and accept all that you are taught as truth.

Everything that goes on around you is faithfully recorded from day one. You record everything that you are told and experience, just like a tape recorder. This goes on until the age of seven or eight. Before this age, the mind is not mature enough to make a judgement about what is true or false because it has limited experiences with which to compare and contrast. Thus, it has no choice other than to simply record all data as truth and fact.

These early programmes become your root programmes which then get continuously reinforced throughout life, creating cycles of repeating experiences. You may think about these root programmes like the roots in your garden that perpetually produce weeds, no matter how many times you pull the weed up. Until you can remove the root, the weeds will continue to grow. Similarly, until you update or delete these root programmes and beliefs within you, you will continue to have patterns of behaviour that repeat in your own life.

Consequently, in our domestic violence example, the baby will see that type of relationship in the future as the norm. In essence, it will feel like 'home'. This is why people from abusive backgrounds will often find themselves in repeating abusive patterns. They may unconsciously look for a similar relationship with an abuser or become an abuser themselves. This is the same as someone unconsciously marrying a person that mirrors their mother or father. If the files are never updated or cleaned out, this is all that you will have to reference what a marriage should look like: that of your parents. How often have you found yourself repeating the words or behaviours of your parents, with your own children?

The content of your files informs your expectations.

By puberty, (let's say eleven to eighteen), the brain has too much data to hold and so will start to archive things that it does not need any more. Brain capacity is critically important and so nothing will ever be wasted or left unused. However, the criterion that the brain uses to decide which files to store is based on the information that will keep you safe and alive or avoid pain in the future. I believe this is why we end up with relatively negative brains.

For example, my happy fifth birthday party has no evolutionary use and so will be 'let go of' by the brain into the deep, unconscious warehouse of stored data. As an analogy; these files get boxed up and sent to the company archives in the basement. The memory of putting my hand in the fire when I was six will be kept in the near consciousness because it is future protective. Let us say that this file gets kept in the draw of your desk as you may need to quickly access it again at some point. Notice the file is not currently open on your desk. Files that are open on the desk are analogous to the conscious thoughts that you have in the 'now' moment. The brain continually needs to make room for new information and so within the sleep process; it will be efficiently doing its filing for the day.

Let us return again to the child's experience in the domestic violence household. As we have discussed, the child would be directly and vicariously experiencing fear in that household everyday. Consequently, they would develop a programme of victimhood that would sit at the forefront of their mind and experiences. Their expectation may be that no-one can be trusted. Love and hate may become entangled together.

The more any file is accessed within the brain, the more it will become the programme of choice. The more that you access particular neuronets, the stronger they become. Just like on your computer, the programme that you use the most will appear top of the menu list. Therefore, as the brain is programmed by language, the things that you say, think and feel the most will become your strongest beliefs. Then, in this case, the child can and will only see people and experiences which reinforce their victimhood. The Bear cycle continues onwards.

Your computer can only display what has been programmed into it. Your brain can only play out the programmes that you or others have programmed into it. If you only have Windows 7 on your computer; that is all it can display. If you want Windows 10 then you or someone else will have to programme it onto the system, or update Windows 7.

This is pure physics.

Take a moment here to ask yourself about your early programming, home environment and most habitual responses to situations. Are these still serving you today?

Sigmund Freud, the grandfather of psychoanalysis, proposed that behaviour and personality arise from the continuous interactions of three levels of awareness or the mind. He termed these levels: the preconscious, the conscious, and the unconscious.

Freud compared these three levels of mind to an iceberg. His analogy was that the conscious mind is the tip of the iceberg that can be seen above the water. The preconscious mind is analogous to the part of the iceberg which is submerged yet still visible below the water-line. Finally, the unconscious makes up the remainder of the iceberg which is completely below the water-line; unseen and unknown.

Using this analogy, he proposed that the conscious mind was 5% of the total mind, the preconscious mind was 2% and the remaining 93% made up the unconscious mind.

He argued that the tiny conscious mind included everything that you are actively aware of in your moment-to-moment experience. You may think about this as the aspect of your mental processing that deals with 'what is in front of your face'. Shockingly, this only constitutes about seven pieces of information and is usually what you are experiencing through the five senses, plus what you think/feel about it. There are millions of 'bits' of other available data that gets recorded but remain unconscious to you. The mind thus creates a perceived reality that is finely filtered **just for you**. In short, the conscious mind experiences only the 'now' or if you prefer, represents the file on your desk that you are currently working on.

The preconscious mind deals with our shorter term memory. So if I were to ask you what you had for dinner yesterday, the answer would not necessarily be at the front of your mind. However, you would think for a moment and perhaps reply "Erm…sausage and chips!" 'Erm' is the sign that you are searching for a file that is not yet buried too deeply or sits just below consciousness. This is akin to the file that is still on your desk but underneath the one that you are currently working on. The preconscious is only concerned with the past.

Thus, the remaining 93% makes up the unconscious mind. repository of everything else that you have ever thought, experienced in the past. This includes all of the things that you forgotten, denied, repressed or suppressed about yourself. It is a res of feelings, thoughts, character traits and memories that are outside of not immediately accessible to your conscious awareness. These are the archived files that are still accessible but are not kept on the desk top. The unconscious is only concerned with the past and longer term memory.

Many of the traits and qualities that you have, but deem unacceptable or unpleasant, are hidden in the unconscious deep beneath the awareness. Freud's theory is that things within the unconscious continually try to influence your behaviour and experience. You are oblivious to this, but eventually you will get to see them in your everyday experience when you have projected them out. You project them into the external environment and on to other people or events so that you can see what is held in *your* unconscious. The environment then is akin to the display screen of your computer. You see the contents of your own mind presented as your reality. We will discuss this in more depth in the later chapters.

From Freud's iceberg analogy, you can see that the majority of your thoughts, beliefs and programmes operate from below the level of your immediate consciousness. This explains why it can often feel like everything is out of your control, that life happens *to you* and that you are powerless to change it. This is absolutely not true. You may feel like you are powerless simply because the interplay of unconscious projection was previously unknown to you.

It is by the mechanisms of sight, hearing, thought and feeling that you not only experience but manifest your life. By following a path that unveils all your hidden traits, the barriers to knowing your True Self are removed.

In my classes, I like to use this simple analogy for how the mind is programmed.

This is how you can change from being a pessimist to an optimist.

Suppose that you have a mud path leading from your front door to your garden gate and that this is the most obvious route out of your property. Because it is a mud path and you cycle down it, you create a very deep rut in the mud by its continual use. Let's say this is representative of the habitual, negative belief programmes running in your mind. We shall call this the 'rut of negative thinking'. Continually accessing negative thoughts makes you a pessimist.

If you no longer wished to reinforce the negative, mud rut then you would need to find another way to leave. In this analogy it would be to ride your bike across the lawn to leave the property. Eventually you would make a rut in the mud underneath the grass. Let us call this the 'rut of positive ninking.' Continually accessing positive thoughts make you an optimist.

If you continue to avoid using the negative mud path then eventually due to the wind and rain, the mud will displace itself into the rut and the rut will eventually disappear.

There is a phrase that is just as relevant for the brain as it is any other muscle in the body and that is: 'use it or lose it!' If you suddenly stop going to the gym, that bicep that you trained for six months to develop will entropy very quickly. If you stop using the negative neuronets they too will come apart on their own, over time.

Albert Einstein said *"Nature abhors a void"*. So, in the same way that nature will never leave any ground devoid of life, the brain will never leave such valuable space unused. Therefore, it is important that when the negative neuronets come apart that you consciously replace them with new and positive ones. The negative, habitual programmes will cease to run as long as they are replaced by new, positive programming. This is the same as leaving any part of the soil in your garden without plants; the weeds will soon take over. Therefore, you must plant some beautiful flowers to keep the weeds at bay.

Making a resolution for positive change is easy, but the most important part is completing the new action and actually peddling across the grass!

You may have heard of mantras or affirmations and really these are simply reprogramming tools. The brain programmes by language. A mantra or affirmation is a positive and powerful sentence repeated over and over in the present tense. It is pure mechanics to change the brain's programming because a mantra builds and reinforces positive neuronets. In fact you will be using the same process of repetition that built the negative pathway in the first place! A belief is simply a thought that you have practiced well. No more and no less.

Change is easy as long as you programme the belief that it is.

A thought that is a repeated, well-practiced belief will mean that no other way of thinking about that subject seems possible. If you remember back to my analogy of continual use of the same path every day creating a rut in the mud, you can see that it is the continual repetition that strengthens the neuronets in the brain. How many times have you programmed yourself with the idea that change is difficult for example? The computer at home doesn't say *"She was only joking, she didn't mean that!"* Like your computer, whatever you say is a clear instruction to the brain and *every* instruction is acted on until another instruction overrides it. Therefore, you must listen to yourselves. It is vital to know and understand that *everything* that you say and think is an instruction and is received neutrally by your brain! It will be acted on and sent to the body, which we will come onto later into the book.

The mantra that I find the most powerful is *"I am in control of my thoughts.*

I am in control of my behaviour". If you sit and think about this mantra, you will see that it would make your life very happy, very quickly because it puts you in control of your life. If that was the strongest programme running it would have to be displayed on the screen of your life.

If you change the belief programme with the affirmation *'I am in control of my thoughts. I am in control of my behaviour'*, you must also allow time for the new belief to take hold via the process of repetition. This is why the band exercise at the end of this chapter is so very effective at changing belief programmes.

Be aware though that any affirmation must be positive, powerful and spoken in the present tense. General phrasing also ensures that you do not activate any negatively associated programmes that may be surreptitiously linked to this issue. It is vitally important to recognise that every word has a unique vibration and every thought has an effect, not only in the mind and environment but also on the body.

And if your Ego starts to protest that any affirmation is untrue then simply tell yourself 'yet!' 'Yet' infers it is only a matter of time and I am on my way. 'I can't meditate.' and 'I can't meditate yet', say very different things. The addition of the word 'yet' changes the vibration from one of being stuck and powerless into one of hope, of control and moving forward.

Peddling across the grass means reprogramming the mind. By repeating the positive thought often enough, it becomes the immediate thought of choice. You are building new positive neuronets by repetition of a thought, until it becomes strong enough to become a belief. This is how you change from being a pessimist to an optimist. Remember, the phrase use it or lose it. As someone once said "Positivity is a muscle that needs working out every day". This is the most important part of the process, but is the very thing that most of us fail to do.

The brain is very plastic and is always creating new pathways and associations.

It happens every time that you think and speak about something new. It is said to take around fifteen minutes of concentrated thought for the brain to build basic neuronets. The brain will then start filtering for evidence of the new thought and within thirty days of dedicated focus you will have made a permanent change.

It is an established fact that you experience the world via your five senses. The discipline of Neuro-linguistic Programming (NLP) supports this theory, and argues that unconsciously you will delete, distort and filter any data that you do not want, or need to pay attention to, in the moment.

Thus, you will create the world that you expect to see that matches your particular belief system or programming. This is important to be able maintain a sense of security and safety.

If you are newly pregnant for example, your brain will start to filter for other pregnant women, babies and prams. If you are thinking about purchasing a certain type of car you will start to see it everywhere. This is because the brain is filtering out or deleting information that is not relevant to you in that moment. You therefore get a worldview that is heavily biased towards your personal preferences and interests.

People who are depressed and paranoid will be able to find someone laughing at them wherever they go. This is not because it is true, but because they will seek to interpret some innocent person's laughter as being directed at them.

There is in psychology two things called attention bias and interpretation bias. That means that your mind is biased to only bring things to your attention that you are interested in. It also means that you will interpret everything to match your current emotional state. If you have a spider phobia, for example, your attention will go first to the spider in the corner of the room whereas someone without that phobia will not even notice the spider.

You seek to make the world personal to you; we all do. You will delete or distort any other pieces of information available. As American writer Anais Nin deftly points out that "Often we do not see the world as it is but as we are!"

Perception, as you will discover as we progress through the book, is not about truth or knowledge. These are whole and unchanging.

Your perceptions shift and change constantly which creates instability and conflict in your life. Perception is subjective and therefore you can never actually see the truth. You can only see what is **true for you**.

Part of the problem is that when you are in an emotional state, the less control you have of your thoughts. Doc Childre from The Institute for Heart Math (IHM) states that *"Emotional processes can work faster than the mind"*. So if emotional processes work faster than the mind, then you need to ease your emotional state before clarity of thought in the next moment becomes possible. It is your emotions that tell you whether a thought is positive or negative as thoughts and emotions are inextricably linked. Emotion then can help you to see where you are and to choose something better.

Once you have realised that you have gone down the negative mud path again, you have to make a conscious decision or intention to change. You must also be attentive and aware so that before you even open the door, you know that you will have to aim your bike for the grass in order to leave. This becomes your choice-point.

The choice-point is the moment in which you become the deliberate selector of that next thought.

This means making the right choice of responding in a positive way as opposed to automatically reacting in a negative way. As every event is neutral, you have a choice about the message that you will take from it or how you can frame it. If you define something as positive you will have a positive experience of it. If you define something as negative then you will have a negative experience of it. You can easily redefine an action or event to mean something different because there is only what is true for you.

For example, if you are going on a first date and have taken a lot to time to get ready but you get drenched in an unexpected downpour on the way, you would be very upset! If there had been a drought for 40 days previously but on this night it suddenly rains then you would be very grateful for the rain. The rain itself is a neutral event and so the story that you tell yourself about it, will define your emotional response. It will define whether you suffer and for how long.

The Dalai Llama reminds us that *"Pain is inevitable but suffering is optional"*.

Therefore, the choice-point allows you to redefine, not only your thoughts about a certain thing but your emotional/vibrational state too. This is how you can immediately become a powerful creator in your life every minute of every day. If you take responsibility for your thoughts and actions then you are able to change these. If you accept that you are the problem, then you also become the solution. In my previous book **'Tour the Core'**, I describe in more detail about the choice-point.

The aim is to be aware of your thoughts which lead to your emotions and to consciously make another choice. Emotion is actually energy in motion and so in and of themselves they are as neutral as the thought that induced them. The emotions, however, can be used as your navigation system to tell you where you are. A positive emotion shows you are on track to get your needs met. This will improve your vibrational state because again, emotion is energy in motion. Any negative emotion is showing you that this is not the way to get your needs met and so will lower your vibration.

According to the Doc Childre of the IHM *"It is not commonly known that the heart actually sends more signals to the brain than the brain send to the heart!"* So, as I think about this, it is akin to 50 emotional voices shouting out from the heart and only a mere 5 rational voices attempting to calm you down. Therefore, your emotional thoughts will be heard as louder than the quiet voice of reason. Your emotions seem more difficult to control and consequently you will be unable to reason or talk yourself out of your emotional state. You may know this if you have ever tried to talk yourself out of a panic attack; it is impossible to do.

One useful tool that is extremely helpful in this regard is Mindfulness. Mindfulness is about being awake, aware and present in your life. It means deliberately paying attention to your emotional state: pausing, breathing and coming into the now and then allowing that energy to dissipate. By removing the story or judgement about the event, it is neutralised and one can then make a more considered and conscious choice.

In some ways you are only ever experiencing the past because, for example, by the time you have acknowledged your anger, you are already angry. A quick example would be that you may receive the wrong change in a shop. This causes anger within you as you may believe that the shopkeeper has cheated you.

As you look for the belief that is causing this reaction, you can see that you must have defined this event in a negative way. Henceforth, you are now allowing someone or something to affect you negatively. Happily though you can now reframe this choice-point for a more positive *response* rather than a negative *reaction*. You can redefine this event as just a mistake, politely point out the error and receive your change. The event ends there and you are both happy. Even if the shopkeeper refuses to believe you, as long as you do not allow any negative emotion such as frustration or injustice to arise you can still leave happy - if *you* choose to let it go. This would avoid getting into an attack spiral which we learn more about in the coming sections. *"You will not be punished for your anger; you will be punished by your anger"*, as the Buddha states.

Throughout the next few chapters I will give you the practical tools to do this in a variety of ways. But for now, let it suffice to say that it is always your choice in how to react or respond. No-one can affect you unless you allow them to. Your job is to realise that your emotional/vibrational responses create your next positive or negative actions, which will reinforce your empowerment or anger!

Every single act, thing and person in the universe is neutral. Nothing has meaning other than which you ascribe to it. Therefore, you create your own suffering from your definitions and perceptions of what the meaning of any person, event or object has for you personally.

Those definitions come from *your* stored files only.

You are likely to believe that memory comes from the past because most people believe in linear time. We shall be looking into this later in the book but for now let us just make the point that when you access a 'memory', what you are doing is accessing the thought called a memory now. You have to use a part of the mind to re-create something that seems to be in the past, now. This is done by a powerful part of our consciousness called the imagination. When you remember, it is actually a re-creation. To 'member' is to put together and so to 're-member' actually means to put back together again. A memory will be multi-sensory. Therefore, if you remember the day when you started school, not only will you see an image but you will have an inner experience and a sense of how it felt. There may also be a recollection of sounds, tastes and smells.

The body like any piece of hardware is operating only in the now, reacting to current data and instructions that are being given now. The memory then is an event happening now for the brain. Consequently, it will have a physical effect on the body in direct correlation to the strength of the emotion present at the time of the original event. This is why in therapy people will shake and cry as if they are re-experiencing the event now.

Memory is very susceptible to error and manipulation because it is based on an original perception, which itself is unstable. You may have had the experience of several people disagreeing with something that you thought that you remembered well. The more they say things like *"Yes you remember, Jill was there with that guy"* and someone else will chip in *"Yes the one with the red jacket"* even though you was sure that Jill was on her own that night. Your memory will start to become unreliable and begin to be coloured or even completely changed by other people's influence. You may start to say things like *"Well now you say that, I vaguely remember"* or *"Yes it is coming back to me now..."*

I am taking advantage of the fluidity of the memory all the time in Hypnotherapy, to help the client to see things differently and be released from their past trauma.

Now most of us dismiss things that come from the imagination as not being real, but in truth all things come via the imagination. Imagination is just another arbitrary compartmentalization of the one mind. Even that chair that you may be sitting on started as an idea in someone's imagination. Every concept that you have ever thought about uses the mechanism of imagination. If you are thinking about your mother for example, you will create an image of her with your imagination. A person has to have a certain amount of creative input to be able to put any concept into a future perspective; you have to imagine *'how does this fit with this'*, for example?

The imagination is really the creative mechanism of the mind. Learning cannot take place without the use of visualisation and thus the imagination. Imagination and visualisation are also key elements for the Law of Attraction (LOA). On some level, you must visualise how to create the future desires and outcomes that you want to manifest.

It is important to realise that imagination is key to be able to create new files. It also plays a part in overwriting old, unwanted ones and helps to envision the consequential changes that will ensue.

Now the LOA is a huge topic and there are three chapters which cover this in **'Tour the Core'** so here I will just give you a basic introduction to it.

LOA states that what you put out, you will receive back and what you ask for is immediately given but that you must also be able to receive it. So if you are radiating a vibration of happiness, we could say that you are broadcasting on 'radio happiness'. Only vibrationally-matching experiences and people can tune into that station; people or events that make one happy. On 'radio anger', only negative people and experiences which make you angry will be able to come into your environment. Those emotions are generated from *all* of your thoughts and therefore you will attract what you are thinking about both consciously and unconsciously.

You may really want a Ferrari but your unconscious says 'no way because it will only induce more fear; you have nowhere to park it securely, you won't be able to handle the power' or even 'you can't afford the insurance'. Because the unconscious is 93% of your mind, it will have the biggest effect on your life. However, you won't necessarily put the puzzle pieces together because the root belief programmes are unconscious to you. A bulb that is hidden underneath the soil looks nothing like the flower it later grows in to. If you do not remember planting the bulb, you may not make any connection to the flower that appears in your environment. And so if you do not manifest what you say that you want, your Ego will likely tell you that the Law of Attraction does not work rather than the unconscious beliefs are stronger than the conscious wants!

As we have already said, the brain is the computer hardware and the mind is the software. In the same way that you cannot access the internet without a computer or some form of hardware, as a physical human being, you cannot express consciousness without a functioning brain. If you are brain dead is it not true that both body and mind cease to function in the physical environment?

Your life is your consciousness projected out on to the computer screen of your environment. We will go into more detail about this throughout the book but once you understand the nature of projection, you can see this it is actually a gift. Projection allows you to see what programming is hidden in the unconscious and have an opportunity to bring it to the surface. It is how you can get to see what old files you have and decide what to keep or discard.

Buddha once said *"The path is clear. Which rocks do you throw before you?"* and it is your responsibility to start deleting your old programming; clearing out the heavy rucksack of 'rocks' that you carry around so that they do not overspill onto the path and trip you up!

In the next chapter we will look at the split mind and programming from the perspective of the Ego *and* the Spirit. But before that, there is also a distinction that we must now make between awareness and consciousness.

In meditation for example, you can be *aware* or have knowledge of sounds around you but they do not engage you. They can but simply flow with you and you can remain as one with them. However, if you become *conscious* of these sounds, you have had recognition of, and make a judgement about them. Thus, consciousness is a duality as you must become conscious *of* something. There is the sound *and* the person conscious of it. If I wanted to make this very simple I could say that with awareness you have no opinion but with consciousness you make a judgement or have a story about the said thing, no matter how small or trivial. In fact, you project a meaning onto the sound. Our limited language makes this difficult to describe in words on a page but hopefully this gives you a sense or a feeling for the distinction we need to make. You only need to know this because perception is an aspect of consciousness but **not** awareness. Spirit has awareness and thus access to Truth but your conscious mind within the body which we shall call Ego throughout the book, only perceives and judges and so has no access to Truth. Awareness is out of time and space but perception is bound and limited by the narrow constrictions within them. This is why you perhaps do not believe that you can change the past or tell the future; you judge it to be irrational and thus impossible.

In my book **'Tour the Core'**, I recount the story of how I first heard the Voice, which I now refer to as 'Spirit'. I mention it here because the Voice told me exactly what was about to happen in the future. It foretold that my computer was about to shut down for no apparent reason - which it did - and I should save my work. My Ego didn't believe it, as it saw no reason for this to happen. My response was then *"I'll just finish this page and then I'll save it"* by which time it was too late and the computer closed down. It was a clear voice but I still managed to ignore it, thanks to the counter-voice of the Ego that doesn't believe that it is possible to know the future.

As you can see, a split mind leads to conflicted opinions, wants and wishes and which part dominates will dictate how happy or unhappy you will be.

So which one should you listen to?

Quick Summary

1. Your brain performs exactly the same way as a computer. Whatever you have programmed into the computer is the *only* thing it will display. You see what is in your unconscious as it gets projected onto the screen of your external environment. You create and perceive it through the filters of *your* beliefs and programmes.

2. Your brain is programmed by association and repetition of thoughts. A belief becomes so because you have accessed the thought continuously and built strong neuronets for it. All files remain in the memory cache exactly as they were recorded unless you have taken a conscious decision to amend or overwrite them.

3. If you are awake and aware you can catch the choice-point at which you can choose a different file and halt habitual programmes running.

4. You will judge incoming data as negative or positive and react accordingly. You thus become the creator of your reality by whichever story that you decide to tell yourself.

5. Only the conscious mind deals with the now. The unconscious deals with the past and the future.

The Band Exercise

This is a really effective technique, from the school of Neuro-Linguistic Programming for changing habits. It is a powerful exercise with which to use your new understanding of how the mind works to create positive and powerful change.

This exercise focuses your mind really quickly on how your thoughts are running but also makes you aware of your negative thought and speech patterns. It also addresses each stage of the thought process and so can amend your behaviour quickly and efficiently.

Begin by selecting a belief or programme that you would like to overwrite. (You can also use this to aid in habit-breaking such as snacking or smoking).

Firstly, you must wear a band on your wrist and to change it to the other wrist each time that you catch yourself doing, saying or thinking something negative or detrimental. As you change the band to the other wrist and break the train of thought, you can then replace it with the new positive affirmation, repeating it constantly, with feeling. This is indeed a vibrational universe and so it is important to *feel* this is true, even if you do not believe it fully *yet*. Then, I suggest that you distract yourself by doing something practical.

Now let us break it down a little.

You will notice that you never have a single thought. You have a run of thoughts, one after the other until you consciously choose to stop the thoughts on that particular subject. The band exercise gives you impetus to stop the run of negative thoughts or to break the state. When you catch this choice-point and decide to reaffirm your new mantra by changing the band to the other wrist, you are coming out of the head and into the body. It is this physical action that interrupts the pattern of thought. You are ceasing to activate old, negative neuronets that you do not want to reinforce.

As we have already said, there is a phrase that is just as relevant for the brain as it is any other muscle in the body which is 'use it or lose it'. Thus, if you stop using the negative neuronets they will come apart over time.

However, you must replace the old one with new positive neuronets and this is achieved by language. You now have an opportunity to activate and build the new belief programme of choice by stating your new mantra, thus overwriting the old. Once the band has been changed to the opposing wrist you repeat *'I am in control of my thoughts. I am in control of my behaviour'* (or another mantra of choice).

Let us say that you wish to have more control over your tendency to snack. You are struggling not to give in to your craving to eat a packet of crisps. The problem is not the crisps; it is the unconscious beliefs such as *'I have no self-control'*. By stopping the run of thoughts, changing the band and stating the new mantra you have addressed all aspects of the cycle. I then suggest that you immediately go off and do something practical in order to distract yourself. Singing a song will do if this is not possible.

If you remember our bike analogy, the only way to build new and different pathways in the brain is to keep cycling over the grass. That is to keep practicing the new affirmation repeatedly until it starts to feel like the truth. Once you have repeated this new mantra so many times, it will become the automatic pathway of choice. *'I am in control'* will then become the absolute truth for you. Then, you must see evidence on the screen of your life which reinforces that. The mind will start filtering for evidence to confirm that you are now in control of your thoughts and will search for confirmation of that around you.

The new belief becomes your new reality. To make sense of the transition period however, you will start to see that you are craving food less or that you may suddenly discover that you can go a whole day without even thinking of crisps.

From the LOA point of view, this technique redirects your focus on to what you do want and builds the new pathway in the brain!

Quick guide:

1. Catch the negative thought or behaviour.
2. Swap the band to the other wrist.
3. Repeat the new mantra "I am in control of my thoughts. I am in control of my behaviour".
4. Distract yourself.

Warning

If you do not choose to do any of the exercises presented throughout the book, remember that it may be because your Ego doesn't want you discovering this information and improving your life with it. However, free will means that it is always your choice.

Chapter 2

What is the Ego?

"Everyone who is seriously involved in the pursuit of science becomes convinced that a spirit is manifest in the laws of the universe - a spirit vastly superior to that of man."
Albert Einstein

Before we can begin to look at the question of the Ego it is vitally important to understand that we all have what is known as a split brain.

Scientific evidence that the brain is 'split' can be found in a wonderful book by Frederick Schiffer called 'Of Two Minds'. In the book, Schiffer discusses the results of a procedure called a Commissurotomy, which was developed for debilitated temporal lobe epileptics. The aim of the operation was to prevent an epileptic seizure spreading from one hemisphere of the brain and causing damage to the other. The operation involves the cutting of the Corpus Callosum (the communication bridge between the two hemispheres).

In the book, Schiffer recounts the doctor's amazement as this procedure resulted in the temporary creation of two different but intelligent and autonomous minds within the patient. Each 'personality' had different wants and wishes. In one patient, the left logical 'personality' wanted to be a draftsman but the creative, spiritual 'personality' of the right side wanted to be a racing driver!

Now in reality, we have a whole brain and our lives work best if we can use it in this way. Ideally, the two sides work together to give us the best possible outcome in every situation.

The left hemisphere processes sequentially and the right is a parallel processor. Put more simply, the left thinks in logical steps and is detail-orientated, whilst the right sees the bigger picture and thinks outside of the box. The right hemisphere is thus considered to be more creative and open to new ways of being and thinking. Therefore, by the two sides working in harmony together on a single problem you would get the best of an analytical and creative mind.

There is a fantastic book called 'My Stroke of Insight' by Jill Bolte Taylor who was a Neuro-anatomist until she had a severe stroke aged just 37. The stroke severely damaged her left hemisphere leaving her as if a baby in a woman's body. She had to relearn even basic skills including numbers, reading and walking. However, because the left side went 'offline', the right hemisphere was allowed free-range and what she experienced was a sense of Oneness, expansion and Nirvana or Heaven. She speaks so eloquently about those feelings of greatness that she experienced only once, the critical voice of the Ego in the left hemisphere had been silenced. She realised that the Ego was just a story about who she was, and when she lost the story she was free to express the glory of her loving Spirit. Gradually, she lost full access to that bliss once the left side of her brain had fully come back online. See my You-Tube channel Positively Joyous to watch her amazing Ted talk video.

Therefore, to some degree, the Ego and body are reality-focussing mechanisms. The Ego is the thought system of left brain and through it you focus yourself into time and space. It develops a story about who you are. It creates a small-self persona and then differentiates you from other people and things in your environment. *(Please note that when we refer to the Ego throughout this book, we will be personifying it, but try to remember that this is just a teaching aid and not intrinsically true. The Ego is a thought system.)*

Jill describes her awareness as feeling completely expanded when her right hemisphere was the only part of the brain online during her stroke. She feared that she would never be able to squeeze the greatness of who she truly was back into a seemingly tiny body. I imagine that her consciousness became like a microscope that had its focus dial turned onto a wide view. Then gradually, it was turned the other way; down into a very narrow focus when the Ego returned. This demonstrates perfectly why we feel so small, limited and obsessed by trivia when the Ego is active.

I like to think that the work that we are doing together throughout this book is akin to turning the dial back to that wide angle view that can eventually lead us to our own Nirvana. This would create the positively joyous life, free of any negative story about ourselves and allow us to become fully realigned with Spirit. This can only appear once we have silenced our own Ego and stopped falling for its tricks.

Now, as I said previously, I will be talking about the Ego as if it is a consciousness in its own right. But this is not fundamentally true. It is actually a complex thought system that we have lost control over. The book 'A Course in Miracles' makes the distinction between the wrong-mindedness of the Ego and right-mindedness of the Spirit. So I will borrow this terminology for the two parts, whilst emphasising the need to remember the greater Soul that we really are. I imagine all of us as coming from pure Love and our work is returning to the Light of Creation: the Soul and God.

Unfortunately, to help you forget what you really are, the Ego has made a little cardboard cutout of a body and stuck it over the Light. You then proceed to collect a range of stickers with labels of name, age, sex, this quality and that quality, which becomes the definition of who you think you are. You create a small-self 'I'. By adding to these stickers via your experiences throughout your life, you eventually cover over all of the Light and then disassociate from your act. To disassociate basically means to separate yourself from the act or to pretend that you didn't do it. As you have to have known about something before you disassociate from it, on some deep, unconscious level you must remember that you created this new 'I' through your act of play. However, many of you may have completely lost touch the Light that you still are and will always be.

It has now been so long since you disassociated from the Light, that you may have forgotten that this was just the act of an innocent child at play. The Ego prefers you to believe that you deliberately turned your back on your Creator and now you must be punished. The only choice left is then to hide from 'His' wrath in the darkness of the physical body.

Obviously the Light still shines pristinely behind the façade of the body and remains untouched by anything that you may believe that you have done. It is just that you are somewhat frightened to look behind you towards the Light. If you do, the Ego will react violently. It wants you to fully associate who you are with the cardboard cut-out. However, you are the Light behind the façade, or perhaps better stated, you are the Light and not the shadow in front of it.

The Ego will sabotage or try to dissuade you from any act, therapy or alternative way of thinking that could help you find your way 'home'. Home for now, you can think about as Heaven on earth or the positively joyous life. The strength or severity of the Ego's sabotage will depend on the likely success of your chosen escape plan. We will be discussing more of this later in the book.

I am reminded of the Greek philosopher Plato's Cave allegory that is at the beginning of the book. Plato suggested that we are like the men chained together facing the back of the cave and believe that this is all there is. The other men actually threaten to kill the man who dares to suggest otherwise, such is the strength of their fear that they could be wrong. The Ego will fight tooth and nail out of fear to maintain its cherished view of reality. Your realization that there is something greater than this world is what the Ego fears most, because as I said, once you have seen the Light who would choose to remain bound in the darkness? Thus, the Ego fears its own death should you find *'en-light-enment!*

With all that said, I would like to propose that the intelligent minds as exposed by Jill's experience and Schiffer's research is in fact what I will call the Spirit residing in the right hemisphere of the brain and the Ego in the left.

The left brain is concerned with logic, planning and analysis whereas the right brain is more concerned with our artistic, creative and spiritual side. You may have experienced the ensuing head-heart battles from this relationship.

In **'Tour the Core'** I discussed the findings of the American research foundation 'The Institute of Heart Math (IHM) which discovered that the heart receives information before the brain. The left brain mainly controls the right side of the body and vice versa. It therefore seemed obvious to me that my heart which is associated with being towards the left side of the body would communicate directly with my Spirit in the right hemisphere of the brain.

I believe that the heart together with my Spirit is actually responsible for the positive decisions that I am consciously trying to make *despite* the controlling mania of the Ego.

Throughout psychology, from Jung to Freud, there have been many different ideas and definitions of the Ego. Psychologists will often refer to the Ego as the part of the human personality often experienced as the "Self" or "I". The Ego is the part that deals with the external world through information that has been recorded by the senses. The Ego remembers everything, evaluates, plans, and is responsive to the physical world or environment. But the Ego watches the screen of the computer (your life) wondering where the internet is coming from. Therefore, it can only *react* to events. The Spirit is still connected to the Soul (internet) and so can be so much more proactive in creating your life because it has more knowledge and the fully-encompassed view.

Often, it seems the Ego has become a self-appointed protector in our lives, allowing us to hide from or avoid difficult and negative experiences, or parts of ourselves that we do not wish to own. This arises *because* there are two separate thought systems at play that are diametrically opposed. The Ego teaches that the rule of reality is that 'seeing is believing'. Spirit knows that the truth is that 'believing is seeing', because this is a thought based reality.

The Ego can only perceive what is going on and perception by its very nature is a subjective interpretation by the observer. Only the creator of a thing or event can know the true intention behind it. Therefore, there can be no *objective* truth ever known by the observer. A good example of this would be in the case of an assault. The Police will receive many different descriptions of an assailant and event. Each account will be different dependant on the locality, viewpoint, and quality of the person's eyesight and level of stress of the witnesses. They may all have a different concept about why the assailant did what he did. They can only see their own perceptions.

You may have been watching a film with someone who saw things that you did not, or perhaps they had a completely different view on what happened than you did. Therefore, perception will always be unreliable or incorrect to some degree and therefore unstable and potentially wrong!

Perception is the product of a personal evaluation or judgement about some-thing. It has the quality of duality (two parts); the judge and the judged. The judge makes a judgement or evaluation of something's worth: better/worse, higher/lower, desirable/undesirable and so on. When you judge something there is a natural rejection of the other part. This sets up elements of division and separation that the Spirit cannot see as it only recognises Oneness and Unity. This is also where the differences of opinion between the two sides of the mind arise as one has knowledge and the other only perception.

Spirit has the qualities of Oneness and Awareness which allows for Knowledge and Truth. Spirit knows that you, as your Soul, are the creator of this reality and thus, why you are creating a situation or event. Therefore, it does not *perceive* because it already knows the Truth. There is no doubt or questions in Truth. This means that for all intents and purposes, perception and knowledge at best do not understand each other and at worse are directly opposed to each other.

There can be no middle ground to Truth and perception is not its opposite. Perception is something completely different. The Spirit is not perturbed by this fact but the Ego becomes fearful of what it knows to be a force more powerful than it. Fear arises because it cannot understand the Spirit. It thus feels obliged to take steps to guard against what it sees as an intruder that is more powerful than it, in its body temple.

In its development, the Ego has pushed to become the sole independent master of your life. When you are too left-brained and the right brain or Spiritual Self is ignored, you can become too fearful, limited and feel out of balance. You often reflect this in your life by living an extremely controlled, safe, and sometimes materialistic existence that lacks spontaneity or creativity. The left brain wants you to take the safe, rational path whereas the right brain is fearless and so wants to take risks and live in the moment.

Language, of which only the left side has access in the physical world, has become so powerful in defining your world, that for some of you it is not only the loudest voice but the *only* thing that catches your attention!

Your lives may be increasingly filled with music, TV, tasks, technology, work, chatter and anxiety. Your ability to quieten the mind and hear the Spirit has likely become nigh on impossible. This is why, in my experience, so many people struggle initially with meditation. The thoughts (or the Ego) do not want to quieten down or to let go of its control through chatter!

In truth, the Ego will feel just like who you *are* because you are probably so used to associating with this part only.

So let us know think about how and why the Ego has become so dominant and controlling.

On a retreat I was teaching in Kent some years ago, someone asked me where the Ego came from and I was a little flummoxed as I had never really thought about it. As usual I just began talking and to my surprise a fully formed analogy flowed from me. I began to draw the analogy of a sole trader, business owner. Like myself, as the sole proprietor of my therapy business I have to complete all the required jobs myself: payroll, media, marketing etc. In short, I have to take care of the details. As my business grows and I take on more staff, I will naturally delegate these jobs to my employees. This involves developing my organisational and communication skills. But eventually, I may struggle to retain personal oversight of the whole company on a day to day basis.

Once my business grows to become multinational, I will now have various offices or departments all over the world. Although they are all part of the same company, each department will be fully autonomous and have its own goals and required practices. I will no longer be able to have personal oversight and have to trust that each department, led by a fully autonomous manager is doing its job correctly.

Now let us imagine that I say that I want more therapists. The Human Resources department says *"Yes Ma'am. We will get straight on it."* However, the Accounts department may step in and say *"No sorry. We cannot afford it."*

Each department is completing its job perfectly for the task that they have been given, for the greater good of the company. Although they represent one company, each department may often find themselves in conflict with the greater wishes of other departments or the CEO.

So which department takes precedent?

This is often the kind of conflict that you will find yourself in within your split mind. This would be where you have the two hemispheres wanting different things or two different belief programmes pulling against each other. E.g. I want to lose weight but I also want a slice of that cake. You will recognise this as I said earlier as the head/heart battle.

This analogy, I later realised, really describes how we developed as humans into social beings with language and the need for organisation.

When we lived individually there was no need for language or organisational skills. We lived in the moment by instinct. Once we realised that there was safety in numbers and begun to live in groups, the ability to communicate and organise became paramount. Consequently, the ability to organise ourselves and the tasks in hand, rapidly developed.

Thus, the brain had to adapt very quickly to handle language, numbers, and sequential information coming in and going out. Subsequently, the compartmentalisation of tasks within the brain occurred. Now, as life has become so much more complex, so has the brain.

We have three different layers of the brain each with its own tasks and abilities. Like my multinational company it has now become a daily experience of conflicts and battles amongst the departments or the Ego and Spirit. Sometimes we are in such turmoil that we literally cannot think straight and become paralysed or stuck in life.

The difference now is that the Ego has become like the micro-managing CEO who will want to make the final decisions on everything. It has become tyrannical and fearful and has lost sight of its original purpose. It doesn't trust its staff or you! Again, it realises that there is another part of you, which it cannot see or understand but recognises that it could possibly stage a takeover of the company and usurp its control. Henceforth, it can become vicious and punishing against anything or anyone that threatens it, including the Spirit.

That is why now, you must diligently guard against the Ego's wish to always be right. The Ego will do all it can to convince you that being right is crucial for your happiness and safety. It will always value being right over your happiness.

However much this is true though, you must not lose sight that you have allowed this to happen. The Ego is still a valid part of you that believes it is doing what is best for the company. It has been overloaded with responsibilities that it cannot handle and has become dazed and confused. It has projected itself 'out there' in order to convince itself that there are other Egos. Safety in numbers is one of its mottos. It then disassociates itself from its own projection. In this way it can convince itself that it is not alone, affirm its own reality and then compare itself favourably against other perceived Egos. Once projected and disassociated, this becomes its fundamental perception of the world.

So let us now look more at projection.

I like to think about us living within a mirrored, glitter ball. These are balls made of hundreds of individual, reflective pieces of glass. Because these tiny, mirrored tiles are all at slightly different angles and positions, if you look into the ball or move around it, 'pieces' of your reflection appear differently in each of the tiles. In each segment, you will see different aspects of the whole. You do not see a whole reflection as you would with a normal mirror.

Mirrors actually do nothing other than reflect back the light that is coming from you. The brain then interprets that light into a matching pattern that you will recognise as your *idea* of you. Anorexics will see a 'fat' representation of themselves and not their (often) true skeletal form, for example.

Were you to imagine that you lived inside the mirror ball, it would be your light in the form of your deepest emotions, rejected character traits, thoughts and beliefs that are projected outwards. This is the contents of your unconscious mind. You would then see them reflected back to you slightly differently from each tile. Thus, you only ever see *aspects* of your psyche that you may have forgotten, reject, deny or do not own which makes it then difficult to recognise them as yours! However, these reflections are all aspects of yourself.

This mechanism of projection essentially allows you to see what is going on in your unconscious mind by externalizing it. You must understand though that these mirrored tiles are analogous to actual people, objects and your own physical body within the environment. So you unconsciously project on to people your own ideas about them and then pretend that you have not done this. In reality then, you see your own self-created story about them *and yourself*. We will explore this in depth in the chapter on relationships.

Now, let's use another example. A cinema projector beams images from the film inside the projector, onto the screen. Note that the film on the screen is a separate object, in a separate place to the actual film and projector. The important thing to remember is that you may not know about the projector in the backroom of the cinema, just as you may have not realised that as a child. You may only be aware of the screen and thus believe (like the Ego) that this is the source of the images. This is analogous to believing that life is a hard and fast reality of matter or that you have no choice about what film is on the screen.

The images on the film roll, never actually leave the projector itself. This exactly mirrors the fact that whatever images you see on the screen of your life never leaves their source; which is your mind. Like a computer, if I send you a file the original stays on my computer too. It is only your thoughts and ideas that play out in the external environment. Your brain is the projector, the Soul is the director of the film and the Ego is the only the audience member! Other people and objects in your life are actually the 'cinema screen' on to which you project your film. Other people are also projecting on to you but you may never know exactly what they see of you.

The process of projection allows you to both see and experience a relationship with all aspects of your true self, both objectively and of course subjectively. This means that if you want to see any change in your external experiences, whether that is with people or events, then you have to change your thinking. It is your film playing out. By changing your mind about the world, you create an effect on everyone else.

If you do not like the growling face in the mirror then you must be the one that smiles. The mirror simply cannot change first.

I play tennis and I was always worrying about my shot being good or bad. As I am only an average player, I was mostly berating myself for poor shots. When I realised that the opposition was simply a reflection of me, I also recognised that I should always be focussed on celebrating their good play. In this way, I am really celebrating my own good play but it makes the game more friendly and uplifting. Paradoxically, by complimenting the opposition I started to play better because I was more relaxed with my own game. Also, my Ego quieted because the fierce element of competition had been nullified. Less pressure equals better play and a better game for all.

This is a clear metaphor for life. You must take the focus off yourself and focus on the positive qualities of others. They will then be reflecting the positive qualities in *you* which then you can appreciate. This will change your focus on to feeling better about yourself; raising your vibration. Law of Attraction will then only be able to bring you more positive people and events. As Mahatma Gandhi said *"You must be the change that you want to see in the world."*

Whilst we are discussing projection it is important to keep in mind that you project *meaning* onto things as well as people. You ascribe money, for example, much more power and meaning than the little bits of metal and paper actually have. You may give money the label of 'root of all evil' for example. That coin or piece of paper is, however, meaningless and neutral. It is your story about them that will define if you have a positive or negative experience with them.

In order to get the best out of the whole brain you must acknowledge that you have the two *valuable* thought systems in operation. Remember it is an integrated system that when working in harmony, gives the best of both types of analysis. It is however, a question of you deciding how you can do that. I suggest that like a judge, you listen to evidence that both 'sides' are presenting and then decide which one meets the demands of your current intention. In this way you become the driver of the car and not the passenger of a self driving car taking whichever route it desires.

Because the Ego is your creation it comes under the same laws as all of God's creations. God in the Bible is referred to as All That Is; as Energy that is everything. If you remove the arbitrary labels of me, you, chair, table etc all that would be left in the room would be Energy. Energy has no boundaries and cannot be divided. It is like we are; One. You are part of that energy and cannot be separated from it. However, you can have an experience of appearing to be divided by creating the idea of a boundary, such as a body.

God loves, protects and honours all of His creations. In like manner - and quite paradoxically - you love, honour and protect your Ego. This occurs on a deeper, unconscious level but this is really why you do not just drop it once you have realised all of its tricks and turns. It is still your baby. Sometimes you may not like the behaviour of your children but you still love and protect them. Spirit understands that nothing exists outside of All That Is, including the Ego, and will love it because you, as one of God's creations loves it too.

Especially early in this work, it may seem as if I am continuously blaming and putting responsibility on the Ego for all of our woes. But as we move deeper into the book, you will see why this is no answer to our problems. You cannot reject any part of yourself then claim to Love yourself fully. If you do not Love yourself wholly then you don't really Love yourself at all. Love as a Truth is whole. If you do not Love yourself fully then you cannot extend Love, at least on this level of creation.

Thus, the Ego has to be integrated and accepted but absolved of its power over us. When all choices become equal: whether you choose the Ego's thought system or the Spirit becomes irrelevant.

I like Bashar's analogy of a jigsaw puzzle.

A puzzle begins whole; All That Is. It is a whole piece of cardboard onto which an image is depicted. The puzzle is then cut into a number of pieces. The four corners may look more special than the more common inner pieces but in truth every part is of equal worth. Every part has its unique place where only it fits. You and I are merely puzzle pieces that now appear separate but in essence are still part of the whole puzzle. Without you owning who you are, exactly as you are, the puzzle can never be completed.

You can imagine that you are having the experience of being separate from the whole. You, as the Ego, can identify yourself as 'piece'. However, you can see that despite what the Ego wants you to believe, you are and will always be part of All That Is: unique, special and valuable. In truth, your meaning and purpose only becomes clear once you are reunited as the whole. Once the puzzle is completed you can then see the bigger picture of who you still are.

Spirit in the completeness and Awareness of the Truth sees no reason to shout and scream or try to wrestle back control from the Ego. The Ego believes you are the puzzle piece. The Spirit sees only the completed jigsaw and gently guides you back to your unique spot.

This is because the Spirit sees the world for what it is: an illusion, Maya or a dream state. If your child is having a nightmare you do not seek to go into the dream to rescue them from the perceived dragons. You stay gently by their side, calling them back from their sleep. The Spirit knows that this perceived nightmare is just a dream. It knows that God or our Source is calling us back to the Real World or Heaven, in my terminology. Spirit doesn't recognise the perception, only Truth. The truth is that you are the dreamer, not the character in the dream.

When you finally awaken the *real*, whole You will realise that nothing 'real' ever happened.

It is only through listening to the quiet, calm voice of the Spirit that the

Ego can be unravelled and you can see the Light again.

In a return to simplicity, unity and whole mindedness the rule of the Ego can be overcome forever. This allows you to finally hear the Voice of Spirit and the ability to choose another way of thinking and being. Just like Jill Bolte Taylor, we can all experience Heaven on Earth.

Whether it is projecting onto people or things, the mechanism of projection gives us a valuable opportunity to accept and heal all aspects of our personalities. Because you will see the world as you are; this mechanism allows you to see what is in your files and have an opportunity to clear them out.

As you will see in the next chapter on the body, the Ego now sees the body as its home and greatest ally. It has become focussed on convincing you that you are the body, and that Spirit is just some made up fantasy figure. It has projected God out and away from you in a similar fashion, so that you only have the Ego to rely on. The Ego thinks that it is the god of your world.

You must guard against projecting power on to the Ego and so you must take your projections back from it. *You* have given it its power by devolving responsibility for your choices both in the past and now in the present. This is just like the sole proprietor that delegates to his staff, takes no interest in their management and then berates them for decisions that they make.

Throughout the next chapters in the book I will show you just how the Ego exerts and protects its power. It has become a master magician, using a charade of smoke and mirrors, distraction and misdirection to keep you from realising what it is really doing. It desperately fears your discovery because then the game is up, and it fears its own death.

The Ego needs you and needs your problems. No problems, no Ego. So in this work I aim to keep you focussed on how the tricks are performed so that you will never be fooled again.

Quick Summary

1. There are two hemispheres of the brain joined by a communication bridge.

2. The two parts process differently in order to give a variety of solutions and options to our problems. The brain works best when both sides are balanced and work in harmony.

3. These are two differing thought systems. I refer to the logical, analytical left hemisphere as the Ego and the creative, right as Spirit. The Ego knows nothing about the Spirit and so can only perceive and react to events. The Spirit is still connected to the Soul and so knows Truth and that you are dreaming.

4. The Ego, for many, has become overly dominant and now believes that it is in control. It therefore uses a game of smoke and mirrors to keep you confused and imprisoned and to protect its power.

5. It lives in constant fear of you discovering what it is doing and taking your power back.

6. To live as Spirit means to unravel the Ego by understanding how it sees life through fear and limitation.

The Eyes Have It Exercise.

One of the most profound findings in recent times is that the eyes are powerful component of how we record and remember things. Schiffer's work has shown us how we can access our stored files from each side of the brain. Just like Schiffer's patients, each hemisphere holds information in different ways. This may be akin to the difference between what we think consciously on a subject as opposed to what the unconscious mind thinks about it. Here is a short exercise that I find fascinating but also very helpful in garnering different opinions from my two hemispheres.

1. Select a memory, event or question that you would like to work with.

2. Close the eyes or cover them with your hands if you prefer.

3. Now ask the question, whilst keeping the head straight on but looking to the left as far as you can and holding the gaze there.

4. Do not go looking for the answers but sit quietly and patiently. Observe the images and listen carefully to the thoughts. Do this for as long as you feel able to.

5. Bring the gaze back to centre. Rest for a moment.

6. Repeat from step three but with eyes to the right.

7. Notice the difference between the answers and information that you received from each side.

Chapter 3

Perception, Projection and the Confusion of Cause and Effect

"Genius is being able to put into effect what is on your mind."
F.Scott Fitzgerald

The definition of genius according to Oxford English Dictionary is 'exceptional, intellectual or creative power, or other natural ability.' So, F. Scott Fitzgerald's quote above speaks to me of being right-minded and in the creative right hemisphere, which we know 'thinks outside of the box'. As the Ego deals with fear and limitation, this could logically be a potential block to genius. The choice is then between the risk-taking visions of the Spiritual you, and the limited, risk averse perception of the small-self Ego.

One of the tricks that the Ego uses to create limitation is to reverse or confuse cause and effect in our lives. You will all be familiar with the concept of cause and effect as a basic law of the world that you are living in. You see it so often in your lives that perhaps you may tend to take it for granted. You will not doubt that if you press down the light switch (cause), the effect is that the light will come on.

The reliability of cause and effect is the mechanism that gives us a sense of safety and security in our lives. Being able to predict an outcome allows life to be manageable and for you to function within it. Even if you press the light switch and the light fails to come on, you will simply look for another cause, which is perhaps the bulb has blown. You know that there is a cause for everything. Even nothing happening when you press the switch, is in essence an effect! This law states that every cause has an effect and you cannot have one without the other. They are two sides of one coin.

The Ego, by reversing cause and effect, is able to confuse you so that you will not be able to solve your real problems. It sends you looking for the cause of your problems outside of you by projecting cause on to other people, places or things.

The Ego will centre your attention on the behaviour that appears to be the problem. However, behaviour is the resulting action of a story you are telling about any physical event or your preceding thought. It is therefore an effect and not a cause. In reality, there is only ever one cause and that is the mind. Thus, it is vitally important that at all times you are able to separate (see apart) the person from the behaviour. This also includes distinguishing the intent of the Spiritual you from your behaviour.

We have already (but perhaps only briefly) discussed how reality is a mind-based projection experience. This is your Universe: your *You*-nique version of your reality that uses two different thought systems that appear to cause two different levels of reality. One is the thought system of the Spirit that recognises that the world is an illusion, and you are actually at home in heavenly peace only dreaming that you are here 'alive' as you. It says that this is your dream and you are the sole creator. Just as when you dream at night, you are both the dreamer and the dream's characters. Thus, the only true reality is the internal consciousness. The dream is never out there in physicality. However, the Ego is invested in the belief that there is a hard and fast physical environment and that ensures its existence.

The Egos story is that you are a physical body rooted in time and space and that everything is concrete and made up of matter. The external reality is real, all that exists and very importantly, that you *did not create it*.

The first thought system makes you a powerful creator or the cause of reality and the latter makes you a powerless victim or the effect. The important point to note here is that you can change a cause but you cannot change an effect. This is vital to understand because this infers that you can create change if you live by the Spirit's thought system but not if you are the effect and live by the Ego's vision.

That is how the Ego keeps you trapped.

One of the things that you may have to watch for - in this chapter particularly but also throughout the book - is the sabotage of the Ego. So be aware that it doesn't like change and will try to cast doubt on many of these theories. This is just another way that it tries to direct and control your thinking. The Ego may rally against the idea of the world not being real. It will scoff and ridicule the idea that you are living in a dream or illusion. All I ask is that you stop and question it for evidence to the contrary. Whatever you believe is fine as long as you are well informed with clear evidence to support your argument. Otherwise it is simply opinion and may be totally untrue. It is also likely to be sabotage. When you live in the darkness of the mundane, harsh world of fear and limitation, the Ego doesn't want you finding the hidden door to the light. It will put up every barrier it can to prevent you from even considering that this world may very well be an illusion. Why? Because then it would lose all power over you. As with the men in Plato's cave, only those who are scared or lack knowledge think that to remain in the darkness is the best possible decision.

I always think about Copernicus when he first purported that the Sun, rather than the Earth, was at the centre of the universe. The mainstream thought that it was ridiculous and he was vilified for it.

Albert Einstein said *"All truth passes through 3 stages. First it is ridiculed. Second it is violently opposed. Third it is accepted as being self evident".*

However, beliefs should be formed by clear and current evidence and not simply be what someone else has programmed into you. Any belief should also be regularly examined for its continued relevance and accuracy. Theories and research results are continually changing and changing rapidly.

Indeed, many of the oldest spiritual traditions purport that this world we think we see is not reality. Quantum physicists now agree that everything is energy and there is very little, if any, solid 'matter' out there at all. Atoms, the fundamental building blocks of all life, are 99.9999% vacuum which is obviously not solid! The world as we know it may indeed be a holographic or virtual projection. There is a lot of evidence now showing that how and when physical matter takes form is actually always due to an observation by consciousness. I.e. your house only exists when you are there to see it!

The mind blowing inference of this is that your universe only exists to the extent of what *you* can see, hear, smell, taste and touch in that moment. Before that moment of observation by one of the senses, everything exists as mere potential.

Reality is far less stable and solid than you may think. The taking of drugs such as LSD can produce hallucinations that have no physical reality but are extremely real and vivid for the person experiencing them. I have worked with people with Alzheimer's disease whose reality is as absolutely solid as yours. The only difference is that they are seeing the house that they are in, as it was thirty years ago and you are seeing it as it is now. For them, it is every inch as concrete a reality as yours. If it is as unquestionably true for them as yours is for you, whose reality is the true reality? Just because there may be 'x' number of others seeing the same event as you, doesn't make it any more real. It just makes it a consensus view. It is also important to realise that both realities are true for each individual and therefore the rule is that it is not a 'this or that' reality but it is a 'this and that' reality for us all.

It is also possible to not see things that are actually there and we call these negative hallucinations. Think about the last time that you lost your keys or glasses and your partner picked them up from in front of you! Consequently, nothing except your consciousness receiving and analysing data can really be proven to exist.

Where does this data come from? It is projected from your own consciousness on to your self-projected screen which is the 'physical' environment. It then operates as a self-perpetuating feedback loop, like the

Bear loop I explained earlier in chapter 1.

Everything is your subjective perception and you can have the wide-angled view of Spirit or the extreme focus of the Ego. As Jill Bolte Taylor discovered, the external world seen through our senses and left brain, is an extremely limited focus. That focus begins and ends with you.

If you were the only person who existed in this physical environment, you could only 'see' your physical body fully if you looked into a reflective surface such as water or a mirror. You could never see the back of your head, without two reflective mediums. We often take for granted that a mirror is simply a neutral, honest reflection of the picture that is presented before it. However, as you will know from trips to the fairground, mirrors can be made to warp the view that you have of yourself. Imagine if the only reflective material that existed was warped mirrors, like the kind you find inside a Fun House at the Fairground. You could easily become convinced that this image was truly what you looked like!

So can you ever know for sure that all the reflective mediums that exist are truly reflective? How can you ever prove that you really look anything like that which you are actually seeing in any mirror?

As we shall see, who you are, is merely whatever your senses are decoding you to be! If you feel rough after a heavy night out, that is the reflection that you will see in the mirror. You may not physically look rough but because the rule is 'believing is seeing'; your expectation must be projected on to the screen of the body. Your past experience (cause) is that you look rough after a heavy night out and so the effect must be that the body will create the matching state, as physiology follows thought. You have just programmed into the computer *"I always look rough after a night out"* and that is all that the computer can display. It was a clear instruction.

It is often said that there is no way of proving that your world looks anything like mine. What I see as the colour red, you may see that which I would recognize as blue. In essence, colour doesn't even exist as 'colour' as we know it!

Colour is simply the interpretation or decoding by the brain of certain vibrations and frequencies that your eyes have recorded. The brain then interprets and assigns meaning to the incoming data.

Physicists say that the only thing that exists is light and thus light is actually the only thing that is real. This is obviously a profound conclusion when we relate this to the fact that most religious and spiritual theologies agree on light being the fundamental element of God, Angels, Spirits and so on. (I have earlier put forward the idea that the body covers the Light that you truly are.)

There is a huge electromagnetic spectrum of light that humans cannot even see. In fact, according to researchers *"Our cone cells detect but a small sliver, typically in the range of 380-720 nanometers -what we call the visible spectrum"*. So, you see only a tiny sliver in the middle of the range of light that is actually available to see 'out there'. You are blind to the rest. You are blinkered to what it is possible to see, or I may say, minutely focused into what you expect to see. The same can be said of all of your senses. Think about animals: dogs can hear sound frequencies that you cannot; others have acute levels of smell far beyond human capability.

This means that there must be much more happening in 'reality' than you are able to consciously sense and of which you as a human remain ignorant.

We know that the brain takes in information in many different formats on a daily basis. It is thought that you are subject to two million bits of information per second. However, humans are only capable of absorbing 134 bits of information per second. Your brain filters out everything that is not relevant or useful for the present moment and files the rest in the unconscious mind. The mainstream scientific view is that information and energy is never lost or discarded in the universe, although it may change form. Therefore, conscious information not immediately required may be archived in a more 'nebulous' form: as potential rather than a structured thought form.

When you actually observe something in reality, let us say a bird flying, your eyes are not actually recording a completed scene of a bird moving through the sky. The different 'seeing' areas in your brain have to map the scene generally and then it begins to layer details like movement, colour, depth or shape. It is almost akin to building up an identikit photo. The brain is thought to match known patterns to your expectations. Thus, your reality is a reconstruction by the brain from both your consciously and unconsciously stored past data, which is constantly being compared to the present moment. Your sensory systems allow only incredibly limited possibilities to exist. The fact that you are mostly matching patterns to make them fit with your *past* experiences severely limits the possibility of anything new arising. Thus, you become trapped in the same old world, exhibiting the same habitual behaviour.

So, how can you ever know for sure that you have 'interpreted' correctly that which you are actually seeing? The answer is that it is impossible to know. This is because you filter what you see through the lenses of your perceptions, beliefs, expectations, stereotypes and prejudices.

Recent developments in consciousness research have confirmed that even the sense of you as a physical body is illusory. There is a fascinating experiment which illustrates this point perfectly in a BBC documentary special called *'Horizon – The Secret You'*. This fascinating documentary researched how the sense of the self can be separated from the physical body.

The programme showed Professor De Sautoy sitting in a chair wearing a visor that was linked to a camera situated *behind* him.

The film playing inside the visor from the camera behind him became his eyes, if you like. The visor of De Sautoy was displaying the images of his physical body appearing to be seated *in front* of where he now perceived himself to be. So, because we are so used to believing exactly what our senses tell us, he felt as if he was actually sitting *behind* himself. This was true despite being able to consciously and clearly see that it was his own body in front of him. Later, to emphasise the depth of separation of self, the researcher swung a hammer in front of the cameras behind where De Sautoy was actually sitting, and Dr Sautoy was fooled into reacting as if the hammer was going to smash into his chest! This proves that De Sautoy truly believed that he was where the cameras were placed. Thus for all intents and purposes, his consciousness or sense of "I" was now fully within the cameras. I found this profoundly disturbing because if our senses can be tricked so easily, it means that 'I' could actually be a brain in a glass jar having my senses stimulated artificially!

I could actually be elsewhere being tricked into believing that I am in London!

How could you tell the difference? In some ways, this is what the popular Matrix films depicted (in more dramatized form).

The Matrix is a computer-generated reality programme run by an alien race which is plundering the earth. Each human is 'asleep' in a watery cocoon. They are also wired up to an artificial reality computer system and have their senses stimulated whilst a simulated film of reality is played to them. They are oblivious to the truth and believe fully that they are living a 'real' life with real experiences.

Many years ago, I had the experience of watching 'Alien 4D' at one of the large American theme parks in Florida. I sat in a very narrow chair that vibrated to simulate movement and had on a visor that showed me an extremely horrific and disturbing film of aliens on a space-craft chasing me around.

The experience was so real to me, that to this day, I can still remember and vividly 'see' the drooling fearsome alien, eyeball to eyeball with me. I remember feeling its breath on my face, that was in fact created by steam or spray from a gadget in the chair. Suffice to say, I was truly terrified! The soundtrack was played so close to my ears, it felt as if it really was my reality in that moment. Now of course, on some level I was obviously still in touch with the part of me that knew I had just voluntarily walked into the theatre. Therefore, I didn't have the heart attack that I am sure that I would have had, if, I had experienced this scenario in my regular everyday reality. Nevertheless, I did experience a range of very vivid, fear-inducing physical sensations!

Think about this, however. Had I been born straight into that theatre with no knowledge of any outside world, how could I have known that that experience was not my 'real' life?

I firmly believe that this world is a dream, a Maya or illusion. I hope to be able to demonstrate how fluid and under your control (by nature of your thoughts) this reality really is. If this is all a dream then I believe when you remove the veil caused by fear and wake up from your nightmare, all that remains is Heaven. My idea of 'heaven' is a positively joyous life of peace and unity. Heaven then will reflect that state!

However, what you choose to believe is completely up to you. Free will is God-given but this next little example demonstrates as clearly as I can give it to you, that what you choose will have very different outcomes.

So please allow me to relate the story of my 'Strawberry Moment' to illustrate the incredible importance of choice and the fragility of truth in one's life.

I am a dedicated and unashamed worshipper of the summer sun. Whenever the sun is out, I am out and usually in my small but beautiful garden. In this particular summer, I had sat in the same spot after work, every day that week. On the day in question I had been sitting out for about twenty minutes.

My life was just beginning to emerge from the dark night of depression and I was seeing so many coincidences and synchronistic events that on some days I felt like life was truly miraculous. I absolutely loved that feeling. As I sat there sipping my tea, I suddenly noticed a fully-grown, bright red strawberry hanging over the edge of a flower pot by my legs and to me it seemed like it had literally just appeared out of nowhere!

I was confused because I had never planted strawberries. I had never seen any sign in the preceding days of this fruit growing. And yet here it was: a juicy, luscious, fully-grown strawberry. My favourite fruit too. It was as if it had just appeared as my personal gift from God; my miracle. I became very excited and started texting my friends and family.

Now I am sure that most of them read my text and just rolled their eyes. No-one seemed to understand my sudden excitement about the world or share my new-found delight in everything around me. But interestingly, my oldest but most cynical friend rang me and informed me quite assuredly that a bird must have flown over and excreted the seeds into my pot.

I fell from walking on air to a crash and burn in the space of a few minutes. *"Damn"*, I thought, *"There is a rational explanation after all…"*

However, as I sat there, I began to wonder why I had not seen any evidence of the strawberry growing and developing before that moment.

Then it hit me and I suddenly realised that no-one held the bag of truth. My friend could not prove her case because of the aforementioned anomalies and I could not prove that it was a miracle. This seemingly insignificant incident became a major turning point in my life because I suddenly realised that I could choose whichever version of the story served me best.

I could choose to live in the mastery and magic of life or in the drudgery of physical existence.

"There are two ways to live your life. One is as if nothing is a miracle. The other is though everything is a miracle" as Einstein once said. I realised in that moment that simply because there may have been a rational explanation for an event, it did not necessarily make it true. Sometimes we 'know' something instinctively, but we have forgotten how to trust ourselves. By ignoring our own tremendous sense of intuition, we often end up living the beliefs, fears and values of everyone around us!

The difference between how the two worlds felt was enough to ensure that in that very moment I made a life-changing shift of focus. I decided that I would always 'believe' the explanation or point of view that was most beneficial for *my* health and well-being!

I now choose to live in the mastery. The truth, I now realise, is only ever a matter of my perception, as is everything else in life.

The Buddha Siddhartha Gautama advised us all to *"Believe nothing, no matter where you read it, who said it, unless it agrees with your own reason"*.

So let us now look at the very nebulous subject of perception and how it works with the Ego's trick of reversing and confusing cause and effect.

As I previously said by reversing cause and effect, the Ego is able to confuse you and consequently, you become unable to solve your real problems. It sends you looking for the cause of your problems externally towards other people, places or things, when really there only is ever one cause and that is the mind. The tool that allows the Ego to use the confusion so well is projection. By projecting blame - which is really cause - on to other people or objects, you will suffer the effects.

A practical example might be when you blame someone else for making you late: you are saying that they are the cause and the effect was your tardiness. They (presumably) did not chain you to their wrist or padlock the door. Thus in reality, you could have left without them. Therefore, on some level at least, you chose to be late.

Whenever you blame an outside source you know that projection is in play.

Now the Ego will protest and try to defend itself. Any time that you feel the need to defend yourself you are saying that you must have been attacked. Attack can only come through another body (or thing) and so the perceived attack looks like it is coming from another person. He or she made you late. However, the projection of blame is actually yours to own because you know subconsciously, that you made that decision to wait for them and be late as well.

Again, when you make any decision you must accept that you are always

Mind and Body Effect Exercise

1. Stand with eyes closed, arms by your side and take some deep breaths in and out.

2. Think of a time when you felt sad or disappointed. Run the memory like a film in the mind over and over as if you are there again. Let the same feelings come over you as if it were today. Do this for about 2 minutes.

3. Notice how your body feels. Does it feel a little heavier perhaps? What has happened to your physical stance? Has the head and shoulders dropped? Has the sides of the mouth dropped? Are you slumped a little?

4. Now immediately change the state and think of a time when you felt really, really happy. Run the memory like a film in the mind over and over, as if you are there again. Let the same feelings come over you. Do this for about 2 minutes.

5. Notice how your body feels. Does it feel a little lighter perhaps? What has happened to your physical stance? Has the head and shoulders lifted again? Has the sides of the mouth risen to a smile? Are you standing straighter now?

This exercise is a quick way to show that just by asking you to think about different scenarios I can affect your physicality almost instantly.

Remember physiology follows thought!

Now consider this: if every thought is having a similar effect and grows in strength the longer that you hold onto that thought - what are you doing to your body everyday? More to the point, what are all the news stories, negative social media and horror films doing to your physical health everyday?

honouring your biggest motivator. Therefore, your defence might be *"Well I couldn't leave her behind as how would she get there without my car?"*, for example. So your biggest motivation is to be caring, which is really the need to be lovable, likable or an asset. As we will see in more detail in the chapter on fear, this is our strongest and most primal motivator because it keys into your survival instinct. Therefore, the real cause of the problem is the choice you made to be late and so the lateness is in fact the effect. The issue here really isn't why you made that choice but the very fact that it was you who did make the choice.

Therefore you are the only cause of your lateness, not your friend!

You may be familiar with the story of the scapegoat in the Bible. The Priest would call the community together and everyone who had sinned would lay their hands on the head of the goat. This was a symbolic transfer of their sins on to the goat, who was then driven out of and away from the community. Therefore, the community felt absolved of their sins and would not have to be reminded of them by seeing the goat. In some ways this is how the Ego uses projection. It projects things out and away so you will not have to be reminded that these are your issues. You do not have to face your own guilt.

So where there is blame, you are projecting the cause away from you and creating a scapegoat.

This actually is the Ego covering the fact that you are not owning your decisions, through hidden fear of any unwanted consequences. Again we will explore this in more detail in the chapter on fear.

If you had decided to not be late and leave without your friend, she may be so upset that you left her that she may disown you or verbally attack you. These actions would cause you pain and as I have said, you as a body are biologically programmed to move away from pain and towards pleasure. Therefore, on some level you decided that the consequences of being late were less painful than the consequences of letting your friend down. The true cause of being late was then your assessment of the consequences of your two choices, in that moment.

Now that you have owned that you were late because you chose your friend over being on time, you have become the cause *and* the effect. Thus, there is no problem any more. The friend that you attacked by projecting blame on to them now suffers no attack and therefore there can be no ill effect. Consequently, you have taken an action previously perceived as negative and instead took ownership of your decisions. By doing so, you have strengthened your own integrity. You have also strengthened your relationship with your friend. And finally, you have taken a mighty tool away from the Ego. Therefore you have created a positive and correct order for cause and effect.

Now this is a clear and concise example but we play the confusion of cause and effect game everywhere and sometimes it is so surreptitious that it can easily be missed.

There was a time when I fell into a rage when I couldn't get the lid off of a tin of paint. I had projected the cause of my anger onto the lid when really it was because this struggle was in fact highlighting my sense of powerlessness. I had a belief programme running that DIY is men's work. It was highlighting my belief that I was alone and having to do my own DIY. It was also highlighting an unconscious fear that as a woman, I was physically weak. It didn't help that my son came straight down later and easily opened the lid!

So again the cause of my suffering was the belief that I was weak. 'I am weak' is a clear instruction to the brain that will then instruct the body to act accordingly 'making' me physically weak. If I programme the computer with the belief that I am weak, that is all it can show me on the screen of my life because believing is seeing.

You may project the blame onto alcohol when perhaps you have said the wrong thing, when you are out socialising. You may claim that the dark, rainy morning is the cause of your depression today. You may accredit the cause of your being overweight to your genes. You may think that person who criticises you is to blame because you are now upset.

No!

The true cause is that you are allowing these things to affect you or devolving responsibility for your action and reactions. Nobody can affect you unless you allow them to. Therefore, if you are ever upset it is because of how you perceive the words or action. *You* are allowing the bad weather to stop you doing what you say that you want to do. *You* are taking whatever has been said as truth rather than just one person's opinion. Any judgement or criticism, no matter who it comes from, is neutrally just a few words leaving someone's mouth. It talks of what *they* like, want or think. That has nothing to do with you unless you allow yourself to take it personally. Just say *"Thank you for your opinion"*, assess whether it is good information for you or not and then get on with your life. Or better still, look for the belief programme of victimhood and do something about that!

And here's the big one. You may think that the cause of your troubles today, is because your parents didn't love you.

Yes of course, we have already discussed how childhood programming and old files will affect you today. But that's only because *you* haven't taken responsibility to clear them out. Therefore the cause isn't poor parenting. The true cause is the fact that you are still behaving as a child. The effect is that those parents can push your buttons or open old files that should have been updated or deleted altogether by the time that you are an adult.

Sometimes you may unconsciously want to see those things so that you can blame other people or other things for the way that you are making *yourself* feel. In reality, the unconscious is projecting everything out so that you can see what is still in the archives causing you pain and heal it.

You can also project onto whole groups of people such as: the council, the government, immigrants or the opposite gender. But the truth is the cause is always your beliefs and fears about the subject. The cause is always in your mind. Projection is caused by unaccepted, denied, repressed or suppressed traits that are too painful to face and so you want that scapegoat driven away from you. That is exactly why the worse you think that someone else is, the better that you feel about yourself in comparison. You have successfully used them as a scapegoat whilst denying your own projection!

You may have learned this as a very successful strategy from early in childhood because what did you do when you were in trouble with your parents or teachers? You say things like *"It wasn't me, mum. It was Johnny"*. Or you may come up with any excuse or logical reason that, like the magician, will distract the attention and focus away from where the real cause is. As long as the true cause is inverted or confused, you do not have to face yourself, or more importantly, own all of your choices and decisions.

The Ego is afraid of you knowing that you are always the cause because then the risk is that you will be able to solve the problem once and for all.

When there was water coming through my son's ceiling, the water coming through the small hole looked like the cause of the problem. The effect was a wet floor. I could have plastered over the ceiling and everything would look fine; problem solved. The Ego though would have then been very happy because it had tricked me again. It stopped me looking for the real cause which was the tile missing from the roof. Pull up the weeds in your garden and the garden will look beautiful for a while. A month later here is another problem: more weeds and you must complete the process again. If you had looked for the true cause of the weeds which is the root you could have solved the problem quicker, easier and permanently. The Ego is a master recycler of problems because *you* never empty the bin permanently.

In the same way then, you must always look past the initial idea of cause to what is really behind that cause.

The Ego thrives on problems because our definition of the word problem is usually negative. It thrives on them because it is our perceived problems with outside causes that appear to keep us weak and vulnerable. It uses the law that you cannot change an effect to its advantage.

The Ego wants you continuously doing, running or worrying about where the next problem will pop up. That keeps you unstable, fearful and away from peace. The Ego has no home or function in a peaceful mind and thus fears its own death should your problems disappear. So in some ways it becomes a dog eat dog battle. It's either you play the Ego's game and it gets to survive or it threatens to take you down with it.

The simple solution is to deal with the ultimate cause that is unseen but that you know exists behind the obvious. The real cause is the root. The weeds are only the effect. Dig for and deal with the root and the problem is fixed forever. It's true that the Ego may then displace the problem elsewhere but if you diligently do your self-development work, eventually all those tricks become revealed and the Ego becomes unravelled and powerless. In the same way, if you keep gardening until you have pulled out all the roots, your garden can remain a clear oasis of colour and beautiful blooms.

Let me give you a word of warning though. It is not good enough to pull out the roots, as nature is never wasteful: *"Nature abhors a void"*, as Albert Einstein said, and so we must plant something of choice in its place.

It is not enough just to catch the confusion of cause and effect but you must reverse it back to its proper order. By owning you are the cause or the problem, you bring both cause and effect back together in the mind where they were created. This then cancels out the cause and nullifies the effect.

Be aware that the mind will come up with all types of crazy concepts and stories to hide or confuse why things are happening.

I have watched my mind on so many occasions create all different concepts about why something has happened or is a certain way. The Ego wants me to be occupied with any external story or cause that fits. It is irrelevant if it is true; only that it fits. The Ego is never interested in truth or fairness. The only thing that the Ego is interested in is its ability to control and survive. So the answer is never, ever external. The reflection in a mirror is always the effect. The external world is the screen of your mind. It is almost as if you are watching the shadows on the cave wall and mistaking it for reality just like Plato's prisoners. But really the cause is behind you on the walkway; the freedom of your mind.

The confusion of cause and effect with objects is seen most clearly perhaps in the use of medicines. Hospitals, doctors and some therapies mostly treat symptoms of mental health issues.

Whether it be due to lack of awareness, time or money, it is most unfortunate that the medical profession is mostly geared up to alleviate symptoms presented but not search for the deeper cause. If you have a headache, (cause), you will take a tablet to deal with the pain which is the perceived effect. But what caused the headache? Yes of course take the tablet and the headache disappears but what stress or strain have you been under that may have caused it in the first place? Why have you created this experience? The answer to one or more of these questions holds the key to the real cause. But the Ego doesn't want you to heal the real problem which is the stress because then you could always be healthy and one of its tools to threaten you with is lost forever. Therefore, it tells you that the headache is the problem and when that is gone all will be fine. But the root cause of stress still exists and therefore will you make you ill again in the near future.

The cause is always in the mind because that is all that really exists. The body is in the mind, not the mind in the body.

As you will see from the next chapter, the Ego uses the body for control. You will be able to see why it is so important not to fall into the trap of believing there is an outside cause and that you must suffer the effects. This makes you a victim to life. The cause can only be in one place and that is the powerful, creative mind.

Own all your choices with brutal honesty and the sharp sword of the Ego becomes a blunt instrument that cannot hurt you anymore.

Quick Summary

1. Reality is a mind-based projection (dream) that you experience on the screen of an apparently external environment.

2. This is your creation: Your Universe, or *You*-nique version of your reality.

3. It includes two different thought systems that in and of themselves, are almost two different levels of reality. One is the thought system of the Spirit that recognises that the world is a dream and we are all One. The Ego believes in the small, *separated* self that lives in a hard and fast physical reality that happens to you.

4. How you perceive the world is down to your choice of which thought system to believe in each moment of your life. This is your perception and is wholly subjective.

5. In order to make you choose the Ego's thought system, it confuses cause and effect so that you believe that the cause of your problem is external and therefore unchangeable.

6. Your behaviour is the resulting action of a story you are telling about any event or your preceding thought. It is therefore an effect and not a cause.

Exercise - Owning your Projection

1. Take a current or recent situation in your life where you have blamed someone or something for a negative feeling or behaviour that you have experienced.

2. Accept the cause is how that you perceive the problem and that this is your projection. Spot how the Ego has confused cause and effect by blaming.

3. Own any decision that you made and understand the motivation that caused your choice.
E.g. Choosing not to upset the friend over the consequences of being late.

4. Look at the belief programmes in play. (Be especially aware of the Ego trick that if you are not lovable, likable or an asset then you will not survive.)

5. Decide whether or not the belief programmes or old files opened, need updating or deleting. Use the band exercise perhaps to overwrite an old belief pattern.

6. Decide what will be your strategy for success the next time this situation or one like it, occurs again.

7. Keep practicing catching your projections and the reversal of cause and effect over both people and things in your life.

Chapter 4

The Ego and its Temple

"It is sown a natural body, it is raised a spiritual body. If there is a natural body, there is also a spiritual body." Corinthians 15:44

A few years ago, on a retreat that I was leading in Kent, a student asked me where the Ego came from. I had never really thought about it and the first thought I had was *'How am I supposed to know?'* But to my amazement, a whole story unfolded as I began speaking. This was the idea of the business model as I explained in the last chapter. I should just explain that for many years now, I have believed that teaching and healing is completed through me, by my Spirit 'side'. I know that I, as my small-self 'I' am just the means through which the communication is delivered.

I am continuously amazed by what comes through and I now trust it implicitly.

A Course in Miracles teaches us that the body is merely a tool of communication between bodies that appear to be separate. I use the words 'appear to be' separate because, as I have explained earlier, even mainstream science is leaning towards the fact that this is a thought-based reality. Therefore, the physical body would have to be just another thought or idea. Thoughts can never be separated (seen-apart) from their source and every idea is inspired to fulfill a need.

It is possible for the world and the body to be a thought projection whilst your experience of it is still very real. Amputees can experience phantom limb syndrome where they still feel pain even though there is no limb there to feel the pain. When my son was little and had Quincy (a very severe form of throat infection), he experienced hallucinations brought on by a soaring temperature. He was absolutely petrified by tigers that he could clearly see. However, these were just projections from his mind. They were not real but his *experience* of it certainly was.

For him - in the only moment that was important or real - tigers *were in the room*. That's why I respectfully remind you to keep questioning everything that you take for granted. Look at the evidence of your experience or of what you actually know. As I said previously, the Ego will want to sabotage any movement towards a more expansive, freeing view of yourself or life. It wants everything just how it is and you just where you are: small and controllable. So if it says, *"I can't believe that"*, ask it to produce hard evidence to the contrary, and *"Everyone knows…."* is not an acceptable answer!

Whatever you believe about reality, let us just say that it is beneficial to accept the notion that this is a dream so that we can take back control of it. Remember from the last chapter that whatever you programme into the computer is all that it can display. Remember also, that you see *your* Universe. You can *only* see your Unique Version of the world. If you programme *'My Universe is concrete and life happens to me'* then that is what you will experience. This creates a sense of powerlessness. If you programme or believe that *'The Universe is made up of my thoughts and beliefs'* now you must experience that on the screen. If the problem is in your head - a problem of perception - then you become the solution *because* you can change your mind. The solution simply means correcting your perception. This is the most powerful state and that is why I recommend developing the belief that you are sole creator of everything.

However, whatever you think, the current, mainstream belief is that we are physical bodies. Therefore, you are much more likely to listen to my message and allow me to help, if I stand before you as a physical body. Bodies then are focussing mechanisms. They not only focus you into time and space, but this helps you to relate to, and differentiate yourself from, other people and things.

Think about your 'Wise Inner Advisor' or guidance that you receive via your heart or as a voice in your head. You may experience this guidance as instinct or intuition. But what do most people do with that insight? If you are like most people you will not trust it and probably ignore it! There is a common belief that if you cannot see it then it doesn't exist. Obviously there are those people, like myself who are open to information gleaned from their own Spirit voice or by another's ability to channel information. We appreciate such knowledge as being just as valuable as that delivered by a 'living' physical body. However, we are definitely in the minority.

Therefore, I think that it is generally true, that most people wouldn't be able to benefit from anyone's help or teaching if they couldn't interact with them as a body.

It is also true that you would not be able to function in the world. The body allows you to differentiate yourself from other people and things. In this way you become able to experience your thoughts, wants and wishes 'out there'. If you remember from the previous chapter, the brain filters to produce what *you* want and expect to see. As we also discussed, what you are actually doing through the mechanism of projection is interacting, not with other people per say, but with other aspects of yourself. That is not to say that there are not other people 'out there' as such, but that you will see them as you wish to see them.

Again, I reiterate that there are two levels of reality that I am dealing with here. There is the level of the dream and the other people are dream characters in your head. But as you are currently engrossed in the dream as being totally real, other people are 'real' and appear separate from you but you will still see them as you wish to see them because of projection.

On both levels the idea of bodies is a useful one. Bodies are an idea that fulfils a need of the Ego. Bodies are ideal to project onto and to be in what appears to be, separate relationships with. Bodies are akin to the tiny, mirrored tiles of the glitter ball. It is easier for us to hide from and deny our unwanted traits if there is someone else to blame. That someone has to have a body, especially if you want to drive it away. This is where the Ego does its best work because only another body can attack. There is even the saying *'That guns don't kill people; people do'* that demonstrates this well.

Something that is whole cannot attack or be attacked. Attack needs a duality: a perpetrator and a victim. Someone that is sane would not attack themselves. Therefore, the thought that we are all One, just energy and Eternal beings cannot co-exist with the idea of the physical body. We have to make a choice on some level which story we are going to believe. In reality, the choice is impossible whilst we continue to deny or suppress the knowledge that we are projecting out on to others. It becomes impossible to accept that injury to the body comes from our own projections, to continue to do it *and then to claim to be sane!*

You appear to experience pain in the body but it has been proven that pain is experienced in the brain once the sensors from the site of injury have informed the brain of what is happening. The brain finds a story or tries to make sense of the data from its cache of past experiences (oven, hot, burn) and instructs the body to act accordingly (move the hand off of the stove).

There is a powerful condition called the Placebo effect. A new drug coming to market must beat the relief recorded by the placebo test group if it is to get a license. In tests, the placebo group believe that they are taking the drug but actually take a sugar pill. More often than not the healing or recovery of the placebo group is equal to or better than the group that are actually taking the real drug. Such is the power of the mind in facilitating healing. Why? It is because all illness and pain is of the mind. Believe that you are healed and it is so. *"This will heal me"* is a direct instruction from the mind. Physiology can only follow thought as every thought is an instruction to both mind *and* body.

Just think about the word disease. 'Dis' to me indicates 'distanced from'. Therefore, disease I believe occurs when you are 'distanced from ease'; which is stress. So the words dispirited or disheartened are really describing how you feel when you are distanced from your heart or Spiritual Self. This is experienced as stress, anxiety or depression.

How do you in fact experience stress? It may lead to effects of heart palpitations, sweaty palms or headaches but the cause is in the mind. You have to be stressed *by* something. Therefore, the cause is your negative story or definition about said thing. If you have a negative definition then you are not thinking with the Spirit mind and are then distanced from Spirit or dis-spirited.

Therefore, it is clearly your thoughts about your life that are causing physical symptoms in the body. The body cannot do anything without an instruction from the mind. The body cannot think for itself, move itself or decide anything. The brain and body are hardware. That is why when the brain stops working (when you are brain-dead), so does the body! The body is merely part of the screen of your reality onto which you project your thoughts. Therefore, it is pure logic that any ailment or sickness must have a mental source. I will show you the evidence of how your mind affects your body at the end of this chapter.

Thus it is important to remember that healing goes one way, like the parent-child relationship. A mother gives birth to the child but the child cannot give birth to her. Therefore, the mother makes the child in the same way that the mind creates the body. It is a one way relationship and so the body cannot make the mind. As I said earlier, mind can continue with a broken body but a body cannot continue without consciousness.

It is demonstrated by the placebo effect that the mind can heal the body but a body does not heal the mind. The body cannot tell you how you feel. The body is innate hardware. It can only send sensory information to the brain which then interprets that information. This interpretation comes from comparing old information and matching patterns. Therefore, for all intents and purposes you will always have the same pain and the same reason for it. The brain simply matches old patterns from its files.

If the first time that you drank alcohol you had a hangover, then your file includes the belief that alcohol gives you hangovers. This actually would likely already be in your unconscious files before you took your first sip because it is likely that you will have seen the effects of alcohol either in your own life, been taught by family members, through media or even anecdotally. The belief is activated, (or the file opens), every time you drink alcohol. The brain notes that you drank alcohol and so instructions are given to the body and then - hey presto - your hangover is created. In some ways then this is a self-inflicted attack due to you not being careful about what you allow to be stored in your files. It simply cannot be only the alcohol because otherwise all people that drink it *must* have hangovers but we know that is not the case!

The only way that the Ego can get you to continue to ignore your own self-attack is to convince you that there are real people and things out there. Alcohol is the cause and hangover is the effect. However, as we know, it is the belief that is the cause and not the alcohol. The Ego is using the body, which has no mind of its own because it is a shadow reflection, to project on to.

Because you know that you can attack others, there is no reason to expect that other people and other things will not do that to you. And of course they will, not because they are real but because it is actually your expectation being played out onto the screen. All attack is of your mind; your perception and thus is self attack.

After all, you are likely to believe wholeheartedly that it is the physical body that needs defence, can become ill, injured, experience pain and be killed. These are all things that allegedly come from an external source. You project onto a myriad of things that could harm the body apart from other people: viruses, cancer, germs, toxins, etc.

Consequently, the Ego tricks you into seeing just two choices of belief. One is that you are a truly separate body that can be injured by an external source; or the other is that you are mad and you are allowing your own thoughts to attack yourself. Neither of these options leaves you with hope of escaping suffering. You are either mad or vulnerable. You cannot do much about madness but you can protect yourself if you are vulnerable, and so you choose the latter.

The Ego vehemently believes that the body is real and it has become its home; its temple. The Ego will defend it to the death, attack to protect before any threat is made real and rules your life providing for its every perceived need and want.

If you stop and think about it, it is shocking to see how everything you do is aimed at meeting one of the aforementioned aims.

You get up and cleanse the body, dress it, feed it; you entertain it; work to get money and pleasures for it. The chair is there for you to rest it on; the light allows it to see and the scent of your mate's body make you feel good. You get angry at drivers that threaten your body, and you become angry, attack or get defensive at any perceived criticism, negative judgement or threatened loss.

Scarcity and lack are irrelevant without a body because it is only the body that needs 'things'. Fear is impossible without a body because it is seemingly a body that can experience pain or die. You have to continuously fight off illness, lack, danger and death. The Ego controls your life via the body and you do not even realise it.

The Ego manages to hide its ploys in two ways. Firstly, the Ego confuses pleasure and pain. It will often present something that appears beneficial but is actually a loss. Let us imagine that you have been inspired by Spirit to give up smoking. The little nagging voice or nudge towards making the decision yourself, has been heard. As nothing can overcome your free will, the Spirit can encourage but the decision has to come from you. The inspiration is not really about smoking but about showing you that you are a powerful creator and not the body.

The Ego wonders where on earth this idea has come from and starts to try to override it because it fears you being happy, healthy and empowered. So the outraged Ego tempts you with 'cravings' for cigarettes. It will aim to make you believe that you are too weak and worthless to succeed in overcome the craving for the cigarette. *"Don't bother trying"* it whispers, *"You will only fail and then feel worse about yourself..."* It will suggest perhaps that no-one can overcome cravings as tobacco is addictive and that addictions are of the body and you have no control over your body. It may suggest that you need cigarettes to keep your stress levels down or even that you love the 'draw'. It will suggest that there is a gain to keep smoking and you will lose so much more by stopping.

So having made a strong case for the benefits of having that cigarette, it sits back and laughs as you now suffer the long-term effects of proving how weak and worthless you really are. It knows that it has got you back smoking and in a low vibration which is exactly where it wants you. It has also just reinforced to you that cravings and addiction are of the body and thus out of your control. It has just reinstated its power and your vulnerability as a slave to the physical body.

At first glance you may say *'That doesn't make sense as the Ego would want a healthy body so that it can live longer'*. But the truth is that, sabotage of its own temple is more important than - or should I say it feels like a safer option – the risk of losing any of its control to the unseen force of Spirit. The Ego doesn't really fear death because it knows the body is not real and consciousness *will* go on with or without a body. We will look into this a little later.

The original beliefs that you are weak and tobacco is addictive are simply belief programmes running in your mind, otherwise how can anyone give up immediately without any physical effects-which they clearly do? The computer can only play out the programmes it has stored. Therefore, by opening the file on smoking, associated files on the body must open. This is because you are likely to want to give up because of the negative and life threatening effects on the body. Your file of beliefs about the physical body is going to be huge unless you have taken any time to clear it out, which most of us do not. If you have tried to give up previously, then in your file labelled smoking, all of those past failures get activated too. In some ways it becomes inevitable that you would fail as your old files will project the same beliefs onto the screen. You may fail not because you are weak but because you opened the failure file. This may be full of other examples of your past failures not only with smoking but at school, with lovers, who knows!

Often we are not doing things for the reasons that we think we are and this is a fine example. Whilst you have set the intention to abstain, the Ego will tempt with the cigarette as a temporary relief from the cravings and stress. It presents these as a gain but then swiftly swipes that gain away by the resulting and more painful loss of self esteem (and health) now you have failed-again!

The Ego has successfully heightened your own sense of guilt that you let yourself and perhaps even your family down. As you may know, guilt is inextricably linked with punishment which must follow somewhere. Guilt - the Ego's sharpest sword and can cut you to the quick on even the most trivial of matters. If there is no-one to punish you, you will punish yourself by holding on to the painful notion that you let yourself or others down. Guilt feels so bad because it taunts you with the idea that punishment will ensue even if it is not here now. Thus, the expectation of the punishment can be worse than the punishment itself.

This is the Ego's second ploy.

Have you ever thought about the consequences of not doing those morning rituals for the body, for example?

Take a moment to answer that question.

Usually the answer given is something like this: if I don't do all the cleansing and care of the body I will smell, be unattractive and eventually be alone and rejected. This then brings up a deeper question: Why do you care about what other people think about you? What's wrong with being alone?

No matter how much you protested that you did not care what people thought about you, you would always do your morning cleansing ritual. When you ask why, you will see this revelation:

You must be likable, lovable or an asset or you will not survive.

Here is how I like to make this idea relevant to people. Let's imagine it is early in our development and we are alive in the 'cavemen' days. Life is very simple and is focussed on surviving threats and having our basic needs met. This would be things like having enough to eat and drink. We have very primal brains.

Later in our development we begin to work out that there is safety in numbers.

Q: If I am out alone and a tiger appears, what are my chances of survival?

A: Very low to non-existent as I'm unlikely to be able to outrun it or fight it off alone.

Q: If I am out with other members of my tribe, I am the best hunter and feed them all and now a tiger appears. What are my chances of survival?

A: Well my odds increase greatly because the tribe is going to fight tooth and nail to keep me alive because I am feeding them! I am an asset and they need me. Presumably they like and love me for that too.

Q: If I am out with other members of my tribe but I am the lazy person who sleeps all day and no-one likes. A tiger appears again. What are my chances of survival now?

A: Well my odds decrease greatly because they are not going to fight to save me because I am not an asset to them! I am a liability. Presumably they will not like or love me either. They may even feed me to it to escape!!

Conclusion: We have deeply engrained, primal programming which says:
You must be likable, lovable or an asset or you will not survive.

We still have that very primal, reptilian brain that runs our fight or flight system. Its main focus is to protect the body. Remember that the brain was formed from the genetic material that came from your parents, which came from their parents and all the way back to the start of the conscious form. No information is ever lost, especially if it is of evolutionary benefit. All knowledge remains in your DNA and so the history of the Universe is in every cell. Therefore, on a deep unconscious level, you have primal programming that says you *need* to care about what others think about you.

Or so the Ego would have us believe.

The irony is that you do not live in those times and conditions any more and there is absolutely no reason why you could not survive on your own. It may be hard or even unwanted but most of us could get a job, feed and protect ourselves.

Often we run ourselves ragged trying to take care of everyone else and fall into the trap of over-caring. You may waste your time trying to prove how lovable and likable you are to the extent that you are never able to be assertive or make the right choices for you. You will often end up living the limited life you think that you *should*, rather than the one that you really want to live.

This is a great example of why it is important to review and update the files of your mind because you are not doing things for the reason that you think you are. Things that appear to be a gain are masking a more painful and usually longer term loss. What are a few days of being uncomfortable when compared to the long term health gains of quitting smoking? When you bring cost versus gain to the light the answer is clear.

This concept is vital to understand because if you can expose the tricks that the Ego is playing then you no longer need fall foul of them.

The Ego presents what you are doing as a positive thing when really it is tying you in to the belief that you are a body. It stalks you with death by seeding that there are other bodies that can attack and kill you. Therefore, you must do everything that you can to make yourself acceptable to others.

Does this sound like how to have a peaceful life to you? This is a crippling fear programme that you probably didn't even know that you have running. It requires a lot of tiring work, the completion of continuous rituals and eternal scanning of your environmental feedback to keep the body safe. The Ego loves to keep you running, endlessly doing and too tired or overwhelmed to change. Thus you end up actually feeling dispirited and disheartened.

Part of that running and never ending work must be presented as positive to keep you engaged.

Even life enhancing activities such as learning, growth and evolution are presented as obviously positive but are essentially tricks. These are just ploys by the Ego to again reinforce the belief that you are a physical body that can and must always improve. It will pretend to go along with things as a ruse to cloak its never ending mission to control you. How many self help books have you bought but not done any of the practical exercises in them? Why? It is because the voice of the Ego gently whispers *"Ok I'll humour you. Buy the book and I will activate the 'you are too lazy to do the exercises' belief"*.

No! You are a perfect Spirit. You are part of All That Is which is already complete; all knowing and unchanging. What else could there be to learn, to evolve into, if you are not a physical body?

The Ego has tied you so closely into believing that you are the body; that you are a physically defined piece of matter with an unchangeable identity, that *will* die, that most have lost all hope. Remember the body can 'die' but consciousness is Eternal otherwise *every-thing* would cease to be.

Whilst in the dream, unless you can identify with yourself as the *creator* of the dream, *and* as a dream character *seemingly* in the body, you remain trapped. Unless you can identify with your self as Spirit or turn to a higher source such as God, you remain at the mercy of a ruthless dictator whose only aim is to protect its own survival via the body. That is why the Ego doesn't want you believing that you are Spirit and cannot die. It fears God and so will continuously seek to show you that you cannot be 'His' powerful Son. If this becomes true; that you are Eternal, a powerful creator and that the Universe is just an illusion or dream then the Ego has lost all of its power over you. However, if you have no identification of yourself as Spirit then there is nowhere else to turn. You will gladly retreat back to the safe and comforting arms of what you have always known - the Ego. You will continue to be grateful for the small crumbs of comfort that it appears to offer.

You will be grateful that you are still alive, whilst all the time being stalked by death. That surely is existing and not truly living.

However, the good news is that the body can become a tool of learning for the mind, through which you unravel the Ego and overcome its tricks.

Therefore, you don't necessarily have to stop your morning cleansing ritual or start taking unnecessary risks. But learning and then knowing why you are doing something, allows you to access the choice-point and to make a positive choice about *why* you are doing it. Completing a ritual through unconscious fear has a very different vibrational effect on the body than completing it because you want to. Want and need are very different vibrations and affect the body (and consequently your life) in different ways due to the Law of Attraction (LOA).

I have already given you a brief introduction to LOA and so here I will just discuss it from the perspective of how it affects the physical body.

Basically the LOA states that 'what you put out you will receive back'. If you put out angry words you will attract angry people and negative events into your life. If you are on radio station Angry 194 then you will only attract other 'listeners' from Angry 194. You are continuously transmitting a vibration. This output is through words and thoughts. It is important to realise that any action is first a thought form from the mind. Every word, thought and action has a different frequency or vibration.

Say to yourself and think generally about the idea of 'getting'. Then do the same with 'receiving'.

Which feels lighter to you?

For most people I have asked the latter feels lighter or better. Why should that be as they look like the same act in reality? This is actually because we have a file for each word with a specific definition and related beliefs and experiences. So your file for receiving is slightly different for your file on getting. The opening of every word file brings with it an emotional resonance that has an effect on the body and its vibrational state. This is often unconscious and so you are unaware of the continuously changing state unless:

A) You stop and reflect on how this situation made you feel.

B) It is such a change in vibration that it catches your attention and this will usually be because some action is required afterwards.

C) You catch the choice-point and choose with Spirit which may include no response whatsoever.

Now again, I have discovered another insidious ploy of the Ego in regards to our emotional system. I have noticed that when things are going well and the emotion present is happiness for example, my mind is very quiet. As soon as any negative emotion comes up I want to move way from it very quickly. As I've said, that emotion comes from the definition or story that you are telling about said event. But, because you believe emotion is *in* the body, the only options to deal with negative emotion apart from healing it are to suppress it or project it out and away from you. Therefore, you may make someone or something else the scapegoat. They get the blame for the reason you are upset: *"If only they would be or do something different then I could be happy."*

However, by suppressing, running away from or projecting the cause out, you lose the opportunity to choose with your right-mind. You lose the opportunity to learn from what the negative emotion is trying to show you about your beliefs. This is important because if you could overcome the Ego without attack or conflict, you would be able to reclaim control over it.

You can do this far more easily after an event, with the obvious benefit of hindsight and objectivity; when the emotion has cleared.

However, in the moment it is experienced, the negative emotion has already been expressed, recorded and has dampened your vibration. You have already fallen for the Ego's ploy. Consequently, it becomes a case of one step backwards remedied by one step forward again. You have not moved. Once you have done some self-reflection and healing work, you can recover the drop in vibration. However, you missed the opportunity to use it, like everything else that occurs, only as an opportunity to raise your vibration. By focussing on the cause of the emotion and not the effect felt in the body you can use it as a positive thing.

The best option was to not allow the event to affect your vibration in the first place: *'To turn the other cheek'* as the Bible says.

Now I am definitely not saying that to catch what happened with the benefit of hindsight is not important. At least you are not going backwards. But what I would say is that it is far better to not make the mistake that needs correcting in the first place.

As you will see in the chapter called Attack Spirals, the Ego ultimately wants you to blame other people and things for everything. It can then fully reinforce your fear that you as the body are vulnerable to attack.

The Ego doesn't want you to be able to stop things in the moment and choose with your right-mind. It will begrudgingly allow you to reflect afterwards because it knows its almost shutting the gate after the horse has bolted.

Another of those devices that the Ego uses the body for is to lock you into time and space. It limits your ability to travel, to achieve things and be all that you can be. More importantly it can be used to keep you away from things and others. It can become your prison rather than the vehicle of freedom.

Your unhappiness with your physical appearance for example, decreases your confidence and then limits your possibilities. The Ego will remind you continuously of the lacks and weaknesses of the body: you are a woman, you are too young, too old, not strong enough, the wrong colour etc. It also is a clever ruse to keep you away from your true beauty and magnificence as Spirit. The body is simply a piece of hardware that follows and more importantly, can only follow the instructions given to it from the mind. If this was not true or if the body was able to create for itself, your limbs would be doing whatever they wanted, whenever they wanted. Your body could take you off to the shops even if you as the mind decided that it wanted to go to the cinema instead. You perhaps tend to believe that the body has a mind of its own and is separate to your will but that simply does not make sense. The body can do nothing without an instruction from some level of the mind.

The stunning realisation about this though is profound. That means all sickness manifests with an instruction from the mind: on some deep level, it is a choice. Now obviously this will be unconscious to you and so we are not talking about blame. However, that doesn't change the fact that it still comes from you.

Now the first thing the Ego will interject with is *'I didn't choose this disease'*. However, it is true anything that you create has a perceived gain. You are biologically programmed to move towards pleasure and away from pain. Everything represents a choice and it will be the greatest motivator in the mind, in that moment that will be chosen.

Here are just a few of the gains of sickness: it brings you more love and attention, days off work, Social Security benefits, and gets you out of social commitments. If you think about it in terms of projection, would you really admit openly to any of these, especially if you have friends and family running around that are worrying or caring for you?

I used to do outreach work for the Alzheimer's Society and would often see carers become ill because they did not feel that they could live with the guilt of putting their husband or wife of 20, 30 or 40 years into a care-home. By manifesting (unconsciously) illness themselves, there was now a *valid* reason to move the partner into a home and escape the guilt. Now obviously I am not saying this is what happens in every case. However, I saw it happen often enough, after I had spent weeks trying to convince them that the move would be best for both of them, to recognise the pattern.

Again the fear of any negative judgement by others often ensured that the carer remained in an unhappy and health-destroying situation by what appears to be a positive act. In fact, the fear of being judged negatively was a bigger motivator than the care of themselves.

This is another of the Ego's favourite tricks which is to make an action appear to be positive whilst actually bringing on long term loss. We will look at this in depth later in the book but for now understand that all sickness helps to reinforce your belief that you are weak or deficient.

There is never a real or lasting gain that is worth the price of your health.

Because of the LOA, all sickness keeps us in a self-perpetuating cycle of low vibration which induces more sickness. If you are always in a state of powerlessness or victimhood you will attract things that make you feel that way, such as illness or attack. This is partly because you will believe that illness happens to you. A virus attacks you for example, from an external cause and therefore, the illness looks like the effect. The true cause is your *belief* that a virus can affect you, ensuring that is what you will experience.

Happy people are rarely ill. A high vibrational state means that illness, which is fear-based and of a low vibration, cannot be on the same 'high vibrational level' as them. A low vibrational state (someone that already feels low or down) will attract the virus because illness is low vibration: like attracts like. The current thoughts and beliefs about their life, affects the physiology (and thus vibration) and then make illness possible, if not more likely. If the virus is the true cause why does every *body* in the vicinity not become ill?

Again, this is another reason why the Ego loves you being unhappy. An unhappy person is more likely to be ill and therefore vulnerable, which only serves to reinforce the belief in the body.

That person is totally on the Ego's wavelength and thus controllable via perceived threats to the body.

If I am going to buy into your beliefs that you are physically sick then I have just reinforced the reality that we are bodies, for both of us. I have just reinforced both of our Ego's worldview. That is not to say that we should not be compassionate, but if we think about this on a vibrational level, the reason becomes obvious.

When you are ill you are saying that you feel low, down or blue: you are saying that your vibrational state is low. I then agree with and reinforce your illness by saying "*Oh poor you. Yes I know how that feels. I had that last year*". Remember that every word and thought creates an immediate vibrational effect in the body? The focus of my mind has now turned to my past pain too. So now all I have done is taken my vibration down to where yours is. Now we are both sitting at the bottom of the well together. Someone now has to come and rescue us both.

You would serve them and yourself better by putting your hand down and pulling them out of the well. That means by offering solutions to their problems but not focussing on the problem. The premise of LOA is that what you focus on you will attract more of. So keeping their spirits up with distractions, laughter or offering ideas for cures perhaps would serve you *and them* much better.

Sometimes illness becomes 'who you are' when you have bought into your own story about your body. If you have been continuously ill since childhood, you may have a definition or file about yourself as always being weak. As we have already said this becomes a case of 'believing is seeing'. Again this is not because it is necessarily true but because you are running the belief programme. This is then the only programme that the computer can display.

Sometimes feelings of guilt, frustration or the need for control can be used by the mind to bring on illness. Perhaps there is a belief that you need punishment, emotional release or you need to feel empowered in an area where you have little control. Eating disorders are an excellent example of the latter. If a young person has no control over their lives they will often use food to take back some control. This may be the only way that they may feel, they can control anything. Even if you were to force feed someone, they can choose to throw it up again later. The Ego's need for power overrides the natural instinct towards wellness. It becomes a case of cost verses gain to the Ego, which values control over everything.

There is a huge increase in auto-immune diseases. This is where the body essentially attacks itself.

I believe that this is perhaps a sign that knowledge about what the Ego is doing may be coming up from the unconscious and being projected out on to the body. I have already said the body as hardware, is simply a screen to project on to. Once people's awareness starts to grow about how all of this works, they can see what their root programme is and deal with it.

What do you instantly pay attention to and act on immediately, in life? The body! If you have any pains or illness you may immediately look for help or a remedy. However, you may suffer for years with a general mood of unhappiness, malaise or depression before you seek help. When you do not get the message that something in your life needs to change: the job, the relationship, quit smoking then the mind will try to get you to act by demonstrating it through the body.

When will you immediately quit the 60 hour a week job? The answer is only when you have nearly died from a heart attack.

When I was married, for a few years before we actually split I went through a phase of one illness after another. These ranged from recurrent sties to severe conjunctivitis and finally a detached retina. I was lucky not to lose my sight. The point is that if that happened to me now, I would immediately start looking for what it is that I am not seeing here? If I had known then, what I know now - that the cause was in my mind - I would have seen how unhappy and stressed I was. I needed to be out of that marriage. As soon as I left my husband my health improved overnight.

Louise Hay and others have clearly shown how most ailments have a direct correlation to the area of the body that reflects the negative or distorted thoughts in the mind. The newly emerging field of PNI-Psycho Neuro Immunology is also showing clear connections between the mind-body inter-faces.

So if the mind is choosing illness, it is also choosing aging and even death. Ageing for example, doesn't make sense if the whole body, as we are reliably informed by medical experts, is renewed over every two years. How does the same problem last three years unless we are recreating the same

The Ego Unravelled

problems from the same template in the mind?

I strongly believe that we choose, maybe not consciously, our time of passing. It has to be that way as nothing, not even God, can overcome your free will.

I have read extensively about people waiting to clear the hospital room of worried relatives before they passed. There are a multitude of stories of people waiting the arrivals of loved ones, or the next anniversary before they chose to let go. I witnessed my own Grandmother wait until all her responsibilities had been sorted and her son stayed overnight for the first time in decades before she chose to let go in peace. But the question remains why do you then die? We will explore this subject later in the book but for now let it suffice to say that death isn't what you may think it is.

I will leave you to just ponder this until later.

But just let me say this- All That Is, by its very nature must be complete and all inclusive. Therefore, it cannot change. You are part of All That Is. If you are a physical body that could die and cease to exist, All That Is would cease to be complete. It would now be less than it was and would have changed. That is impossible and so you cannot die or at least cease to exist in some form.

Now I fully realise that to stop believing that you are a body is extremely difficult and is contrary to all that you think you are. It flies in the face of your everyday experience and logic. But all of the ideas in this chapter are here to allow you to feel a sense of empowerment over the body. Once you see the tricks and games of the Ego you can stop falling for them any longer. Some self-reflection and honesty about how you use illness is urgently required. To question your beliefs about aging and dying can start to unravel the confusion of cause and effect that the Ego uses to maintain its control.

A Course in Miracles tells us that health comes about from inner peace and we all know that inner peace comes about from peaceful thoughts.

The understanding of how benign the body is and that sickness is of the mind, can free you from the grip of the Ego. You can then return the body to its primary function as tool of learning and communication for the Spirit.

In truth the body is a giver and receiver of messages in a physical environment that we believe that we live in. You can then see that it should be used merely a means to an end whist you still believe in a solid reality.

However, it is vitally important to reiterate that you should not seek to deny the need for the body or its value. It is more important that you only use it for the job that it was designed to do. It is crucial not to project any power or value onto it that it does not have. It is too easy to give it power because you do not want to take responsibility for your thoughts and behaviour.

You must never reject any part of you. That idea shifts your vibration up towards one of perfect love where health and happiness actually abide. To love the body and even the Ego is the only way to overcome their perceived power over you.

You must accept that we as humans are naturally predisposed towards rejecting and avoiding negative emotions and feelings. The Ego wants them out of the body. Although honouring and expressing your negative emotions may feel counterintuitive, it is vital for your physical health and wellbeing to be able to do so. In this way you also rid them from the mind.

Great peace can be found in the acceptance of your own power and creations. Never forget that all problems arise in the mind first and if you are the problem, then you are also the solution. There is nowhere to hide - not even in the body - from the fact that you are the creator of your reality.

You cannot cherry pick only the positive scenarios to own as your creation. Nor can you run away from the problems that you or the Ego are creating because wherever you run, you take you, and it with you. It is not good enough to just catch the tricks of the Ego. It is not enough not to look at the dark. You have to actually bring in the light instead. You have to choose to overlook the Ego's tricks and choose with your right-mind. Otherwise your illusion may become a little bit less unpleasant but you are still caught in the illusion.

The only way to escape it is to choose with Spirit. You must buy fully into the fact that the body is a thought construct and has no power in and of itself. Then it follows logically that the body cannot be harmed or die. As most of the Ego's tricks require that you believe that you are a body, then by refusing to believe in that reality, you become freed from the illusion itself.

If you are no longer seeing illusion then you must start to see Reality.

The Ego cannot afford to let you listen to Radio Spirit and get to Heaven. It wants you loyal to Radio Fear.

Once you have tasted peace and empowerment who would want to return to fear and limitation? The Ego would have lost its audience for ever.

So, as we shall see throughout the book, the Ego uses many tricks and devices to keep us locked into its limited worldview and confined within its body temple.

However, the simple truth is, as we shall see, that you are sitting in jail with the door wide open!

Quick Summary

1. The mind creates the body but the body cannot create the mind.

2. The body is itself a benign tool of communication. It is the giver and receiver of messages about which it has no opinion.

3. The Ego wants you to believe that you are a body because it keeps you separate from others. Once 'others' exist you start to fear their attack and your death.

5. The body becomes a tool for projection onto, and from, other things and people. It can also be used as a scapegoat.

6. Pain like sickness is caused by and experienced in the mind only. The body is the screen that these thoughts are played out on.

Physiology follows thought.

7. In order to hide this, the Ego reverses cause and effect. Then you believe that illness happens to you. You are then powerless to stop it as you are the effect not the cause.

Physical Discovery Exercise

This is a short exercise to help you to discover what sickness of mind may be causing the ailment in the body. Sometimes it helps to think about phrases that you already know for that area of the body. The mental issue will be reflected in the appropriate area of the body. I know someone who had four Kidney infections that were so serious that he had to be hospitalised each time. My first question to him was "What are you so angry (pissed off about)?" at which point he collapsed in tears.

Here are some examples that may help:

Who or what is being a pain in the neck/bottom?
Who has stabbed you in the back?
Where are you shouldering the blame?
Who or what do you want to give the elbow to?
Constipation- what are you having difficulty letting go of/want to hold onto?
Eczema/anything inflamed or sore = anger
Urinary problems- Who or what is pissing you off?
Need to get a grip on something-hand problems
What am I not seeing/hearing?
Broken limbs- What do I need a break from?

1. Find a comfortable place and takes some long slow, deep breaths in and out. Do this for around five minutes until the mind settles.

2. Take a current ailment or a recent one if you are currently healthy and just hold the attention on the specific area of the body for about five minutes.

3. Keeping the attention there, ask the question of Spirit, (that means that you ask and then patiently wait until the answer is given *to you*)
Why did I create this? What is/was the gain? What is/was this for?

OR

4. Start to think about the phrases that you know for that part of the body (see above). Think around that time in your life: What was going on before it started? How were you feeling and behaving? Were you angry, frustrated or attacking the self in some way?

5. Offer gratitude for any new information or revelation received and

then consider the following:

A) What could/should I do or have thought differently in my mind? The body is following instructions if you remember.

B) What could/should I do or have done differently in my external life? What action needs to be taken now?

C) How can I make sure that issues of the mind do not have to be reflected through the body any more? What programmes need updating or deleting?

Fail to prepare and prepare to fail!

Thank the mind and the body and forgive yourself for this unnecessary creation.

N.B. *The questions at 5 come from the worksheets used in my first book* **Tour the Core - The Pathway to a Positively Joyous Life**, *available on Amazon.*

We shall be using this as the chosen tool of focus for healing at the end of each exercise and so it may be useful to read up on how to do the TOUR work in that book.

The Tour acronym is:

T - The reality mirror – What are you seeing? What is the problem?
O - Owning – Accept that you have created this.
U - Uncovering – Why are you choosing something that you say you do not want?
R - Reprogramming – ABC- An immediate Action, a new long term Behaviour and Choosing a new belief programme.

Chapter 5

Case Study of the Ego

I thought it would be beneficial here to offer a practical example of a situation that happened to me. I am using this (but I could have used anything in my life) because it was so trivial in some ways and yet so revealing of all of the Ego's tricks. I will highlight the concepts in action that we have discussed so far in the book. Then later I will present it again and highlight all of the other deceptions that we have not yet covered. In this way, this one example can reveal in the totality of the antics, of the Ego at work.

It was just after Christmas 2017 and I was going for a short break to do a personal silence in Spain. I was travelling alone and so had my earphones on, shutting out the bustle of the world. I was immersed in an inspirational download and completely isolated in a peaceful world of my own.

I had a wonderful feeling of just being in the now and at peace from the moment I got up. I was clearly in my right-mind, had a high vibration and was in joy with Spirit. I got myself ready and went to the airport and everything was flowing beautifully. There were no queues at check-in or passport control. I had a wonderful peaceful breakfast that ended just in time to flow easily through to the gate.

Then, out of the blue, things started to go wrong.

Now before I go on I want to deal with that phrase 'out of the blue'. I suggest you stop using it because it is one of the Ego's favourite phrases and it suggests that life is unpredictable. This is a clever mechanism to make you always feel unstable and fearful. It is also a belief programme that is unconsciously going to sabotage any happiness that you do have. This is because you are programming into the computer that all of a sudden it can all go wrong for some external reason that is out of your control. I suggest that you erase that file from the computer! If you are the creator of your reality how can that be true? It can only be true *because* you have the programme running, like a background virus.

As you will see, what the Ego is cleverly disguising is the moment that it took back control.

So, out of the blue it seems, things started to go wrong.

We almost took off on time but had to return to the terminal as a member of the crew was taken ill. This caused an hours delay. When I got to the villa where I was going to stay lots of things were not working. Trying to sort these things out with the owner was very stressful. I had been on the phone to my sister who was desperately trying to help despite being unwell (unbeknownst to me). When I discovered this, I felt very guilty at causing her this stress.

I ended the day tired and fed up and wondering what on earth happened to my bliss.

The next morning, once rested and back in the flow of my right-mind, I begun to self-reflect. When I traced it back I could pinpoint the exact thoughts that changed everything. Before I show you what pushed me from right-mind to wrong-minded thinking let me just give you something else that is important to understand about what went on.

I love a TV programme called 'The Dog Whisperer' with Caesar Milan. He has an amazing gift of understanding and thus correcting a dog's behaviour. Well actually, he corrects the owner which is why I love it. His 'dog' psychology mirrors what I believe about humans when dealing with energy and vibrational states. We rarely pay conscious attention to energy but it is being read and then reacted to by us all, unconsciously all of the time.

There was an episode in a dog grooming parlour where the groomer wanted Caesar to help with his toughest cases: dogs who hated being groomed and would attack him. Caesar watched him at work and then asked him at what point he felt his energy change. The man was oblivious to his energy changing. Caesar deftly pointed out that he was happy and confident outside with the owners but almost the moment he went into the grooming area he started exuding fear in his energy. We call these 'tells' in psychology. Tells are very subtle unconscious movements and gestures that give away how you are really feeling. As soon as there is fear, you are attracting 'attack' and if the communication breaks down, then attack almost becomes inevitable.

Also, think about this - if you saw a surgeon coming towards you with trembling hands and you sensed his fear, would you want him or her touching you? If you were also unable to verbalise that resistance, what would you do? You are going to struggle and resist as soon as the surgeon comes near.

Caesar understands that bodies are simply tools of communication and so do dogs. Dogs are reading energy, not listening to our words. To the animal, this nervous man is doing unnatural, invasive things to its body (that it hasn't chosen and probably doesn't understand). Consequently, it is going to be defensive and/or attack. The important point is that this is not the dog's problem. The behaviour of the dog is only caused by the groomer's energy. Once Caesar teaches him this, the dog calms and submits to being groomed.

The thing that Caesar does most of the time is to 'own' the space energetically (without words or actions) and become pack leader so that the animal instinctively becomes submissive.

The reason that I find this programme so interesting is because the level of projection that goes on between man and dog is so hilarious. The owner will often think they know what the dog is thinking and feeling. (There was one episode when I thought Caesar's eyes would pop out of his head as a woman projected all her needs and beliefs on to the dog!) Caesar explained that dogs live in the moment and don't have stories the way we do. Their stories are simply 'am I the pack leader or a follower here?' They don't hold grudges. However, if they think they own you, they will fight to protect their goods and territory which might be your bed! This is not because *'He is lonely on the floor'* (owner's projection) but because he believes he is pack leader and you have allowed him to 'own' the territory.

I digress; back to the airport.

So what I recognised at the airport was that there was an exact moment when my energy changed and because this is my Universe, it had to change everything around me.

I noticed that people were gathering en-masse around the gate entrance. In that moment I had started seeing others as separate from me and in competition with me. This is a clear sign of the Ego at work.

Up until then I had been just mooching around in La La Land. Now suddenly the Ego brought to my attention other people who had their own agenda and suggested that their agenda would negatively affect my life. No-one had said a word but I felt the energy of 'attack' brewing. The Ego did this by reminding me that I am separate and vulnerable to others. It brought me back into being a body.

Now I have no objective evidence at that point that these 'others' had an agenda that would affect me. This was my Ego's story or projection designed to bring up a fear based vibration but was cleverly cloaked.

I was travelling just with hand luggage as most people now do with short, budget airline flights. This causes a rush to get on the plane first to ensure that you can fit your case into the overhead locker where you are seated. Excuse the pun but it becomes dog eat dog, because there is never enough locker space. Or at least, that is in my Ego's version of the world.

The Ego believes that story and can successfully buy me into it because it loves to use the past against me. There is no reason why anything that has happened previously should repeat. (Aside from the fact that because of memory, I have an active file opened about airports and passengers now). I had to put my case in a locker far behind me on my last flight which meant I had to wait to get off the plane last in order to retrieve it. It caused no problem really because I caught everyone up at passport control. Therefore, there is no logical reason for it to even be a problem this time, should it occur. But oh no, my Ego had become fazed by my bliss and needed to find a way to sabotage it at the earliest opportunity!

I had started seeing myself in a body (Ego wrong-mindedness) instead of part of the flow (Spirit right-mindedness) as I had when everything was going well.

Fear had arisen over the potential (not even real yet) lack of locker space. The Ego, by means of its projections and stories about other people out to get me, had now thrown lack and scarcity into the mix. It is when we feel that we will lose out by another's action that we behave badly. Because the Ego believes that it is possible to lose out, it will fight to protect what it sees as its goods and territory (like the dog).

There is no-one else out there to take away from me, unless I play the Ego's game and project it out! I had also fallen into the attack/defence cycle. (This will be explained later in the book).

Finally, the Ego's other favourite thing to enslave me with is time or the perceived lack of it, which was now chasing me again. What would it really matter if I was last off? The belief was that everyone else would gain time by getting off first. My belief in time as short can be used to enslave me, induce fear and then put me into a negative vibrational state.

The interesting thing was that I remember feeling the shift in vibration, but didn't catch its meaning. I also heard the quiet Voice of Spirit say "*It will all be ok*", but I allowed my Ego's voice of fear to override it. Author Neale Donald Walsch said *"The Soul speaks to us in feelings"* and it certainly didn't let me down. It gave me the message that I needed to maintain my bliss, which I felt but did not heed.

Wow, what a learning experience this was for me once I had carefully unravelled the Ego's trick! If I had listened when I felt the energy change I am sure there would not have been the downward spiral I experienced for the rest of that day. I clearly heard the warning about the initial thought: *'There are a lot of people here and you won't get a locker space!'* If I had not listened to that, my bliss would have continued.

It is true that you never have a single thought. From that first mad idea, my mind went on from there to create stupid strategies. These were defence strategies about how I should queue up now, not let latecomers get in front of me and on and on and on! There had been no attack, except in my mind but here I was on the defensive.

It was my responsibility to catch the shift but I failed miserably and paid the price. Those other passengers and what they did or didn't do was irrelevant. It was my wrong-mindedness that was the only cause.

And finally, notice how the crazy strategies were actually put forward as a gain? Rushing to get ahead would mean I gained a locker space, time and peace of mind. I would also gain power and a boost in energy because I was quicker and smarter than the other passengers.

Sadly the opposite is true. I gained a locker space but lost a day of my precious life to wrong-mindedness which only boosts my Ego's power. I will never get those precious minutes back again - ever! I also suffered emotional pain in the form of guilt over upsetting my sister. Whenever, we tread over others to get our own needs met then guilt must follow. I felt guilty over my selfishness and, worst of all, lost alignment with my Spirit and bliss.

It was my own judgement and subsequent condemnation of the other passengers, which was undeserved, that served to injure me.

Was it a price worth paying?

As always with Egotistical behaviour - a resounding No!

However, as always, the Spirit will re-interpret what the Ego creates. Thus, by my self-reflection and courage to look at myself honestly I could see what programmes were running and update or delete them. I could forgive myself for my errors of thought and aim to do better next time. I will now be given another opportunity to practice better behaviour next time, which in this case will be on the return journey home…

Chapter 6

The Unchangeable Belief

"Man is what he believes." Anton Chekhov

I was amazed to read recently that gravity is just a theory. According to the Oxford English Dictionary a theory is defined as *"A supposition or system of ideas intended to explain something."* Einstein's theory of general relativity is used to explain gravity. According to Science News*, gravity is *"A distortion of space caused by the presence of matter or energy".* I always believed it was like a magnet that kept us all stuck down. Yet this quote seems to be suggesting that you cause gravity by being the presence of matter and it is your energy disturbing the field around you. I.e. you are the cause and gravity is the effect!

This got me thinking about how many other things that we have been programmed to believe are proven certainties in the world but may just be theory.

We accept at face value whatever we are told by parents and teachers who are only able to repeat whatever they were programmed with. The experts, researchers and scientists may be doing the same, unless they have actively discovered or researched these things themselves. It is well researched and documented that scientists find and interpret the results that they receive to fit their own biases and purpose. In reality, unless you have done the actual experiments yourself, you can never know if you are being told the truth about anything.

Yet, no doubt, you will continue to live your life as if gravity is real because you perhaps do not have the time or expertise to find out for yourself. Thus, it will remain a firm belief reinforced every minute of every day - even though it may be a complete fallacy. Does so much of what you live by become unconscious because if you were to start questioning everything you would discover so many anomalies that you couldn't operate in the world any more? If the body is a thought structure it stays on the Earth because you want it to, not because of gravity. If you do not believe that and you believe the body is physical then you may think that there is a reason that you don't float off into space. Your mind will then create a concept that fits. That's why gravity can only ever be a theory.

As I said in chapter one, a belief is just a thought that you have repeated or heard often enough that neuronets in the brain have cemented this notion. This then means that such a thought comes to the top of the 'menu' and becomes the first thought of choice on that subject. To choose is essentially to create and thus every choice of thought will be projected out on the screen of your life, and cause some emotional/vibrational change in the body. Seeing it on the screen then reinforces its reality (the Ego's seeing is believing) and it becomes a self-perpetuating feedback loop.

We each have many differing levels of belief programmes that affect our behaviour, but these can roughly be divided into three categories. These are:

1. Core beliefs—these are the accepted, unquestioned and deeply held beliefs that come from parents, educators, society, culture, history and the collective consciousness. These will form the world that we believe we live in.

2. Experiential beliefs—these are beliefs that we have picked up from personal life experiences and relationships. These will usually have some kind of personal emotional tie to them. They are likely to influence our judgements of who we think we are.

3. Background beliefs—these are beliefs based on things that we have heard, been told, seen in the media or on the TV. They are likely to be running as low level background programmes. They may appear on the surface to be fairly innocuous and not directly related to us personally.

As we said earlier, there is a fundamental structure that creates your experience as a physical being that I call the Bear cycle. It is a self perpetuating, feedback loop that unless understood, creates the same life everyday and every year. It is worth repeating here: (Read clockwise)

Beliefs

Reinforcement　　　　　　　　Emotion

Action

Your beliefs cause an emotional and vibrational effect that then determines your action or behaviour. This then, reinforces your original belief. Thus we have a cycle of 'believing is seeing' and not 'seeing is believing'. Essentially it is a loop and so theoretically you could start anywhere within it. However, the first makes you empowered but the latter makes you a victim. Your power lies in being able to change the content within the loop but not the mechanism itself.

You are continually creating and sharing your thoughts, both consciously and unconsciously. Thoughts never leave their source and can only be shared and extended: like a secret can be shared. However, you still retain the secret too. You are never separated from your thoughts and it is through them that you and other people come to know yourselves. By giving or sharing your thoughts they are strengthened. That sharing and strengthening is fantastic if they are positive but not so healthy if they are negative. You are in a relationship with your thoughts and beliefs and that is essentially what your life is made up of.

I often catch my mind arbitrarily putting two and two together and coming up with concepts, theories and stories about why and how a certain thing has happened. For example, I awoke to find a small dead bird on the lawn. It had no sign of injury and so my mind started to come up with a whole host of concepts about what must have happened. I laughed when I caught myself doing this because in some ways it was just an example of the Ego occupying my mind with trivia. I couldn't ever know the truth but I had to feel satisfied that I had come up with the right (or at least most feasible) option before I could let it go.

Why was that necessary I wondered? Finally, I realised that it made me feel safe and secure to know that there was a rational reason for everything. Remember, I suggested in the case study that we don't like things coming out of the blue. This is exactly because it makes you feel unstable and as if things happen to you and they are therefore out of your control.

If you fear things being *out of your control* then you must on some deeper level know that you control everything - you can only lose something if you had it in the first place!

It is only our beliefs that make the world functional. A belief by its very nature stabilises reality. If we take the example of gravity, if you were not sure that it worked all the time, your life would be very unpredictable.

Your behaviour reflects and is reinforced by, the belief that originally motivated it. By your knowing that it is totally reliable, you can operate safely in the world. Without the firm belief that gravity always worked you would not leave the spot. By trusting and walking without doubt the neuronets are continually reinforced by your continuing experience and those of the collective around you.

One of the Ego's tricks is to use smoke and mirrors to cover what is really going on and that is why it must reverse cause and effect. As we have already discussed this creates confusion about what is really happening in your life. More importantly it also makes you feel powerless to change it.

An event appears to have an outside cause and your emotional reaction is the effect. The virus makes you sick or the partner dumping you makes you sad and the lottery win makes you happy. But we have already established that the only real cause is the mind. Therefore, external reality is the effect and is displayed on the screen of the external environment.

How can the computer screen be the cause of the internet, for example? The internet is the cause and the effect is shown on the screen. Therefore, it is your beliefs about the spouse dumping you that is the cause of the sadness, not the partner actually dumping you. If you had had enough of them anyway, you would have a different thought about it and so the effect would be different; relief rather than sadness. We said earlier that behaviour is the result of a thought and so the behaviour is the effect. You can change a cause but you cannot change an effect. Thus, by bringing the cause back into your mind and owning that you are the creator of outcome, the effect is nullified. No-one and no-thing can affect you unless you allow it to. This makes you self-empowered. Believing your happiness is dependant on the actions of another (cause) makes you a victim and an effect.

An effect must have a cause to exist but if you have nullified the cause there can be no effect. We will be going into this in relation to how the Ego uses this alongside attack and defence later.

Life is actually a series of quantum 'now' moments or frames that you experience as a sequence that appears to you as time (more on this in future chapters). So every nanosecond you are choosing to recreate the mind (world) on your screen. The reason that you don't realise this is partially because of the speed that it occurs but also because you habitually choose what you already know. You get what you expect. Therefore, the next scene looks so incredibly like the last. It will run automatically until you consciously decide to choose again. Now this is actually great for positive beliefs. However, what that means for negative beliefs is that once you have chosen the belief it appears to come with its own built in limitations of what else is possible. What is possible appears to be based on what has happened in the past. The belief then will appear to have a powerful quality of being unable to be changed. This is to protect the Ego's view of the world and keep you imprisoned within it.

Before we get practical and explore the unchangeable belief, I just want to give a nod to the work of Bashar who offers a similar framework on which my version of the unchangeable belief is based. This is simply how I have made sense of the teachings and added to it with my other knowledge directly gained from Spirit.

Imagine that a tourist asks my friend Johnny for directions in London.

Johnny believes that he cannot help as he is only visiting himself. The whole file on London roads opens and sure enough there is not much information in it. Therefore, this belief plays out on the screen of his life in the only way it can: he is unable to help the tourist.

The structure of reality is set up so that you are always proved right. So Johnny is reassured that he can operate safely and securely in his world because he was right *'See I told you I know nothing about London roads'*.

Now because this is a fairly innocuous belief neither Johnny nor the Ego thinks any more about it.

In this example, Johnny's belief seems quite rational, acceptable and justified. But let us take another example that will demonstrate how that very rationality and need for justification can be used to trap us into unwanted negative behaviours. We are now going to look at the structure and mechanisms that perpetuate negative beliefs in the mind. Like our computers, if you can understand the basis of how they work you can overcome malfunctions and get the best out of them.

Let us now say that Johnny believes that he is clumsy and stupid. If I were to ask him why he believes that, he no doubt will open the huge file in his memory bank. This file will include all the times he has been told and shown that he is clumsy or stupid. A lot of that will most likely be from childhood because your root programming or most ingrained beliefs are from your earliest experiences. Please note, that this is only his past programming and doesn't necessarily mean it was, or is, intrinsically true. When it was seeded, all through his childhood he was completely different in mind, body and Spirit to the adult that he is today.

Anyway, after relaying all of his past evidence that he finds in his old files, perhaps we too would agree that on the face of it this belief is rational, acceptable and justified.

Now, as I have said previously, whatever has been programmed into your computer is all that it can play out. Therefore, Johnny believes he is stupid and clumsy not because it may be necessarily true *now* perhaps, but because his expectation and belief about it will activate the Bear mechanism. Because this is a self-perpetuating mechanism it can *only* prove that he is stupid based on his current beliefs. No other new or different information has been provided to update his files. Consequently, he can only continue to create or tell the same old stories.

We have learned already that the physiological state will follow the belief. Subconsciously, Johnny will always be aware that his clumsiness could arise at any moment. Even though he may not be consciously thinking about his clumsiness before the party, his file labelled 'party' has opened and in it are other experiences when he has looked stupid or been clumsy at parties. Therefore, on this social occasion for example, Johnny may be shaking with nerves so badly that he spills a drink over his friend called Danny. Even though the drenched Danny now reflects back to Johnny his own frustration about how stupid he is, Johnny will believe that Danny thinking of him as clumsy is now the problem. Therefore, and quite irrationally, the Ego has proved Johnny's beliefs right (that he is clumsy and stupid) by physically causing his clumsiness and then projecting the blame on to Danny for his hurt.

You are always showing others what you believe you are and sharing it. Thus, you must separate the action from the person. It was inevitable to some extent, that with his past programming affecting his physiology (nervousness) that Johnny would become clumsy. However, you must understand it is not Johnny that is stupid. His lack of knowledge of how the mind works and that physiology follows thought, simply allows old programmes to run unchecked. This actually reassures him unconsciously that he is sane and safe and the world remains a reliably predictable place. The Ego uses this need for predictability, to make it appear that no other choice of belief is possible in order to keep him imprisoned. Even though this looks like a negative programme the Ego has rewarded him with a safe world by choosing the same belief. This encourages him to choose it again.

The world is no safer in reality but Johnny's unconscious perception of it is now, that it indeed is. Thus, perception can only ever give a limited view from a conflicted mind. Perception then cannot be trusted.

Earlier in the book we touched on the way that the mind will delete, distort or generalise information coming into it. Therefore, to ensure the continuation of the belief, Johnny's Ego will have deleted examples of times and situations when he has shown intelligence and ability. He will not remember all the social occasions when he hasn't been clumsy and has not spilled any drinks. However, even if some examples are available to demonstrate this, the Ego may seek to distort or undermine them claiming *"Yes, but that was different because...."*

Now it is vitally important here to recognise that the Ego will also try to delete or distort any advice coming through from the Spirit. The Spirit obviously has an opposite or contradictory view on whom and what Johnny is. It knows that he is buying into the Ego's trick and will try to 'salvage' the situation. One of the best things that Spirit does is reinterpret what we have created and correct the information that the Ego has distorted. There is always the opportunity for change or a flicker of light in the darkness, if you will. All of his friends and family (or other external sources) may be continuously trying to persuade him that his belief is not true but the Ego will always ignore any assistance and reject any evidence to the contrary. Assistance will look like someone suggesting deep breathing or calming techniques, for example. The Ego may not even have a decent excuse why not to take this advice and so will offer a response such as *"Well you don't understand. I've tried ...I can't...I don't know why...."* etc. In short, the Ego will keep him away from any therapy or other ideas that could help.

Finally, the Ego will make huge swathes of generalisation to make the situation unchangeable with statements like *"I always mess everything up."* The two words always and everything are all inclusive. When you programme a computer it takes everything literally. If you type 'send to all' into the computer or phone it will email or text *everyone* in the address book. The phone or computer just activates the programme as instructed. Therefore, Johnny's brain will now display on the screen of his life, experiences where he messes *everything* up in *all* ways. This again has just reinforced the neuronets and the Ego's mantra of 'seeing is believing'. It becomes a self-fulfilling prophecy.

Another aspect of the mechanism that perhaps you have already spotted is projection. The body is already being projected onto as an instrument of clumsiness. As we have said the body is also a screen in your environment on to which you project cause. Johnny may project blame on to his sweaty hands or even something like Dyspraxia (a disorder that causes difficulties with co-ordination or movement) for the spill.

Johnny may also be projecting onto Danny, by blaming Danny for making him feel nervous. Danny also reinforces Johnny's original belief of stupidity by becoming annoyed at him.

But Johnny may also project agreement with his belief onto others in a seemingly positive way. Humour is often a double edged sword. When his friends laugh and say *"Oh don't worry about it, I've done that before"* they think they are helping. In reality, all they have done is say that the belief, which is actually detrimental and limiting, is normal or acceptable. Johnny has just been made lovable and likable again and so will unconsciously take the message away that being stupid is actually ok. Johnny now unconsciously thinks that he doesn't need to do anything to change that programme because he has been rewarded by confirmation that he is lovable and safe. How insidious and devious is that?

Remember you are free to choose any thought in any moment. Johnny can choose to listen to the rewarding thought of Spirit that reminds him that he is a perfect creation of God and thus, that he cannot be stupid. This would create a new programme that could then be reinforced.

So, as we have said the reward of security is one of the mechanisms that encourages you to continue to pick the negative belief. There is another element of reward that the Ego tricks you with in order to ensure that you always pick the negative belief; you get to survive.

Why is it so bad to be a stupid person? The answer is, as we discovered earlier, the Ego dictates that you must be lovable, likable or an asset in order to survive. Danny, the drenched man certainly doesn't like him now and Johnny doesn't like himself. However, in reality if Danny ended their friendship over an accident (which isn't likely) then he wasn't a friend anyway. Most importantly though, Johnny could still survive without him. These are just the crazy fear-based ideas that the Ego stalks you with surreptitiously.

Even if Danny had been so mad that he had killed Johnny, the projection of Johnny's body may end but the Spirit cannot die. The Spirit and the Ego both know that the death of the body is not a real death, more of a scene change. (More on this in the chapter called Father and Son). The Ego knows on one level that it isn't the body as such, because it knows that it is merely a creation of the mind. But it has enlisted the body as its ally and uses the body to separate itself and you, from others. Once you feel separate and different from others, attack from someone or something else is now possible. So being lovable, likable and an asset becomes vital to ward off attack and death.

Therefore, as long as you know you cannot die (which is what Jesus demonstrated with the resurrection) or that you can survive on your own, you could give up this belief that you must be lovable, likable or an asset at all times. We will look more deeply at the impossibility of death later on in the book.

When governments are working on top secret projects they will often outsource separate pieces of the work out to different companies. No company will know who is working on the other parts of the project or what those parts are. This is so no-one could put all of the pieces of the puzzle together and know what the final product is.

So by dividing and separating negative ideas, thoughts and beliefs the Ego ensures that you can never discover its final plan. It compartmentalises beliefs, like my business analogy from earlier, so that you cannot see the correlation between them. Thus, it is difficult to see the connection between believing that you are stupid and being a vulnerable physical body that can die. This ensures that you are powerless to change the faulty thinking and break the hidden associations. Unless somebody teaches you the way the mind works, it is impossible to break the connections.

Be aware that the Ego also compartmentalises knowledge and solutions too. Whilst writing this, I realised that what I am presenting here has come to me, piecemeal, through a great many books and teachers.

Not one teacher has all of the answers for me. These are many and range from the likes of Louise Hay to Abraham, Bashar to my beloved A Course in Miracles. If I were to have found all the answers at once from one teacher, the Ego would have gone into overdrive and had to take drastic action to stop that teacher 'saving' me. Therefore, by the Spirit directing me slowly and carefully to the right materials, I have been able to negotiate with the Ego down a gentle path. It is important to work *with* the Ego to undo the framework of your current beliefs and fears.

But you must always look deeper to find the real issue at hand. It always comes out as the same thing which is the Ego's wish to keep control by means of fear. Apart from compartmentalising beliefs, the Ego also cloaks everything with smoke, mirrors and distraction in order to keep the status quo.

How does a magician perform his tricks? The magician encourages you to look over there whilst something else that is more important happens over here. Thus, the main event is hidden by the distraction of some other seemingly more urgent or important event.

The Ego is a master magician.

The problem is not that Johnny is stupid but it's that the Ego is masking Johnny's belief in himself as a fallible and thus vulnerable, physical body.

Logically, it would seem that this belief is actually a dangerous one that you would suppose the Ego would want him to get rid of. But instead the Ego warns that if Johnny goes looking for the belief that he is stupid and actually discovers evidence that it is true, then he definitely will not survive. So the circular thinking is that *"The best thing is not to even go looking. Just stay as you are, with the possibility that it may not be totally true (doubt is the key) and I, the Ego, will keep you safe"*. This ties him down, keeping him stuck and afraid to even look into the possibility of changing because if Johnny finds out that he *definitely* is stupid all hope is lost!

So the elements that ensure that beliefs feel so rigid and unchangeable are *rationality* and *justification*, *projection* and *rejection* of other ideas, rejection of *assistance*, and the most difficult to deal with *reward*. The Ego will then link these to survivability.

With this mechanism, the Ego gets to use negative beliefs, sometimes presented as positive gains (and sometimes not), to reinforce its control over you with fear and vulnerability. Because we are not very good at questioning old programmes or understanding the deeper meaning, we live as if today is the past and this creates our expectations of the future. The reason this mechanism works so well is that negative energy separates and divides and so negative beliefs are used by the Ego to divide and conquer.

So just before we move on to how to use this mechanism to our advantage let me just do a quick summary.

In order to make you absolutely believe that no other belief is possible (and if you chose it, it would be totally catastrophic) the Ego uses these seven tricks. It disassociates their connections in order to mask what it is doing. I have changed a couple of the terms used earlier to make it easier to remember but you can use the originals if you prefer.

Here are its tricks: **RISPARRS**

1. **Rationality**: How does believing that this idea is rational help to make it appear acceptable and unchangeable? Here you will hear/look for

all the *objective* evidence, almost like saying 'well everybody knows that....' The Ego is likely to come up with whatever event has raised the issue in the first place as this evidence.

2. **Is Justified**: How does believing that this idea is justified help to make it appear acceptable and unchangeable? This will bring up a more *subjective* evidence and old programmes and experiences as evidence.

3. **Projection:** How does projection help to make this belief appear to be acceptable and unchangeable? Who or what are you blaming and thus projecting on to but not owning? How is this belief presented so it appears that the cause is 'out there' and thus not your fault or out of your control?

4. **Assistance:** How does receiving assistance or reinforcement from other people or society help to reinforce this belief as acceptable and unchangeable? What are other people around you saying and suggesting to you? How are other people reinforcing it positively or negatively?

5. **Rejection:** How does rejecting any other way of thinking/being make this belief appear unchangeable? How/why do you ignore or reject advice to solve the problem and/or get over it? E.g. If someone suggests therapy or a certain book would you act on that? Think about what is being deleted, distorted or generalised to keep you away from any other choice of thought. What is the evidence contrary to the belief?

6. **Reward:** How does the Ego reward you for choosing that belief again? What is the gain to keeping this belief? Remember if you stay small, vulnerable or in fear it loves and rewards you with its protection.

7. **Survivability:** How does the Ego guarantee your safety and survival by choosing that belief again? Explore how the Ego links this belief to continuing to keep you as being lovable, likeable or an asset.

So just to make this clear, let me offer a really brief example. (I'll present the Ego's version first and then the Spirit's reinterpretation afterwards.)

It is likely that there was a lot more coming up for the person (Jenny) in this example but due to time and space I'll just present the highlights.

Jenny was upset because her four brothers were messaging each other but everyone appeared to be ignoring hers.

The negative belief is: **No-one listens to me.**

1. **Rationalise**: It is obvious that they are online and answering each others messages so it is obvious that they are ignoring mine! It's because no-one ever listens to me.

2. **Is Justified**: This is justified because ever since I was a child I learned to keep quiet as no-one listened anyway. I was always excluded by my brothers because they were all older and didn't want a girl hanging around. I work and they don't, so they are together all the time. It's the same at work, I offer great ideas but the others act like no-one even hears my words. I can't change the past. The evidence is all there.

3. **Projection:** It is other people that are not listening *to me* and my frustration comes because I cannot force them to. It is rude and unfair as I listen to them.

4. **Assistance:** Other people tell me that it is all in my imagination. My brothers say that it wasn't intentional. They say I am paranoid. They say I should work on my self-esteem. People at work claim that they didn't hear me and say I should speak louder or be more assertive.

5. **Rejection:** This is who I am. I have always been this way. I'm too old to change. I don't have the confidence to stand up for myself. I am too afraid to do a course to improve my self-esteem. There is no hope. Why should I change when they are the problem?

6. **Reward:** It is all too much. I like the way I am. It's too difficult to change. I don't know what life would be like if I become assertive so I'll stay here in my comfort zone.

7. **Survivability**: No-one will like me if I stand up for myself. I don't like bossy, aggressive people so they won't like me either. I'll end up sacked or with no friends.

Remember that the Ego's premise is: *"Don't go to disprove the belief because what if you find out that it is true? Then there is nowhere left to turn and you are now doomed to be ignored forever. Stay as you are then at least there is doubt in the authenticity of the belief".*
If you believed the Ego's story from the sections above would you be able to just drop this belief? It now appears to not only be unchangeable but a life-saver if you understand the warped and twisted rationality of the Ego. It ties you up in knots with all this projection, confusion of cause and effect, emotional blackmail and fear. The most insidious thing is that you do not even know that it is happening!

The Ego Unravelled

However, we are blessed with the right-mindedness of Spirit also and when we complete this process, the other voice will participate also. So let's hear how the Spirit will guide Jenny gently away from this.

1. **Rationalise:** If family members don't reply when you WhatsApp them they must be ignoring you.

Spirit: There could be a multitude of reasons: WhatsApp conversations move very quickly and easily get out of sync and some messages get lost or missed. This has happened to you before! It's not personal. Let it go.

2. **Is Justified**: This is justified because ever since I was a child I learned to keep quiet as no-one listened anyway. I was always excluded by my brothers because they were all older. I work and they don't, so they are together all the time. It's the same at work, I offer great ideas but the others act like no-one even hears my words. I can't change the past. The evidence is all there.

Spirit: That is old programming that is easily cleared from your mind. It may be just your perception, your brothers claim it wasn't how you remember it. Listen to what they say. They were a lot older and had different interests. They were also going to places that you could not go due to your age. You are acting like a child. At work, as everywhere else, it is the same belief running and being observed. It is just one problem in essence. The problem is that you are playing victim again and if you blame others you cannot change the situation. You are not a victim because you are at source Spirit. Take responsibility for your reactions. No-one can affect you unless you allow them to. Update your old programmes with the band exercise so that tomorrow can be different. You do not need anyone to reaffirm your value. If they don't listen then they will lose out.

3. **Projection:** It is other people that are not listening *to me* and my frustration comes because I cannot force them to. It is rude and unfair as I listen to them.

Spirit: You are projecting the real cause outside so that it appears that it is unchangeable, in that it is other people that are not listening to you. Remember that the Ego reverses cause and effect to confuse you. The cause of your upset is really that you have not looked at these old files and so they keep playing out on the screen of your life. It's not about being listened to, it's about your victimhood and not owning your power and taking responsibility. If you own the problem you can become the solution. No-one will change their behaviour and nor do they have to. If you want things to be different, you must change. Let go of this false belief and work on your assertiveness. You are allowing others to affect you. Take back your projection. What you have to say is valuable whether people listen to you or not but if you do not value it neither will they. The Ego has disguised this as attack from outside so that paradoxically you will turn back to the Ego for safety and protection. This is also reinforcing your belief in yourself as a vulnerable physical body that only the Ego can protect. No-one is out to get you and so you do not need the protection of the Ego. You are not a body you are an Eternal Spirit and your worth is established by God and no-one else.

4. **Assistance:** Other people tell me that it is all in my imagination. My brothers say that it wasn't intentional. They say I am paranoid. People at work claim that they didn't hear me and say I should speak louder or be more assertive.

Spirit: Look how many great people are around you who are prepared to listen to you complain! Love and be grateful for them. Always listen to other people's good advice. Listen to what they are telling you objectively. Read the books they suggest. Do the exercises. If you claim not to have time it means you are not prioritizing. Why? Because you are listening to the Ego, and it fears the guidance that made you buy the book. You are living the effects of a split mind. Look for evidence of how you have always been supported by the Universe. Look for all the times when you are assertive, with the kids for example. Look at what the difference is and do more of that. If you do not, or feel that you can't, then ask yourself why what are you worried about? What is the worst thing that could happen if you did? Could you handle it? Question your Ego and its fear just once and see if you can face that fear. Practice assertiveness and loving the self.

5. **Rejection**: This is who I am. I have always been this way. I'm too old to change. I don't have the confidence to stand up for myself. There is no hope. Why should I change when they are the problem?

Spirit: You may have shown those qualities as a child and it may have served you then. Now you are an adult, equal to everyone else and you have the right to speak out. There are lots of people who listen to you and highly respect your opinion and advice. It matters not if anyone listens. Everyone has free will. Accept this and you will find peace. Make anyone else wrong, like your brothers though and you will feel attacked. No, you are causing your own suffering because you are defining this as a problem. Let it go. Is this really worth wasting life on? It's your choice. Work on your own self-esteem. I am here and I will guide and support you. Push past your doubts and examine any lack of motivation.

6. **Reward:** It is all too much. I don't know what life would be like if I become assertive so I'll stay here in my comfort zone.

Spirit: Know that this is a false security that the Ego is offering. You were created by God and your value was established at the point of creation. No-one is out to get you and the Ego cannot protect you anyway. The only problem is old files opening that should now be updated or deleted. There is no real reward for causing your own suffering. If you cut them off you are the only one that will suffer. That is increasing the problem, not solving it.

Survivability: No-one will like me if I stand up for myself. I don't like bossy, aggressive people so they won't like me either. I'll end up sacked or with no friends.

Spirit: Nobody is universally liked by all and that is ok. You will not lose friends because you are assertive as long as it is done in a kind, loving way. Start to honour yourself. If you do not love you, who else can? Besides which, you are not a body and cannot die therefore, you will always survive. Understand that this is an empty threat of the Ego.

Once this exercise has been done Jenny must then be vigilant for the sabotage of her efforts to change. The Ego giving a little away on one hand then sabotages Jenny with not letting her do any of the exercises advised in this book. If she does do them it may only let her put into action some strategies for change but only for a short while. Then the Ego will make her forget to do them or reject by suggesting that *'This is going to take so much work you are going to fail so don't bother'*. It will tell her she has no time; she can't do it or a myriad of excuses that rationally make sense. Ego will then bring up fear of failure or fear of looking stupid etc. More importantly she dare not go against the Ego whom has by means of projection, and as you see reward, convinced her to not look further.

So as you may notice, you would never see all the connections here unless you did this exercise to examine each aspect of the mechanism. The more that you do look at beliefs through RISPARRS the quicker you can spot the elements. They are all covertly interconnected and weave a web of deceit for Jenny. This makes the negative belief for all intents and purposes, seemingly unchangeable.

So how can poor Johnny and Jenny ever change their behaviour for the better? The answer is to really listen to the voice of Spirit and friends and family who are giving guidance and assistance. For Johnny, it simply was an accident that could have happened to anyone. Another person without that same programming would just apologise and carry on with their evening.

A good example of this was when I had the negative belief that my son was disrespecting me by refusing to clean his room. I was very strict and controlling back then so it used to really make me angry. From a teacher I heard the phrase *'Is it better to be happy or right?'* I later discovered that it actually comes from A Course in Miracles (ACIM). I decided to make my son the first thing I would practice this with, as I was sick of continually arguing over this room and I just wanted to be happy.

Now through those years when we argued he would say things like *"Close the door if you don't like it. It's my room. Don't come in here."* but all I heard was disrespect which of course made me even angrier.

So I decided to choose happiness instead. I decided to close the door, not to go in and honour his right to have a personal space however he wanted it to be. It was a good few years later when I was recounting the experience in a class that I realised that all along, he had actually been telling me the solution to my problem (which unconsciously I already knew). If I hadn't heard it as attack, or if I listened to the quiet Voice of Spirit, I could have saved us both years of unnecessary stress. The cost of being right was not worth the price paid in unhappiness and the stress-causing illnesses that came from it. You cannot put a price on health and happiness.

If I hadn't met that teacher and received that timely advice the situation would have at some point come to a head. He would have either got old enough to escape, I had a heart attack or the situation was never resolved. The cost of being right would have completely ruined the relationship between us, not to mention my health. It is often only when a situation gets intolerable that someone or something will give in, either voluntarily or nudged by Spirit in order to save you.

The easiest question is to ask: what would Spirit say here? For Johnny, it would remind him of the practical evidence (it was an accident, let it go) and that he is not his beliefs or actions. He is perfect Spirit and it will direct him to the real root of the problem by reminding him perhaps, how his Mum always used to call him stupid. This is really telling him to remove that old programme from the computer (by the band exercise) because it is out of date and irrelevant to whom he really is today. Then the old programme will be overwritten and then cannot be displayed on his screen any more.

Johnny can then look at how the Ego was using the mechanisms to make him believe it was unchangeable. He will be able to use the same awareness to catch the Ego in action with other negative beliefs he may have. Be aware however, that as soon as you heal one problem, if you haven't addressed the real underlying issue then the Ego will just reflect it somewhere else. If you don't get the root up, the weeds will soon be back.

The other option is to use the TOUR system and worksheets from my other book **'Tour the Core - The Pathway to a Positively Joyous Life'**. A quick method from that book is to own that you created the problem and ask:

• What am I giving myself an opportunity to practice? (If I set an intention to deal with a habitual problem I will create opportunities to practice my new behaviour)

• What am I having an opportunity to face about myself?

• What am I having an opportunity to learn?

One of these three questions will give you the answer to what's going on. Then briefly I have the ABC of healing, and by addressing these steps you will be taking positive action towards healing the mind and your life:

1. **A**ction - to immediately resolve or improve the current problem in reality.

2. **B**ehaviour - positively begin to develop a new long term behaviour.

3. **C**hoose a new positive belief (affirmation) to overwrite the old belief about yourself using the band exercise.

I know that the mechanisms employed by the Ego are very complex. It has taken me years to understand this. Therefore I suggest you take a few examples of your own and work through how the mechanisms of rejection, projection, rationality, justification, assistance, reward and survivability are being used against you.

It is true however, that a person must actually want to change. You must have a strong enough motivation to be able to face these uncomfortable beliefs. You must be determined enough to get to the end point where you can see a different way of being. We all have free will and some people are not ready to change. But if the will is strong, this knowledge is powerful to achieve that goal. Remember that it is not you but the behaviour that may be unwanted.

These mechanisms are, as I have said before, innately neutral in so far as they are merely the structure on which beliefs reinforce themselves and run automatically. The goal is not to remove the Ego or the mechanisms. I don't even think that would be possible. The only peaceful solution is to love and understand them but to not choose the Ego's thought system. Once a belief has been examined and brought to light, it will soon lose its power. That is because the Ego can no longer distort and disguise it.

By listening to the different point of view of the Spirit, new information can come in and adjust the point of view. You also have to neutralise the power that it gives the Ego, by simply accepting that the Ego *thinks* that it is actually acting out of love. It is just trying to protect its existence and to stay alive - just as you may fight to protect your life. If you attack it or blame it then you reinforce its reality and power. Also as you shall see later, when you attack, you only injure yourself because all attack is an attack against the self.

If you project all of your problems on to the Ego, you just make it your scapegoat and then never get the opportunity to see what's stored in your old files and update them. Therefore, compassion and understanding should be offered to your Ego.

In order to overcome the structure itself you have to simply bring each facet to the light and see it clearly. What that does is make all choices equal. Once you understand why you believe something, you can choose to keep believing it or not. That ability to choose shows that now, the Ego's view and Spirit's view are both just potentials and thus equalised. That puts you back in the position of being the Creator of your life which is exactly the gift that you received from God and what Spirit would actually remind you of.

Therefore, paradoxically by making all choices valid, you instinctively make the choice for the positive. Positive energy integrates and increases things like synchronicity, freedom and joy. The high vibration that making a choice for the Voice of Spirit begets is only more positivity and joy and then that becomes a self-fulfilling prophecy.

Often you will be caught up in a run of events that seem to spiral in severity but are often the same underlying belief being brought up for healing time and time again. If you catch that and do your work, you will profit from the learning and release. But when you do not, you will suffer for as long as you are unprepared to look at the real problem. It is your choice to suffer and for how long.

I noticed that often when I reached the top of the tree in so far as clearing negative beliefs and keeping my vibration high I would suddenly have a 'crash and burn' as I call it. It feels so uncomfortable that I seek to change it immediately.

Sometimes if you have been depressed for a long time your tolerance level for suffering is so high that it becomes 'background'. This is the same as when you move in to a house by a railway and the noise is very loud. But after you have lived there for a while you don't even notice it any more.

Sometimes our levels of expectation of life are so low that again pain and unhappiness is the norm and therefore you don't even notice new pain. The Ego loves this because it says *"Don't go climbing up there because if you fall it is going to hurt a lot more than if you stay down here with me"*.

But my Spirit Voice will begin to reframe the falls as: when you reach the top of the tree and fall it hurts a lot more (and is more noticeable) than if you had only fallen from a low branch. But that is great because now you know how well you were doing and if you climbed up once then you know that you can do it again.

When you start to really take your self-development seriously and have cleared a lot of your emotional baggage, your vibration soars and happiness becomes your expectation and thus the norm. You may have occasional falls but how long that you sit at the bottom of the tree complaining is up to you. I also noticed that when I fell I hurt myself, but I would then hurt others by projecting the cause on to someone or something else. It was as if they had actually pushed me from the branch. This resulted in suffering twice as I got frustrated by the sudden drop in happiness level but also by the guilt that I blamed others.

However, I always have my bag of self development tools and exercises such as the ones presented here. The tools shared here and in my other book, are all I need to start climbing. But the real lesson was to not sit under the tree crying in pain and focussed on the problem. The real lesson was to jump straight back up and focus on the solution. The quicker I did that, the less I suffered and the more empowered I felt. Therefore, your journey to empowerment is to understand how this system works and also to ensure that you are always choosing empowering beliefs.

To start taking full responsibility for your life you have to accept the following truths and act upon them:

- The belief is the initial cause. You are therefore the cause of the problem *but* also the solution. No belief is unchangeable. (Reversing cause and effect.)
- A problem should be redefined as a challenge or an opportunity. (Nullify cause and effect).
- The person who is causing you problems is either the reflection of your traits in the mirror or is giving you an opportunity to learn how to deal with these traits successfully. (Noticing your projection and ceasing the attack spiral)
- You must own all of your decisions. The solution is to stop scowling in the mirror and the reflection that you see will stop scowling back! (Reclaiming your projection)
- Forgive this person, forgive yourself and thank them for playing 'that' role for you so that you could learn and grow. They are your greatest spiritual teacher.

I remind my students that I can only provide them with a set of tools. But just like their toolbox under the stairs at home, if they do not get it out when their house is crumbling then it is their fault only. The problem and the solution are two sides of one coin. If you remember that, and the fact that you have a toolbox, then any problem can be corrected and peace restored. It's all in your control- despite what your Ego may tell you. There is another choice and that choice is simply about choosing the Spirit's thought system over a wrong-minded one.

So if the Ego tells you that you haven't got the right tool, do not worry because Spirit will have it. Ask and the answer will be given.

Quick Summary

1. All events and people are neutral until we project and layer judgement upon them. Everyone out there is a mirror or teacher for you.

2. You create your reality based on your perceptions, beliefs and expectations. You use events, people and objects as tools to help you learn about yourself, your world and your programming.

3. You may accept at face value whatever you are told by parents and teachers who often just repeat whatever they were programmed with.

4. The BEAR cycle then operates as a self-perpetuating feedback loop: Beliefs, Emotions, Actions, Reinforcement.

5. Beliefs will seem unchangeable because of the BEAR cycle and is disguised by RISPARRS to ensure that the Ego stays in control.

6. By looking at RISPARRS you can see all the tricks of the Ego and thus change what appeared to be an unchangeable belief.

7. How long you choose to suffer before focussing on the solution is down to you.

The RISPARRS Exercise

Select a current issue or belief that you are struggling to change or a repeating pattern of behaviour to work on. I suggest that when you do this exercise that you do it as a silent, contemplative exercise that allows the answers to come to you, once you have asked the question or stated each word.

You will also hear evidence to the contrary which will be the opposite view of the Spirit. Make sure that you pay heed to both. However, let the exercise take on its own form to some extent and follow the evidence contrary to what the Ego is showing. Just because things happened before, doesn't mean that you are the same person now and they will happen again.

The belief is……………………………..

1. **Rationality**: This belief is rational and unchangeable because…..

(Here you will hear/look for all the objective evidence) almost like saying well everybody knows that…. It is likely to come up with whatever event has raised the issue.

2. **Is Justified**: This belief is justified and therefore unchangeable because….

(This will bring up a more subjective evidence and old programmes and experiences as evidence).

3. **Projection**: How does projection help to make this belief appear to be unchangeable?

Who or what are you blaming and thus projecting on to but not owning? How is this belief presented so it appears that the cause is 'out there' and thus not your fault or out of your control?

4. **Assistance:** How does receiving assistance or reinforcement from other people or society help to reinforce this belief as unchangeable? What are other people around you saying and suggesting to you? How are other people reinforcing it positively or negatively?

5. **Rejection:** How does rejecting any other way of thinking/being make this belief appear unchangeable? How/why do you ignore or reject advice to solve the problem and/or get over it? E.g. If someone suggests therapy or a certain book would you act on that? Think about what is being deleted,

distorted or generalised to keep you away from any other choice of thought. What is the evidence contrary to the belief?

6. Reward: How does the Ego reward you for choosing that belief again? Remember if you stay small, vulnerable or in fear it loves and rewards you with its protection.

7. Survivability: How does the Ego guarantee your safety and survival by choosing that belief again? Explore how the Ego links this belief to continuing to keep you as being lovable, likeable or an asset.

(Remember that the Ego's premise is: Don't try to disprove the belief because what if you find out that it is true? Then there is nowhere left to turn and you are now doomed. Stay as you are, then at least there is doubt in the authenticity of the belief.)

Once you have looked at how all of the mechanisms are being used against you, you can forgive the Ego and forgive yourself for falling for its tricks. Then decide to stop choosing fear and wrong-mindedness!

7. Imagine reality is made up of trillions of lines coming out of you and each one represents a parallel universe, and feel yourself moving into the stream that contains the new version of you with the new programming set. Acknowledge that the old structure is still there but now lies dormant.

8. Use the ABC to change the old behaviour wherever and whenever you can.

1. **A**ction – Something to immediately improve the current problem in reality. (For Jenny- to apologise to her brothers.)

2. **B**ehaviour – Select a new long term behaviour to practice. (For Jenny to be assertive.)

3. **C**hoose a new positive belief (affirmation) about yourself to use with the band exercise. (For Jenny it may be 'I am confident'. Do not use the negative version of the old programme as in 'I am not ignored' as that still opens the file labelled 'ignored'. Jenny needs a new file labelled 'Confident' to be started and filled only with examples of when Jenny is confident.)

Chapter 7

Fear as Control

"Fears only make sense if you believe that someone outside of you is creating your reality"
Anon

Fear plays a huge part in all our lives, but it is usually a very negative part. That is because the Ego uses the mechanism of fear, which ultimately is a negative belief to limit and control us.

The Ego fears Love and empowerment because these are really the antidotes to fear and can be used to restrain its power. But what is fear? Fear stalks you in many more ways than you probably realise.

Let us look firstly at the mainstream view of fear.

If you take the mainstream view that you are indeed a physical body, then a sense of fear is an innate and seemingly necessary aspect of your biological make-up. It is a key factor in your ability to stay safe and alive. It is a protective mechanism.

It is important to recognise that fear appears to be a natural and normal aspect of your everyday life. Therefore, you will never be totally free of things that cause you fear. I personally do not buy into that view because if you are not a physical body then there is nothing to fear but for now we will look into the physical effects of fear. Any fear will set off the freeze, fight, or flight (FFF) response mechanism in the body.

The FFF system operates in this way. If you sense danger, the body either prepares to freeze and hope not to be seen, fights to defend itself, or sets to flee and run away. These were the only options primitive man had.

As the system was originally designed purely as a survival strategy, the body prioritizes sending blood, oxygen and energy to the limbs.

This reduces the amount available to the brain as logic or planning is not necessary at that point. You will experience the FFF system as symptoms such as a racing heart, sweating of the hands and an inability to 'think straight'. Because all the resources are in the limbs, there is a lot less than would normally be available to the logical, rational frontal lobe. This makes it nigh on impossible to calm yourself down mentally until you have calmed yourself physically by turning off the FFF switch. I believe the FFF system—although this may be an over simplification—has an off/on switch. There is either fear or there is no fear, although there are clearly different degrees of fear.

I believe though that a lot of illnesses, particularly stressed-based ones such as Irritable Bowel Syndrome, may have something to do with our unconsciously living in a constant state of fight or flight. I guess this would be akin to having the switch stuck on the 'on' position without your conscious awareness of it.

Thinking about it logically, if you are constantly sending the majority of blood, oxygen and energy to the limbs, what remains to replenish and repair any of your major organs? What resources are there to boost the immune or the digestive systems? Your car will start to break down if you drive it continuously without replenishing it with oil. Thus, the physical body will break down if, in the long term, it doesn't receive the things it needs. With so many millions of people in long term states of anxiety and depression across the world it is obvious that we have become so frightened of life itself.

The obsession with health and safety shows that our lives have become completely overtaken by fear.

Now why should this be true if life is supposedly getting better? You are at the top of the food chain and in some ways your only predators are other people.

Barring accidents, which paying attention and taking care can usually help us to avoid, you should feel happier and healthier surely?

One of the solutions to remedy high levels of anxiety is to teach people how the FFF system works and how to turn it off. It is turned off by slow, conscious breathing. This allows blood and oxygen to return to the other parts of the brain which can then deal with the thought that caused the original fear. Remember from earlier that the physical symptoms (50 voices) have to be quietened first before the 5 voices of reason can be heard.

The Ego, as we have discussed, uses fear as a control device. Remember, that it sees the physical body as its temple and will do anything to protect it. Most fears in some way relate to either protecting the physical body from pain or avoiding death. The Ego wants you to believe that you are weak, vulnerable and mortal so that it remains your protector.

I am always reminded of the film 'The Truman Show'. In the film, the main character believes that he is living in a real community. However, he has actually been born into and grown up on a TV set. He therefore believes that the set is his real life. The programme follows his daily life which is, completely unbeknownst to him, watched by millions of viewers.

Interestingly, the way that the directors manipulate or restrict his movements is by triggering his fears.

As a child Truman witnessed his father 'drown' in open water. This sets up an extreme fear of the sea. He will never now leave the island that he appears to live on for fear of the water. He also has a fear of dogs. When the directors want Truman not to go somewhere, they will have a neighbour or actor appear with their dogs and Truman will move away from that area.

This is exactly how the Ego controls and manoeuvres you into whatever it wants you to do.

At their core then, fears appear to be avoidance programmes; avoidance of loss and of emotional pain. One could argue that the two could actually just be one programme of avoidance of pain since any loss causes pain by its very nature. Even the ultimate fear of death is actually about the pain of the loss of life; not the loss of life itself. Most people that I have asked fear a painful death rather than the ending itself.

Limiting our growth and achievements, these programmes can run consciously or unconsciously within us and will often be disguised as a fear of something completely different.

One of the biggest and most disguised fears is fear of death. People say that they are afraid of flying, heights or germs when really if ever played out to its full potential, it becomes apparent that their true fear is fear of death (loss of life). One of the biggest things that helped to free me from the fear of death was courageously facing death head on by learning all about people who had experienced NDE or Near Death Experiences. This is a very interesting research project because the wealth of data available from sources all over the world is generally telling the same story. Stories of NDE's appear consistent over great swathes of time and distance despite collusion being impossible between the cases. As a Clinical Hypnotherapist, I am performing many Past Life Regressions. Many of my clients are able to correlate information gleaned from their regressions with facts from the history books. All of this research helped me to drop my fear by developing new beliefs and 'knowledge' about what I believe will really happen.

Remember there is no truth other than what is true for you. Whatever you believe, the point is that it should bring you peace.

We will discuss more of this on the chapter on death.

There is a Zen Buddhist proverb that proposes that we should *'Face the fear and walk straight through it.'* This is a wise and successful strategy because most fears include a large element of lack of correct information within them. There is an acronym that is quite relevant here:

False Evidence Appearing Real.

In the film mentioned earlier, it is only when Truman decides to face his fear of water and leave the 'island' that he discovers the truth. What he had been taught (or programmed to believe) all his life was actually a lie. When he faced and walked straight through the fear it disappeared. Then it could only be replaced with the truth-the fact that his was a TV set.

The darkness of any fear is simply covering the light of a greater truth.

Fears, at their core then, are just another form of belief programme. They are beliefs with negative judgements overlaid upon them. However, the problem is that what you fear, you make real and with your heightened emotional attention to it you will increase your attraction to it. The Law of Attraction states 'like attracts like and what you think about is what you get'.

I like to remember this: 'No fear; no appear'.

Eventually as you do not think about the subject of your fear the brain begins to filter it out as unimportant to you. This means that you will not be affected by it any more.

Or as we saw in the last chapter, by actually analysing a fear with the RISPARRS mechanism you can bring the way that the Ego is using that fear to the light. Then you can face the fear and walk straight through it.

Some people, however, will maintain that they do not know why they are afraid of spiders or clowns or whatever it may be. The explanation for irrational fears mostly, and quite reasonably, appears to lie in a scary childhood experience. This is known as an Initial Sensitizing Event (ISE). The memory gets lodged in the brain but has not been archived as a past memory in the normal way because it is future-protective. It will also have been recorded as painful in the body's energy field. The body is always in a state of now and so that emotional tie to the pain remains current.

These experiences can obviously occur in adulthood too. However, as an adult we have enough ability to rationalise events and put them into their proper context. If however, the emotional experience linked to the event is extreme *for you*, in the moment that it was experienced, then a true phobia may still be created.

So let's really analyse fear.

As already stated most types of fear will have an ISE. For instance, I had a fear of wasps after being stung on the hand when I was eating a biscuit aged about four. This was my ISE.

Q: How do I know that I am afraid of wasps now?

A: You first need to grasp that we are only ever seeing the past. How do I identify this creature is a wasp to start with? Well as we have previously discussed, I must have a file about this subject in order to know what it is. I go through a checklist: small, buzzing sound, yellow, long body (longer than a Bee), has a sting in its tail. The brain analyses the patterns presented, recognises it as a wasp and opens the file. Therefore, I only ever see wasps from the past - so to speak - because this is where the current information comes from: old files.

Within that file is my past painful experience. This is how I know that I need to be afraid now as an adult. For there to be fear there must be a negative story in that file. I must have had, or at least interpreted these experiences as negative and made a note on that file that this thing must be avoided in the future. Your biggest motivation is always to stay pain free and alive; to move towards pleasure and away from pain. You may not have had any negative experiences yourself but may have been programmed by the warning tales of others, the media or through witnessing the fear of significant others. I only took steps to overcome my wasp phobia for example, when I saw my young son was starting to develop the same fear. He had never been stung himself but was copying me. You may remember from the first chapter that the cub must copy everything that the mother bear shows it? Well here it was in action!

How many horror films have you watched that may now have made you fearful of caves or ventriloquist dummies, for example? How much of what you ingest or don't ingest whether that be food or medicine, is due to fear-based information programmed in to you through the different media outlets?

The answer is that you can tell by looking at your own programming. It's an old story; it is history; 'his'-story. Even the spelling of the word shows you that the past is just your story about an event. Unfortunately, that old story is now what you are building your current life and future expectations on.

That the past creates the future is the story the Ego has told over thousands of generations and it is a strong root belief. People laugh at me today when I say the past doesn't exist except in their head. However, time doesn't exist in the way you think it does. As we discussed earlier in the book, a memory is a re-creation of an event, thought about and experienced now, but placed in a frame or idea called the 'Past'. Even looking at a photograph of a past event is being accessed now. Any emotional content of the photograph or memory will be experienced now. The body doesn't understand time. The body is always now. So any emotion engendered by thoughts about the photograph or memory are felt now.

Physiology follows thought immediately.

When you reach any point in the future, it will be now. The only moment that exists is now. Therefore fears about past or future events only exist in your head and thus are actually current programmes running now. The file has been opened and is on the desk in front of you. The perceived and feared future then, is a thought presented *now* but appears in a frame called the future.

All thought can only take place in the now although the content can be *about* the perceived past, present or future.

The Ego is obsessed with the past and the future. It wants to keep you moving and doing and away from the now where your real power lies. It has introduced the idea of the present, or the pre-sent, in order to make you believe that the past is responsible for whatever is happening now. Therefore, it suggests that the past wasp sting is the cause of the present (pre-sent) fear which makes the actual fear the effect. We have already learned that an effect cannot be changed. I cannot change the fear. This must mean that I can only change the cause. However, because the cause is in the past - which I have been taught is impossible to change - the phobia seems to be unchangeable.

The Ego *only* wants you to believe that the external world is the cause and consequently, you must be affected by it. In this way your power is seemingly removed from you. This keeps you unstable and powerless in that world.

You are trained to believe that the future is a result of, or caused by, your past or present actions and is therefore inevitable. In this way, the future becomes an unchangeable effect. Consequently, you anticipate an ever repeating future based on your beliefs about what has happened in the unalterable past. Again, fear is always about an *imagined*, unwanted future that becomes seemingly incurable because it looks like the cause is in the unchangeable past.

There is however, no reason that the past is unchangeable if you understand that it exists as a thought now. The real damage comes from the fact that there is an expectation that the same will now happen again. Once you understand this then, the phobia becomes a choice not to update the programming of the past, now.

I was stung in the past when I wasn't doing anything except happily eating my biscuit. Here is that 'out of the blue' problem again reinforcing that at any moment something bad can happen to you. Any moment of happiness can be turned to pain and so consequently I end up with pleasure and pain linked together. Therefore, I must now live in a constant state of readiness for attack, particularly if I am experiencing pleasure. This becomes a root programme from which lots of weeds or matching experiences must come. A weed looks very different from the root. My other experiences through my life will look different but come from the same source – life is scary so be on guard and pain follows pleasure!

My specific memory file says that the sting was very painful; everyone seemed to panic around me as my aunty rushed over to suck the poison out of my finger. Subsequently, I learn that this must be very bad. This seeming panic was linked in my immature brain to the pain. As you may remember, the brain associates. Now I am programmed with 'pain and panic goes together' -which I used to experience consistently.

Being only four, there was also a feeling of not knowing what was going on and that something different had happened to the adults. I needed the adults to deal with this as I did not understand where the pain came from. However, they did not initially know why I had suddenly started screaming and so appeared (in my perception) to be panicking. In reality, they were just moving quickly to discover the cause. Thus, what was recorded was a warped, inflated version of what was in reality an insignificant, non-life threatening and very brief event.

But the obvious question arises: was my phobia caused because I was directly programmed to panic because of the way I perceived the reactions from the adults; or by the pain of the sting itself? Remember that the answer can be both this *and* that. So I believe it was both of these working together. If I had not interpreted the behaviour as panic, would the phobia have even developed? After all, many children are stung by wasps but do not go on to develop phobias. Often it is the reaction of others, particularly adults that defines how the event is recorded.

Every word, thought or belief causes a vibrational and/or emotional effect in the body because, as I have already said, physiology follows thought immediately. So, simply the idea or thought of a wasp fires me into the appropriate action for the emotional state of fear - FFF turns on and I begin playing the Bear cycle out.

Let us say that I am in the garden as an adult eating a biscuit. The belief programmes such as *'wasps come near sweet things, wasps hurt and you must avoid them'* activate because biscuits for me are associated with wasps and pain. Just those thoughts are enough to create a vibrational and emotional effect (fear and nervousness) that in turn creates my actions (continuous alertness and anxiety). This reinforces the original belief that; *'Wasps must be avoided because look how they make me feel: vulnerable and scared'*. Now, just the thought of a wasp has successfully dropped my vibrational state. If I survive eating the biscuit with no wasp present the Ego will chip in with *"Well you were lucky that you were not stung this time but..."* to ensure that I held on to the fear. It then reinforces these ideas with the thought that *'It was only because you were alert that no wasp came'*. Therefore, I learn that being scared and therefore continuously alert keeps wasps at bay. Amazingly, the negative actions are suggested as being positive and future-protective. Again this ensures that I will need to be in a low level state of readiness for attack all of the time.

What all this means is that the Ego ensures that the original beliefs get reinforced even though nothing at all happened because no wasp was even present. The Ego has also succeeded in dropping my vibrational state which is exactly where it wants me.

It is essential to remember that anything playing out is simply old programming. When a wasp is present, the pain and panic association is activated and I begin to run around like a lunatic! This was how I recorded the appropriate action adults take in the presence of a wasp but became more pronounced as the fear became stronger. Paradoxically, as FFF gets turned on I may actually get stung again because my fear-induced panic that made my arms wave about frightens the wasp into stinging me again. Alternatively, I may successfully avoid being stung and reinforce the programme that this action works. In some ways, I am damned if I do react and damned if I don't and therefore the behaviour seems unchangeable.

With every wasp experience, whether being stung or not, the file now has another page added making it even stronger. Even though it was faulty thinking and misperception in the first place, the belief is continually strengthened. If I never look at that file again even though I may be twenty-four I am now living as if I am four years old on the subject of wasps. I know this is true because even as an adult I would cause havoc running and screaming like a child just at the sight of a wasp. This is totally irrational behaviour for a grown adult. This is not because I am a bad, weak or a stupid person but because I am reliving the root experience of being four.

So, how can you overcome these fears and phobias?

As I said, it is important to realise that there is often an emotional tie to a negative past event that is responsible for maintaining the connection to your present experiences. Any trauma (and the smallest thing can be traumatic to an immature brain) gets recorded in the physical, energy-body as well as the mind. Undoing this emotional tie will help the individual overcome the fear thus making it easier to then overwrite the files.

Hypnotherapy works really well for these types of fears and phobias because it can access the programmes within the unconscious mind and use visualisation effectively to change them in the now. There may also be other negative beliefs at play here such as 'this fear is too difficult to overcome'. You may not know (lack of information) that phobias are easy to change and overcome with the right tool such as Hypnotherapy, for example. You may not want to prioritise the time, money or effort it might take to find the right therapist or you may be reluctant to pay the price required. 'I am not worth it' may even be in play. You may be too embarrassed to seek help; after all, subconsciously you know that you may be acting like a child. All these are really, unconscious gains because your action will always be to follow your biggest motivator. Apart from the tricks shown earlier, staying safe and in your comfort zone is the biggest ruse the Ego uses to keep you weak. The problem is that the Ego is so clever in disguising what you really want and why.

It is therefore important to be clear and take responsibility for the fact that you are not willing to pay the price in time or money to get your problem sorted. It becomes obvious then that what you are actually saying is that you value the status quo more. You are actually choosing to keep the problem. You will always protect what you value.

I know I would have said all those years ago that I would do anything to get rid of this phobia. Yet if I look at those words they are a lie because in fact I did nothing at all until my love for my son became a bigger motivator. I also didn't want the guilt of him having to live like this. At this point the gains of teaching my son well become bigger than the cost of staying the same. Cost no longer outweighed gain.

So why would I keep choosing something that I consciously think that I do not want? What would motivate me to do that?

Have you ever thought about where motivation comes from? What drives your every decision and action? It's simply the Bear cycle on autopilot, especially if you are not aware of how the Ego manipulates the automatic aspect of the natural mechanism of creation. Once you are in the Bear cycle, there becomes a point at which you choose what will be reinforced - the old story, or will you reflect and edit the file? This choice-point is like a doorway to the light, an escape hatch.

Sadly I can see so clearly now that I had lived my life so disempowered and under the thumb of the Ego that it never even occurred to me to look for the doorway. That possibility never arose. The door didn't exist for me.

The Ego though will disguise the door because as we have already said, it doesn't want you even knowing it is there. But if per chance you do notice it, the Ego will present a raft of reasons to keep you away from it, such as it's too hard, there's no time, you are not good enough, (and its favourite): it's too dangerous, stay here with me, and I'll look after you... It will use the RISPARRS against you. If you were to do that exercise on any fear, you will uncover a raft of hidden rationalisations, projections and rewards.

So why do we agree to play this game? It is because the Ego is exploiting your belief that you are the body. All fears are about the avoidance of pain or the potential destruction of the body in some way. By making the body appear vulnerable, the Ego keeps you feeling disempowered and that you need its love and protection.

This is why the Ego loves the autopilot aspect of the Bear because it keeps you asleep and a slave to the Ego. Just look at how it gains from my phobia; it is using a threat to the physical body that I think is me. It also keeps me focussed in the past and future where there is no hope of change. This keeps me out of the now where a completely different answer exists and the Voice of Spirit can be heard.

That Voice reminds me that the phobia is simply old programming that can be updated or deleted now. That Voice reminds me that I am not a physical body; be calm and nothing will happen.

As I just said the Ego confuses my true wants and motivation and so I dutifully coalesce. It wants me to always see things through my fear goggles and not have the clarity of the clear, reasonable, adult viewpoint that Spirit has.

There is only now and the Voice of Truth (Spirit) can only be heard in the now. You can only be conscious of the now when you are not doing but being, which requires stillness and silence. It is true, is it not, that you cannot talk and listen at the same time?

Thus, by quieting your (Ego) chatter and thoughts, you can access the quiet Voice of Spirit that has no story about this wasp. Thus, the Spirit can successfully reinterpret the event for me.

If I see the wasp now without the old file then I have a different experience of a wasp. I actually overcame the phobia myself by just keeping calm and showing no reaction outwardly to my son. By telling him positive things like *"It's ok keep still"* and *"It's not interested in you"*, I was actually overwriting my own files too. As you give, you receive because we are all One.

The Ego will often use your negative beliefs to hijack your pleasure through fear or negative consequences. It is able to do that because most of us get programmed early on with pain follows pleasure. How many times when you were happily playing rambunctiously or play fighting with your siblings, were you reprimanded or warned that *"It will end in tears"* or even punished by your parents for having too much fun or being too loud.

Here is an adult example, I love the sun but the Ego pipes up that I must cover up or I'll burn. It reminds me of the risk of skin damage or tries to tell me I am lazy. It believes that I must pay a price for everything good or that this pleasure will eventually be followed by pain. The Ego can only do this with fear.

I was having a lie-in, which is a rare treat for me, reading and meditating innocently deciding whether to have a fourth cup of tea. You would never believe that this thought was a fear-based one would you?

I caught myself in a place of conflict over this and as I watched my Ego and Spirit 'converse' I was fascinated. The Ego was saying *"NO. It is greedy. You won't sleep later"*, which is a fear. My Spirit was countering with *"You are not a physical body. You have free will. If you want it, have it. It can only affect you if you think it will"*.

What I suddenly realised was that the Ego was using old information. Years ago I used to drink a lot of coffee and had trouble sleeping. Consequently, I weaned myself on to tea believing it to have less caffeine. Eventually I weaned myself onto decaffeinated tea and sleep very well. Therefore, four cups of tea will not affect my sleep because there is no caffeine in it to keep me awake. But the Ego was still able to use the fear and threat of lack of sleep as a weapon to control me with, simply because I still had old files open. These files are now providing outdated information. The lesson learned here was that I must keep all my files updated or it can be used against me.

Even though I've had this experience often in my life this was the first time I had actually stopped to examine it. To my horror the Ego stalks me with every tiny thing. When it was super cold and I was debating whether to play tennis or not, the Ego started berating me with *'You're being lazy'*. I play tennis mainly for exercise. Which if you play it through to the end is really saying, if you don't play: you are lazy = unfit = ill health = death! The Ego stalks me with death so heavily disguised as innocuous trivialities that no wonder I end up with base vibrations of fear and don't know why.

As a therapist, I see so many people experiencing an unconscious fear of failure. Fear of failure is innately connected to the realm of beliefs and judgements. It may manifest in many guises like public speaking or as a well hidden self-sabotage programme. If you risk trying to succeed at something but fail, this has the potential to cause you much suffering. Therefore, you will stop yourself before success comes too close. Worse than that, you may even decide not to even start a project because your fear is that you will not succeed, so why bother! Ego wins again.

It is easy to end up believing that if you aim for the stars and fall to earth then it is going to hurt a lot more than if you just fall from a low wall.

Fear of being successful or achieving your desires can also be used by the Ego to sabotage you. If you suddenly became wealthy, the fear of the loss of that money in the future can unconsciously be much stronger than the desire to have it in the first place. The risks of having something taken away from you is much more painful than if you never had it. Therefore, the fear of the pain of loss will often not outweigh the potential gain. Fear is the strongest programme running, but it is well disguised.

I see a lot of people in my work who have been programmed that to not succeed immediately (at a first attempt) or to not be the best at everything, automatically means that they are a failure or worthless. These people avoid all potential trials, tests or any situations where they might be evaluated or asked to compete. Consequently, they usually end up living very small and limited lives. There are lots of people out there, who use many other things as rational excuses or reasons to justify not attempting something. Again, these are just well cloaked fear programmes.

Often a fear can be the tool that the mind uses in order to bring to a person's attention to something that the unconscious mind wants them to deal with.

Let me give you an example.

I know of someone whose fear of driving covered up a very different fear. After repeated but unsuccessful steps to get him driving again we eventually discovered that there was an ISE (a childhood trauma) present that had nothing to do with driving. It was actually fear of being humiliated in public. He had difficulties walking and so if he couldn't drive this meant that he didn't *have* to go out in public. Thus, the ISE was actually his humiliation in public when he was five and he was just manifesting more and more fear based programmes to limit his ability to be in public. Once this was discovered everything else fell into place for him.

The unconscious is projecting out things that make you feel a certain way in order to grab your attention. Any fear therefore will make you feel like a victim. The fear overtakes body and mind which then appears to have complete power and control over you.

But the negative emotion used correctly merely shows you that you are out of alignment with who you really are. You have an emotional Sat-Nav system that is always trying to direct you to Happisville! Fear clearly says that *'You are not going to get there thinking and doing this'*.

The Spirit reinterprets the Ego's desire for you to feel 'bad' into the possibility of finding the cause or root programme of the fear and remove it from the computer. It is trying to help you discover what is hidden in the submerged iceberg of your unconscious mind. But because we do not understand that it is another unconscious projection, we just take steps to avoid the issue arising. My beliefs and programming about the wasp was the issue, not the poor wasp on to whom I was projecting my fear. I must have been the cause because I have never been stung or reacted to wasps since I changed my programming on them!

The good news is that you can use fear for positive reasons if you are prepared to look for the learning.

Fear can also be about not owning your decisions. If there is a particular issue or something that you do not want to do, you may unconsciously create a fear of something else as an avoidance ploy. If you did not get on with your partner's family in India for example, you may develop a fear of flying so that you could not go to visit. If you are completely against doing something then at least choose to a healthier way to avoid doing it. Better still, be assertive and own your decisions. Remind yourself that you are important too!

Most of the clients that I see in my sessions and classes that suffer from stress, anxiety and fear are worried about what other people think about them. They worry about how they are or will be perceived and judged. This can range from being in relation to how they look to what they wear, how they perform at school or work. There is fear about whether they are achieving goals that society values, such as having a good job, qualifications, a partner, children, being intelligent, blah, blah, blah! By remembering that another's judgement or criticism is merely their opinion, this can easily be neutralised. We have already talked at length about the Spirit's true vision of you as a perfect and invaluable puzzle piece. You have nothing to fear about being unlovable, disliked or not being an asset because as an adult you are responsible for your own survival. This is only the Ego's empty threat.

Fear of change is the other programme that the Ego loves. Change is always positive in the end. Staying the same is not positive because anything that ceases motion stagnates, just like water in a fish pond without a pump, for example. Again surrendering to the reality that change is the only constant is the only way to end suffering. A good question to ask oneself when dealing with fear of change is *'What is the worst that could happen and how could I deal with it?'* Every decision has a consequence and thus to face the fear head on and have a strategy prepared is truly empowering. Remember, fail to prepare and you will prepare to fail. But also, if you know that you are powerful and can easily cope with any change, this knowledge nullifies the fear. Acknowledging that even if you do not know how to solve a problem there will always be someone out there that does also removes the hold of that fear. A Google search never produces a blank page if you ask the right question! Non-attachment to specific outcomes also leaves open the possibility for something much better to appear. And finally there is only the space of now and you fill it up. Therefore, if you want something different you have to be prepared to let something else go. Fear and peace cannot exist in the same space!

Now I want to discuss something that changed my whole life when I was early on in this work of discovery. I call it 'Good Girl in Jail'. It is about how the Ego was imprisoning me with fear and I will present it as the exercise at the end of the chapter.

I had a shock when one day I heard Spirit ask me who was I running away from and who was trying to wrestle control from me? The questions stopped me in my tracks because when I examined the evidence, I was indeed running around in fear of people controlling me. I had to admit that there was no-one hounding me. I discovered that I hadn't even realised how much fear I was living in.

This started a profound period of personal exploration mentioned here and throughout the book.

Completely unbeknownst to me, I was living and acting as if some unknown other was trying to wrestle my independence from me. It was also chasing me time wise and seemed continuously out to get me. I live with my adult son and we get on famously. I make my own money and decisions. I have no enemies as far as I know and my life is sweet. But, unbeknownst to me I was acting as if I had to protect my territory, material things and my independence. But from whom? There was no-one trying to do anything or take anything away from me at all. No-one was trying to move in with me, order me about or evict me from my home. No one wanted to control me. Yet I was acting from a deep unconscious fear that this was a valid threat.

When I actually looked for that person chasing me down I realised there was no-one. Then it dawned on me that it must be me! It must be in my imagination, or rather my Ego!

We have already discussed how powerful the imagination is with regard to creation and so here I was using my most powerful tool to chase myself down. More shockingly, I didn't have a clue what I was doing. Now obviously I realise this unseen person is the Ego's thought system and that I was caught up in a continuous attack/defence cycle of victimhood.

In truth, it was just the Ego using all of its tricks to surreptitiously undermine my stability and security with the belief that I must protect myself from imminent attack. No wonder we are all ill or anxious all the time if we are continuously running from imaginary threats. How tiring and stressful is that? But how relieved and enlightened will you feel when you have turned on the light to see that there is no-one there?

So now that we have identified that the real cause is the Ego, it becomes possible to dismantle the walls of our imagined jail. Let me give you an example.

I was having difficulty at work with being 'managed'.

The Ego was illustrating the story of fear: someone is trying to control you. I am completely autonomous in my own life and run my own therapy business. So the couple of days that I was still working for the NHS, being put upon more and more as I saw it, were making me feel resentful and frustrated. Resentment is like acid and acid does more damage to the container it is in than it ever does outside of it. I knew that but I could not shift this feeling of resentment. I kept trying to reframe the situation and told myself *Just leave the extra work; if it's not done then they will have to get more staff*. This actually was what was needed. But I just couldn't leave the work and worried that the patients were the ones that would actually end up suffering. I looked at my beliefs and behaviours about why I wouldn't actually do what was the rational thing. Then suddenly, I realised that my problem was that I was imprisoned by my belief that I always had to be a good girl. My Ego had built seemingly impenetrable walls around me by my super conscientiousness, my strong sense of responsibility, my fear and lack/scarcity principles.

These traits formed my Ego-created jail in which I, as the good girl appeared to be imprisoned. I say 'good girl' because those two heavy, guilt-laden chains of responsibility and super conscientiousness made me a very good girl as a child and a well performing citizen as an adult. However, these had become extremely disempowering characteristics for me as an adult. The first thing is to realise that every thought and every action is exercised from the background; core values and beliefs of your particular prison walls. So every decision of mine was coloured by or measured against my need to be respected for fulfilling my responsibilities and praised for my conscientiousness. These were joined by the walls of trying to evade the consequences of lack and fear. These made up my prison walls.

Now before I move on I want to reiterate that everything and every quality are at their core, neutral. They can have a positive or a negative spin.

Selfishness for example, can make you feel lazy, guilty and disliked but used positively this can make you committed, focussed and successful. In fact to make this clear in **'Tour the Core'** I distinguish between self-is-ness and selfishness to drive the point home. Selfishness is something that you do that benefits you but may cause another person pain. This is the negative expression. Self-is-ness is about honouring the value of you first so that you can then produce positive benefits for all.

Anyway, responsibility and conscientiousness had made me lovable and an asset; caring and reliable. But when my depression was at its worst, these traits started to work against me.

Now in reality the door to the jail was, and is always open. I was choosing to be responsible and conscientious but I was free to choose the opposite also. But as we have discussed before, the Ego wants to hide this choice or keep you away by fear.

Eventually, I realised that I could leave the work and ease my stress if I dealt with that old programming from childhood and school. My parents (as I did with my son) brought me up with a very strict moral code of always doing the right thing and not letting anyone down, Consequently, very deep root files were created. These form my basic moral codes and values, or core beliefs if you prefer. As I had never really looked at the files since childhood I had been simply adding to the original core beliefs.

By looking at those files I discovered that I was replaying my disciplined childhood programming who was/is frightened of my elders or anyone in authority over me, like my manager. This was making me feel voiceless and powerless to stand up for myself lest I be judged a 'bad' girl (who won't survive). No one will protect or provide for me if I am no longer reliable, helping others or acting responsibly. So I continued this behaviour even though to do so, was now causing physical stress and unhappiness. The potential cost of not being conscientious and responsible was not worth what I gained by being a good girl, it appeared.

The other prison walls were made of fear and scarcity. Money is another of the Ego's tools because the mainstream belief is that you cannot live without money. We have projected onto money such power that it now runs our lives. It has become like a god or an idol in itself. When I looked at my life there was so much fear around lack of money, control and disempowerment. But in this example, the fear was that if I didn't please them I could be fired, be put out on the streets and die! Sound familiar? Yes it's the old Ego trick of stalking me with death again.

So the problem was that I had these four huge programmes of fear and limitation running that I had never really looked at and updated. Did these qualities serve me as an adult or did I need to update them? I did not want to completely remove these qualities, as used in the positive spin they are excellent traits. However, they needed to be updated with information like I am now - an equal adult and it is possible to speak up successfully if done with a loving intent and delivery.

So the Ego used them, to keep me small and disempowered, cowering on the doorstep of the jail looking at the open door but too frightened to step out. This was only because of the imagined or perceived consequences. Remember the prisoners in Plato's cave analogy did not choose freedom in the end. They continued to be jailed only by their invalid and imagined perception that the alternative was more negative than the present situation.

Thankfully, I started to listen to that other Voice that taught me that I was equal to my manager (we are all just people doing the best that we can with the knowledge that we have at that time). I started to update my files and worked on easing my fears about money and lack. I had no lack in my life but I was living as if I had. This was due to my mother's issues around money that I had taken as mine and I talk a lot about that in **'Tour the Core'**.

The key is that all fears and old programming have to be dealt with, not only in the mind, but because of projection, you also have to heal it in the physical manifestation of your reality. So I looked at the issue of what programmes I had running on 'conscientiousness' and 'responsibility' through mind maps and the Tour worksheets.

I put the ABC into action:

1. An immediate Action to take to improve the current problem in reality.
2. A new positive Behaviour to begin to develop (in life).
3. Choose a new positive belief (affirmation).

I did the band exercise diligently to overwrite old programming until I one day realised that the old files had changed and I was making self-empowering, right-minded choices. I had begun to value my freedom more than the pseudo-safety that the Ego-thought system was advocating as my only choice. Eventually I spoke up in a kind, loving way making suggestions rather than demands. Once all that programming had been updated I realised that I had no lack and could leave with a peaceful vibration. The fears subsided and my prison walls crumbled.

The Buddhists believe that it is clinging, grasping and striving for a thing, which is the cause of your suffering. You cling to beliefs, strive for control, and grasp at material things to make you feel secure in the world. But you are the creator of your reality and are in control of everything anyway. If you have nothing of value to lose, you cannot suffer by its loss, or even the threat of its loss. It is always the fear of loss that causes the most suffering. When an item is lost you can replace it and solve the problem. However, when it is fear of a possible future, it appears as if you cannot solve *that* problem. So I advise you to surrender and practice non-attachment to outcomes and especially things that appear to be out of your control. Remember the quote from the beginning: *"Fears only makes sense if you believe that something outside of you is creating your reality"*.

It is good to ask yourself this regularly:

What are you attached to in life and thus fear losing? This may be anything from relationships to emotions or material things. Now consider whether this attachment is healthy. If you make your happiness dependant on external things or people then you are always a victim to their potential loss or removal.

The Ego plays on your fear of lack and scarcity to control you. This works so well because lack can only be experienced by the body. As Spirit you are one with everything. You are a part of All That Is and thus must know everything. The Ego can give you an experience of believing that you forget things. It can cover over the door to the light by denying your real Self. The Ego will scare you away from it by planting that seed of doubt that says if you go out there to prove you are All That Is and it isn't true then where will you go from there? The fear of scarcity and lack ensures that unconsciously, all of your actions will be motivated by the need for survival. It both motivates and imprisons you through the ever present threat of paucity to keep doing, running and striving so that you can have all of your perceived needs met and avoid pain.

This is an insidious trick though because the fear of scarcity puts you in competition for resources with me. Remember what destroyed my bliss on the flight? It was the sudden realisation that there were others competing for the few locker spaces available. When you perceive that you are in competition for resources or have to 'fight' others for something, you have fallen into the attack/defence cycle that we shall explore further later. This reinforces that you are a separate, vulnerable physical body. In short, this induces continuous fear based behaviour.

Every decision that you make either reinforces the walls of your jail or removes a brick. The perceived darkness of fear is simply the absence of light; the absence of knowledge.

Overcoming fear simply requires that you search for the old beliefs and programmes and listen to the Voice of Spirit or right-mindedness.

Listening to Spirit leads to a positively joyous life but listening to the fallacies and confusions of the Ego leads only to more fear.

Self-acceptance, trust and faith in yourself as a Creator are the antidotes to the Ego's tricks and ultimately will lead to the unravelling of the Ego.

Quick Summary

1. Fear is a belief about an unwanted and imagined event in the future. Fear will turn on the Freeze, Fight or Flight system in the body.

2. Fears are ultimately avoidance of loss, pain or death. They can be directly seeded by experience or from a learned behaviour.

3. The Ego also makes fear appear to be unchangeable by confusing cause and effect with regards to time. The cause appears to be in the past which is unchangeable. The effect is projected into an unreachable future and the present is merely the pre-sent.

4. By bringing cause and effect into the now, the fear can be examined and old programming overwritten.

5. By making fear inseparable from the bodily reaction (FFF), the Ego reinforces that you are a physical body that can be damaged or destroyed. The Ego uses fear to direct, control and to manipulate you.

6. The Buddhists say "Face the fear and walk straight through it!"

Good Girl/Boy in Jail Exercise

This is an exercise that I developed to help my students discover what limits them and thus forms the walls of their particular prison.

1. Explore a situation that is causing you upset.

2. Think about what your core beliefs and values are and how these are playing out in this situation. Pay attention to what you believe that both you and other people 'should' and 'shouldn't' be doing. Where do these beliefs come from?

3. Explore how these core beliefs and programmes work with the most persistent of your character traits. You should now be able to start seeing the core beliefs that are forming your fears and limitations. Think about how these served you as a child and how they may be appearing to serve you now.

4. Explore how these beliefs or traits of your prison work together or against each other.

5. Now ask: Are these still serving you? How can you turn from expressing them with a negative spin to a positive one?

6. Use the ABC to change the outcome wherever and whenever you can.

1. An immediate **A**ction to take, to improve the current problem in reality.

2. A new long term positive **B**ehaviour to begin to develop in life.

3. **C**hoose a new positive belief (affirmation) about yourself to use with the band exercise.

Chapter 8

Attack Spirals

"Do not ruin other people's happiness just because you cannot find your own."
Buddha

I have two sisters and we are all very close in age. We get on fairly well but as with all families we get into the odd disagreement or get over excited when we are together. My brother-in-law says that we have the guinea pig gene, (i.e. when we get defensive our voices get higher and higher in pitch!)

As all behaviour is motivated by need, each of us learned to get louder and higher in pitch than the other in order to be heard.

Our household, growing up was very combative in that my sisters and I fought verbally and physically. We were all angry people for some reason. Therefore, what we were programmed with is that you have to defend yourself strongly from any perceived attack. To make matters worse, I had undiagnosed coeliac disease for eleven years and so was tiny for my age, especially in comparison to my sisters who are quite tall girls. Therefore, I really had to fight and defend myself, being at a size disadvantage. I also had a lot of the usual middle child rejection, 'poor me' and isolation programming running: not being as special as the first born or as cherished as the baby of the family.

Therefore, my old files were all about being a victim. If you could be attacked where you are supposed to be, and feel safe then there is nowhere where your safety is guaranteed. Fight or flight will be continuously on in the background.

This, now with the benefit of hindsight, is exactly how I have lived my life and one of things I believe, that led to my depression. When you have any victimhood programming running you will constantly see and be attracting perpetrators and attackers everywhere. Consequently, I was overly sensitive and overly defensive. I would switch from being an attacker to a victim in different places and at different times. I was quiet as a mouse at work, put on and walked over but at home I was angry all the time because that was the only safe place to express it. This was displaced anger.

An attacker and a victim are actually both low vibrational states and much closer on the vibrational scale than you may imagine. The best form of defence is attack after all. Obviously happy, healthy people do not attack or feel powerless. Therefore if you attack others you are really projecting your own powerlessness. Attack is never true strength.

Knowing that I can attack *and be* a victim simply reinforces my belief that attackers *and* victims exist, as everyone is a reflection of me. This is not necessarily because there are thousands of people and things out there waiting to 'get' me. This exists for me because I have developed a belief from childhood that this is the world and how people are. Consequently, I am going to expect the future to be the same as the past.

Your brain will start filtering out evidence for the contrary and actively filtering to match your current beliefs and thoughts. Therefore, I now realise that I didn't trust people and didn't think they would like me because in my warped perception no-one liked me at home. My over-sensitivity was really another way of saying that I expect you to dislike and attack me and I am ready to defend myself. Also from the LOA point of view, what you think about is what you get!

Your attention to any subject opens the whole file on that particular subject exposing both the positive and negative contents within it. It also sets your vibrational/emotional state on that radio station. So if you have victimhood running you are always going to be on high alert for potential attack. Therefore, you will only attract things that make you feel attacked or experience the other side of the coin, defensiveness. It is pure physics. You will be actively filtering for opportunities to see attack that consequently reinforces your victimhood.

Returning to our shop-keeping example from earlier in the book, if you are short changed in a shop but are feeling happy and healthy, you will most probably just point out the mistake to the shopkeeper and he will correct it happily. If however, you are in a vibration of victimhood you are more likely to see this as the shopkeeper deliberately trying to cheat you. Your reaction will be more aggressive and thus you are more likely to get an aggressive response back. This simply serves to reinforce your belief that you have been attacked and the spiral of ever-increasing hostility begins. This in reality was the projection of your basic victimhood programming onto the poor shopkeeper.

This victimhood programming will also cause behaviour such as being frightened to make a mistake, fearing criticism or stepping out of line. Thus even up until a few years ago, any time that I had made an innocent mistake or missed something at work, the fear of admitting this was overwhelming.

In my childhood mistakes meant punishment. Thus, as I was still accessing files from childhood I feared the punishment that was bound (in my perception) to follow from management. Thus, I would fiercely deny any error and even project blame onto lack of time, equipment or stress of having so many other things to do. I had to defend myself from all these perceived attacks.

Of course this was all in my mind and the jailor was me. No-one was out to get me or even would be that bothered if I had made a mistake. A mistake by its very nature infers that there was no malintention. We are all human and I certainly wasn't surrounded by perfect people or colleagues. Even though I knew all this logically and rationally I just couldn't risk *not* defending myself from these perceived attacks. This was a very tiring activity to do everyday and everywhere in my life.

Like a wounded and frightened animal, when cornered, I would lash out at people for absolutely no reason and for the most trivial of things. Because I was feeling so powerless and fearful of attack, the best defence my Ego could come up with was to attack first. Often I would lash out at my son because it was safe. He couldn't leave me or retaliate. When you are feeling weak and threatened but you do not feel that it is safe to attack back by shouting back at your boss for example, you will take it out on someone else where it is safe to do so. You may even take it out on things like kicking the car or smashing a plate. The mechanism of displacement is only really another name for projection because you must find some arbitrary reason to lash out at this other person to justify your attack. But again this clearly demonstrates that as ever, you are always cause.

It is important to note here that this is simply a neutral automatic mechanism and the Universe or God or anything else isn't out to ruin your life. The negative behaviour is not you and even this programming is not you. You are the Spirit and so there is no higher authority judging you; it is only you judging you.

Suppose, with the shopkeeper example, that you have defined his error as a deliberate attempt to cheat you. As you fell into attack and he into defence you may experience guilt after this. This is because A) You know unconsciously that this was your projection and B) That you have been horrible to an innocent person and so will be punished. Remember that you must be lovable or an asset to survive so now the Ego will flood you with fear and guilt. This reinforces your neuronets of victimhood, but now with the added power that you deserve to be punished because guilt is always followed by punishment. We will look into this more later.

For now though please understand that it is vital to separate yourself from the actions and programmes. You did not deliberately set out to be rude or aggressive but you merely have old files open, a low vibrational state and fell unconsciously into the attack spiral. All of these things can

The Ego Unravelled

change. As you are an Eternal changeless Spirit, these qualities are not you.

This situation with the shopkeeper then is merely another example of 'believing is seeing' and not the reverse.

As we know, the Ego's favourite trick is to reverse or confuse cause and effect. So here it appears that the cause is the actions of the shopkeeper. This is not true. The real cause is your perception of what is happening. We can see the event is neutral at source. I.e. the shopkeeper did not give the correct change. In the first scenario there is no problem as such. But in the latter, the problem becomes real *because* of the negative story or definition that you gave it. It was also inevitable to some degree because of your low vibrational state. A low vibrational state can only attract low vibrational experiences into your awareness. Your mind can only interpret this scenario one way because of these factors therefore, you are free from blame. It was simply a mistake.

If you ever conclude that the cause is someone or something else then you will have to wait for *them* to change or correct their error, in order for you to be free. This keeps you a victim and powerless forever because the other is actually the reflection of you. If you growl in the mirror it cannot change and smile first. However, if you accept that the real problem is the way that you are *allowing* yourself to feel or be affected then you become empowered. By accepting that this is your projection and returning cause to its rightful source which is your mind, then you are powerful enough to change it. If there was no cause in so far as you never saw any attack by the shopkeeper, then there cannot be any effect. You can only have an effect following a cause.

No attack; no victim *and* no victim; no attack

If you blame anyone, anything or any situation, for your suffering then you have not accepted your own decision to suffer. American Life-Coach Debbie Ford has a lovely way of demonstrating this. When you are pointing the finger of blame at anyone just stop for a moment and look at your hand. You will see that most of your fingers are pointing straight back at you.

You are aware I am sure, that you can concoct a whole, elaborate story about how bad and wrong the other person is. However, you will always come back to the same realisation. That realisation will always be that you have allowed the 'thing' to affect you and thus you are the cause of your own suffering. More bluntly put: you are choosing to suffer.

The obvious conclusion is then that you are attacking yourself. Here lies your power to create peace instead.

Let us now look more deeply into the attack spiral.

Firstly think about this: would the tiny island of Malta for example, attack the USA? The obvious answer is no. Why? Because it would be suicide for the tiny island who cannot match the defence capability of this

Superpower. This is important to understand because if someone attacks you, or least you feel attacked, then you have already subconsciously recognised that they feel safe to do so. It is *you* who must believe that they are stronger than you. Therefore, you have given them that role by default, by identifying them as 'stronger' than you. Paradoxically, you have thus defined yourself as weak! No-one picks a fight they think they will lose. However, if the one perceived as weak suddenly finds the courage to stand up to the alleged aggressor then the aggressor will normally back away. This is because only someone who is intrinsically weak or lacking feels the need to attack. Once you stand up to them, their unconscious definition of you is that you must now be stronger than them – or else you wouldn't attack.

Whenever you feel that you are being attacked, whether that is with words, objects or events, you have three options open to you. You will either retaliate, seek to defend yourself or you will turn the other cheek and do nothing. Any of these options actually constitutes negative behaviour because your first mistake is to define what is occurring as an attack. Once you have defined something as an attack it has become so. None of these options are single action events.

If you attack or become defensive there will be a spiral downwards caused by the consequential actions and vibrations.

Let us look at verbal attacks first. It is a fact that whatever anyone else says is simply their opinion. Any criticism or judgement is simply opinion. You must acknowledge that that person is actually talking about themselves. They are talking about their likes or dislikes; their wishes or preferences. They are simply highlighting their current programming and matching vibrational state.

Let's imagine that you say to your colleague called Mark *"I hate that jumper you are wearing. Don't you have any taste? Who on earth would buy something like that?"* Now depending on Mark's current vibrational state and programming, he will perceive this as either irrelevant or a very personal attack. If Mark has difficulty accepting criticism, is defining his worth on how he looks, or has victimhood playing out, then he will react as if he has been personally attacked. The comment will push his emotional buttons. He will take the criticism as if it is about him personally as the jumper is almost an extension of him. It has been his choice to buy and wear it and thus unconsciously it is a symbol or statement about who he is.

But it isn't really this that affects Mark. It is the same old Ego trick. Mark is now unconsciously running the programme that he has become disliked and so when he needs your help, you will not offer it. The Ego then whispers to him the ultimate fear: that now he will not survive. So again, here the Ego is surreptitiously stalking him with threats of death. I know it sounds dramatic but until you realise this insanity you will never be able to get over worrying about what people think about you is important.

Even if you say that I don't care what others think about me, if you actually question why you are doing things you will see the truth. Remember the examples of why you wash etc.

The only antidote to this is to hear that statement as simply one, neutral opinion. You must also separate what the real subject of the statement is about. In truth, it is the other person talking about their preferences only. It is not about the person or really even the jumper.

If Mark has perceived these words as criticism or negative judgement then to the Ego, he has just been attacked. This will then leave him with the option of retaliating; *"Well look at that dress you are wearing. It looks like it comes from the charity shop"*. Or he will become defensive; *"Oh I've had it for years I just wore it today because I knew we would be getting messy"*. It matters not whether Mark defends, or retaliates; both are negative responses that reinforce that an attack has taken place. Remember that when you attack or feel attacked you have only 'injured' yourself. You are causing your own suffering by allowing the programme that 'I am a victim' or 'others can affect me' to run again.

It is vital for Mark to remember that this is *his* projection of victimhood and that he is the cause.

Be careful also, that you do not think that to ignore criticism and say nothing may necessarily be the best way to deal with it. If you are genuinely not affected by it then of course, to not even acknowledge the comment is indeed a positive reaction because no attack has taken place. However, to 'bite your tongue' even if it is to keep the peace, still reinforces that an attack has been made and consequently is still low vibration and will cause resentment. You can tell the truth of how you are responding by the feeling or emotion that follows your responses. Remember that your emotions are like a Sat-Nav system always feeding back to you where you are in relation to getting to Happisville. The energy of suppression or resentment feels eminently different from peace and happiness. Criticism levelled or received feels bad because it is low vibration and Happisville is on Radio High Vibe!

You can also fall into attack spirals with things. Hilariously, I have realised that I have previously fallen into attack spirals with tins of paint, computers, curtain rails and almost everything in my environment, including the weather!

As I mentioned in one of the previous chapters, I had a huge strop years ago because I could not get the lid off of a tin of paint. It's funny now but at the time I was screaming and almost in tears with frustration as I fought with it for about twenty minutes. Really, unbeknownst to me, I had fallen into the attack spiral with a lid! I was acting as if the lid was doing it on purpose and was deliberately out to get me. It attacked me and I shouted and beat it back. It would then stick even more (attack back) and I would beat it even more. Crazy, crazy, crazy! Once my son had told me to calm down and move away he was easily able to remove the lid. Now this didn't help my old programming about a man doing something I couldn't but it did end the attack spiral. However, the lid had beaten me, according to my Ego! If I had calmly at the beginning seen what I was falling into I could have chosen a different action and outcome. I could have saved myself all that stress. It was a true example of what you resist, persists!

I noticed I did this a lot in my car. Because the car becomes your body on the road, any body (another car) that pulls out on you will make it will feel as though they have attacked you personally. Therefore, when driving you often feel that you must either defend or attack back to survive. This is why even mild rage in the car is so difficult to control I think. It is because unbeknownst to you it's a personal attack on your 'body'. Thus you may appear to have no choice but to take it personally.

More interestingly when someone pulls out it's almost as if you are saying that Joe Bloggs has waited at that junction (for who knows how long) especially to pull out on *you*. Again how crazy is that? When you resolve not to play the attack game on the road and choose to let all this craziness go, you lighten up and laugh at yourself instead. Eventually, you stop defining these minor incidences as attack or personal and you don't even notice them any more.

Probably unbeknownst to you, you are very good at making things about yourself.

Just as part of a very innocent conversation, I was telling a friend about an uncomfortable journey that I had had. It was about my experience on a coach with a gentleman that sat next to me who was so large that I was left with less than half a seat. As far as I was concerned there was no element of attack in this story. The story was about aspects of my journey and not about his size per say. However, my friend chose to see the story from the filters of her beliefs and perceptions and saw what she wanted to see through her fear goggles. Being rather large herself she started to defend the man quite vehemently. She made it personal, because she projected out that this is how people may be thinking about her. It was obvious that she had seen this as a covert attack on her. Her guilt and dislike of her size became projected onto me, via the other gentleman. Why would she do this? Well again I think that the answer is two-fold: A) I pushed an emotional button and activated her file of dislike of self, and B) The Ego then seized the opportunity to reinforce this programming by defining it as an attack.

This was very interesting to me and I started to think about all the things and people I may defend or defend myself against.

I realised that I had done exactly the same thing at the tennis club earlier in the week where I entered into an attack spiral. We had just had expensive new fencing placed around the courts. There is a market that runs alongside the club when we are there playing. The market uses our car park and so we, as players can park on our football grounds. Part of the warranty for the new fence is that nothing is hung on it for a certain period. However, the stall holders continually break this rule. On this particular morning I just couldn't take my attention off all the things hanging on the fence. To make it worse a couple of people visiting the market parked illegally on our field.

I am laughing as I am writing this at how pathetic I now realise that this is but these things were really winding me up. *"Well it's not right is it?"* said my Ego that thrives on righteous injustice! Why was I letting these things that were not really any of my business and not really hurting anyone, ruin my morning? When I did my work on it later I realised that I was projecting all of this deeper meaning onto the fence and field. The thoughts were that it's *my* fence, you should respect it and me, you are breaking the rules, and this will cost the club (me).

Remember also, that the super-conscientious and responsible child in me expects that all wrongdoing should be punished.

I was almost saying: I am going to suffer loss if you ruin my fence and you are not one of us, so don't park on *our* field. How crazy is that? Not only was I seeing this as a personal attack that I must defend, but I was behaving as if the fence and the field were an extension of me. It was as if they were hanging things on my body and parking on my foot!

Now, because I know this is my dream and everything is me, of course I would unconsciously feel that. But surely brought to the clear light of consciousness it is insanity. There is a basic confusion of realities here that causes my problem.

If I am going to live as if I believe the world is a dream, then the other characters are my creation and *cannot* attack me unless I design it that way. Consequently, my belief that they can do anything other than follow my instructions is impossible. There is no-one else when you are dreaming, except you. It also means that the body is not real. To perceive attack and then feel the need to defend it, must mean then that I really believe that I am living in a physical world and other people are real. The two scenarios do not mix at all. This is akin to either living in the Matrix or in reality. In the 'The Matrix' Neo has to take a red or blue pill to make the choice as to which world he is going to reside in. Will he exist in the Matrix and go back to sleep or will he escape to 'reality' and live outside it in an awakened state? Living in both is not possible. You are either awake or not.

However, there is one more option possible.

There is the possibility that I am choosing the dream but then denying this, so that I can have the full blown experience of life. However, this is a dangerous game because once I have denied it for long enough, I may then forget that I chose denial and now I am stuck in the dream forever!

I think that this is exactly what we have done in so far as separating ourselves from God and Heaven, to have an experience called Life. By denying Heaven for long enough, we have forgotten the reality of who and what we are. Albert Einstein said *"No problem can be solved from the same level of consciousness that created it"*. Therefore, we need the channelled information and teachers who are outside of this level of reality to share with us their revelations. They have to come in to *re*-mind us who and what we really are; the Light.

The lesson at the club was in essence like that of the car. I was denying the fact that I am creating people pulling out in front of me so that I would see this paradox and be able to finally grasp how real attack of any kind is impossible. Yes it may be an unconscious creation but it is *my* unconscious creation. Therefore, surprise attacks by things, people or out of the blue situations are also impossible.

This also makes any act of defence nonsensical because you would be defending yourself against your own creation.

You are prone to defend yourself most vehemently against any criticism of anything that you define yourself to be such as: man/woman, teacher, therapist, single mother/father etc.

Like my larger friend earlier, it is unsurprising then that you connect yourselves with everything and everyone around you. However, this should in fact remove all fear and separation from others and not increase it. It is only because the Ego encourages you to disown and disassociate from your creations that the game of attack can be played. The connection to your Oneness should nullify the need for any attack. This is because something that is One or whole cannot attack itself unless it sees itself as parts, which isn't then strictly One or whole. This is what you have done by splitting your consciousness into Ego and Spirit; the whole is now parts that can be in conflict.

Defensiveness is the same as attack. The reaction of defence only arises if you have perceived or defined that an attack has taken place. Attack is merely projection and would be impossible if you did not identify yourself as parts. It is the way the Ego wants to deny your part in the creation in order to keep you small, weak and invested in reality.

Attack needs a perpetrator and a victim. This is why the Ego wants you to believe that you are a body *and* a mind or even that there are two minds, precisely so that the idea of duality can allow you to attack yourself. That is also why the mechanism of projection is a key tool of the Ego. If you believe that there is your body and other bodies out there that can have different opinions, aims and wishes opposite than yours, then there is now the potential for conflict and attack. If my larger friend did not project out (and away from her) that she was being attacked by my coach story it would be impossible for her to see this as an attack. The story would have remained neutral and indeed nothing to do with her. No defence would have been necessary.

The Ego Unravelled

It is interesting to see also that you are continuously being attacked by things in such a covert way that you are likely to be oblivious to it. Time is the most obvious one. Time chases and controls us with its perceived qualities of being short, lacking and limited. The Ego ties in lack and scarcity to the attack and defensiveness spirals so that we are forced to keep rushing, worrying, striving and grasping. I even do this with the sun in summer. Because our weather is very unpredictable in England, whenever the sun is out I feel that I have to drop everything and sit out in it because the Ego fills my head with *"Well you don't know when you will see it again!"*

This consistent feeling of lack and scarcity haunts and stalks you. This is the Ego's way of consistently attacking you.

It may also be meaningful to you with money. The fear of money being scarce or totally lacking is for most one of our main drivers because it keys in to the ability to survive. As soon as you get money there is the stalking fear in the background that at any moment something could happen and it could be taken away. Therefore, you take measures to defend yourself from this attack by saving money for a rainy day or being frugal and tight. The happy consequence for the Ego is that we learn pleasure is intricately linked to pain and sacrifice and that there is a price to pay for everything. Any perceived pleasure will be attacked and destroyed. *'All good things come to an end'* or *'It's too good to be true'* becomes our mantra or belief. Once this has been installed as a belief programme it must be displayed on the screen of your life. Therefore, you will not be able to fully enjoy any moment of pleasure because the Ego will be surreptitiously stalking you with the knowledge that it will not last!

In some ways this reflects our belief in Karma. Karma usually, is interpreted as what you do to others will be done to you. Or that you will pay a price for your deeds. Now, as we shall see in the chapter on giving and receiving, this is true to a degree and certainly Law of Attraction would make this so. However, the difference between the Spirit's use of Karma and the way the Ego uses Karma is huge. Spirit sees it as a learning device. If you are the dreamer and the dream characters then of course, as you do to others (who are you,) you will experience yourself. To the Ego, Karma is an excuse for attack, revenge and payback if you are the victim. Alternatively you will be attacked, if you were the perpetrator previously. The Spirit's Karma eventually ends when all lessons have been learned but the Ego's means endless rounds of tit for tat, which is why I refer to them as spirals.

There can be no winners in the Ego's game. Therefore, Spirit advises to not play the attack game at all.

This is important to understand because even if you are the attacker and appear to win any argument or gain power or control over another, you will not gain anything of value. This is because as soon as you have perceived an attack, unconscious or conscious guilt and therefore punishment must follow. We will look into the whole area of sin and guilt in the next chapters. But for now let us remember that *'As you sow you reap'*. Knowing that you have hurt another actually drops you into the same low vibration as the victim. Like my friend earlier who made the coach story about her, she became angry and defensive thus dropping into the vibration of anger. Attacking me, took her into her own negative emotional state. Making me wrong and trying to make herself right brought up her own disappointment with herself, fear and most likely guilt. These are all low vibration states.

As we are all equal, peace can only be found when we are treating each other as the same, respecting each other and seeing no competition or hierarchy. It is important to remember that it appears to be bodies that attack (even if it comes from the mouth in words) and that you attack to *get* something. This can be demonstrated most vividly if we look at attack in terms of energy.

If we look at the hierarchy mechanism involved with attack, what we actually see is that the attacker perceives themselves as 'above', or more powerful than the victim. Subsequently the victim must see themselves as less or lower than the attacker. However, a happy, healthy person never attacks. A person only attacks another if they fear loss of some kind; loss of power, territory or life perhaps. You attack only when you lack or are in fear.

If we look at this in terms of energy, you want or need what the other has because you believe that it will increase you in some way. Therefore, this act is already coming from a place of low vibration. When you feel as if you have won an argument for example, you may feel a temporary rise in energy and the victim will experience a drop in energy. However, that energy boost will not last long because you have actually made the other wrong and 'stolen' his energy. As we will see in the chapter on giving and receiving, we have this idea reversed so that we believe we gain by getting and indeed lose by giving. However, the truth is what you give you actually keep, because to give is to share or extend. Thus, when you are giving out attack, that is actually what you are extending and sharing. This is low vibrational energy. Therefore, what you are actually gaining is just more low vibration energy. If you are angry at someone, it is *you* that will *feel* the anger. Then, with the guilt and regret that follows afterwards you are just attracting even more low vibrational energy. Thus attack causes downward spirals even if you may feel vindicated and puffed up for a brief moment as the victor at the end of the attack. The energy you have won will dissipate because it is nothing solid or tangible.

Often criticisms are really demonstrations of the attackers own need to increase their vibrational/emotional state by sucking energy from yours. It is almost as if by putting someone down you stand taller. You may feel better about yourself when you criticise, negatively judge or laugh at other's misfortunes or inabilities. However, these can be just as much of an attack as actually striking someone with an object. But what in reality did you gain? Nothing because you just ruined your own peace by attacking another. As an aside, be very aware that humour is sometimes used by the Ego as a covert attack implement. Many a true word said in jest really means jest is a cover for my attack on you. Jest can also be used as a 'get out' clause by adding something like *"I was only joking"* if someone has taken offence.

An apology or forgiveness on the part of the perceived attacker to the victim may go some way to rebalance or lift the energy levels for both. However, an apology only re-establishes the attacker as on the same low level as the victim. Asking for and receiving forgiveness however, elevates the status of the victim to the same level of the attacker in that true forgiveness allow you to rebalance the energy and power into one.

We will go into forgiveness in depth a little later in the book but for now understand that these are indeed favourable acts but the healthiest and most peaceful way to live is not to have taken any offence in the first place. Attack is only attack if you define it to be so. If you reclaim your projection and reverse cause and effect then you can see who really is responsible. If you have felt attacked then know that it is you that has injured yourself by *allowing* yourself to believe your own projection can turn against you.

It is often good to ask yourself: what are you projecting out and why? What vibrational state must you be in to have projected that? If you have made an error and attacked another then do not deny it, simply correct it so that no attack took place. Tell yourself a different story about the situation; redefine or reframe it. There is no objective truth, only your perception of events. If you do not choose to redefine a perceived attack and let it go, then you must be valuing suffering. You must *want* to feel attacked and like a victim. The obvious question then is: why?

Whatever you value, is your treasure and you will be forced to defend it if you continue to perceive attack as possible. There is no peace in this behaviour, neither for victim nor perpetrator.

The whole-minded thinking of Spirit knows that we are all One and equal. It sees no attack or attackers, only misperception and errors.

It is important that you remember that the body is simply a tool of communication for the Spirit. The body can never be used in any form to attack, especially if you emphasize your Wholeness.

The body then can be used to join in harmony with all 'others' instead of allowing the Ego to use the body for attack and division.

Peace begins and ends with your choices.

Quick Summary

1. All attack is made by the mind but is projected onto a physical body or object that will look like the cause. Therefore, all attack is an attack on the self.

2. Attack and the need to defend, can only arise if you believe in a physical reality that happens *to you*.

3. Something that is whole and One cannot have parts and therefore cannot attack itself. Two is required in an attack: a victim and a perpetrator.

4. All events are neutral so attack can only become so if you have defined it as such. No-one can affect you unless you allow them to.

5. If you define yourself as attacked you must now defend yourself which will require the other to defend themselves too and the attack spiral begins.

6. Apologies go some way towards healing. However, the asking and receiving of forgiveness can bring both parties to an equal standing and if done genuinely, it is as if no attack has taken place.

Spot the Attack Exercise

1. Find a situation in your life, or something that happened recently, in which you found yourself feeling attacked. Write a few lines about what you are blaming that person or thing for.
E.g. The shopkeeper cheated me out of my change.

2. Accept that this was your projection. Ask yourself why whatever the other person or object was doing or saying was a problem. What emotional button was it pushing for you? What was the emotion?
E.g. I don't like to be cheated. Everyone always tries to cheat me and it makes me so mad.

3. Reverse cause and effect. Now you are the creator of the problem, therefore forgive the perceived attacker for what he has not actually done.
E.g. I am allowing myself to suffer by allowing him to affect me. I don't know for sure that he was trying to cheat me; it could have been a mistake. (This is redefining or reframing). I will go and apologise.

4. At what point did you fall into the attack spiral and how could you have prevented it?
E.g. I immediately jumped to conclusions and I should have just politely pointed out the error. Then that big row wouldn't have happened and I wouldn't now be feeling this guilt or righteousness.

5. Look for the beliefs and programmes that are being activated and update or delete the files.
E.g. Why do I assume everyone is going to cheat me? It happens only because I have the programme from when my sister stole my piggy bank money. Therefore by having the programme I know that it is going to be displayed and I must change this.

6. Use the ABC exercise to change the outcome wherever and whenever you can.
   1. An immediate **A**ction to take to improve the current problem in reality. E.g. Apologise to shopkeeper
   2. A new positive **B**ehaviour to begin to develop (in life). E.g. Practice trusting others.
   3. **C**hoose a new positive belief (affirmation) about yourself to use with the band exercise. "I am in control of my thoughts. I am in control of my behaviour".

Chapter 9

Significant Relationships

"Whether we choose to focus on the guilt in their personality or the innocence in their soul is up to us." Marianne Williamson

As we have previously established, you are only ever able to see the past. Being able to remember what you have previously learned is an important element that enables you to quickly make sense of the world. By being able to rely on the fact that things, people and events generally follow set rules that do not change day to day, you can to survive in the world.

Let's consider a simple object such as a fork.

How do you recognise what it is, let alone know what to do with it?

The answer is of course, that you know by what you have been taught or programmed with in the past. You have neuronets or a file on it.

In reality, when you see a fork your brain searches for all the elements that you see (silver, trident-shaped, three-pronged, long handle etc) and then it searches for the matching file that has all of these elements. The brain says *"A*ha *a match"* and opens the whole file on fork.

Thus, although you feel as if you are 'seeing' the object in the present what you are actually doing is recognising the fork in the now but as information from the past (pre-sent). To cognise is to know and so to recognise is to know again! It is your past history or relationship with the object that you revisit. If, for example, your little brother Jason had stabbed you with a fork in childhood; because the brain associates things together, in your file about 'fork' you would have not only Jason but emotional and physical pain attached too. Thus, you now have expectations and a story about the fork and what it will or will not do.

Everybody's file about, or perception of 'fork' will be subtly different which is why we all have or see, our own version or experience of the Universe (*your Unique version*) of the world and events.

Now this is also the case for people.

How do you know that it is your mother for example, that has just walked through the door?

Again, the brain looks at all the information that is being received: tall, grey haired, glasses. It finds the matching file which has been labelled in the past as 'Mother' and you now recognise your mum.

Now for most people, their file on Mother is going to be very thick, very detailed and full of huge emotional experiences that form your story about mothers. But it is your story only. It is vitally important to note that this file includes what you think, feel, know and expect from this particular person; let's call her Mary. It will also include all of what you believe that she thinks, feels, and expects of you!

As soon as you have recognised your mother Mary walk through the door the whole file opens. You will be just expecting her to be the same as she always has been because you will be matching patterns recorded from the past. What is an expectation after all, other than something that you are setting in the future based on old information from the past?

Now let us imagine that your file about Mary is full of experiences where, she has let you down, shown she doesn't care or continuously criticised you. In this case your expectation will be that she will obviously do this again.

Therefore, you can only ever see the past about her. Moreover, you will be primed to hear something as criticism or perhaps perceive a neutral refusal of an invitation to visit, as proof that she doesn't care. Then you will find yourself saying *"See, I told you she doesn't care"*. This perceived evidence reinforces your expectations and worldview, which paradoxically makes you feel safe and secure. Unfortunately it has also just reinforced your neuronets that say she doesn't care. Or added another page to the file if you prefer, only strengthening your case against her! However, the truth is that reality operates as *'believing is seeing'* and so it is your expectation that informs your perception and consequently informs your interpretation of what are essentially Mary's neutral words.

Mary may have a completely different story about why she cannot visit. Mary may not see it as a big issue at all and genuinely has no idea why you are upset. She has never seen your file on her! And you have never seen her file on you, which may not include any belief that she doesn't care about you.

It is important to point out that because most of you never clear your files or old programming, you will continue to see your parents through the eyes of the child. Remember my wasp phobia when I acting as if I was still four! A child's eye view of the world is very different from that of an adult. This is especially true for young children. For them, every experience is emotional and potentially on a deeper unconscious level, either safeguards or threatens their very survival. If you remember from the chapter on fear, we have primal programming to ensure that we must be likeable, lovable or an asset in order to survive. When that child sees that parent shouting at them, or being angry it is, on a deeper level, life-threatening to them!

The parent may be just frustrated or having a bad day but the child without the ability to put it into perspective just sees that this parent who is responsible for their survival now doesn't like them and so may withdraw that support! Again, the child believes that if this person who is biologically programmed to love them unconditionally cannot even love them then what hope is there?

Now as always, there is no blame on any party here, just the recognition that unless we have looked at this programming and perhaps looked at it through adults eyes then it is still sitting in your file. So, when you open that file, the information that was recorded when you were five for example, is still there unchanged and so the expectation is that Mary will prove she doesn't like or love you again!

If I wrote a word document in 2003 and opened it again in 2017, all of the information will be the same as when I wrote it in 2003.

So whose problem is this? It's not your mother's…it's yours! It is your responsibility to update your programming or rip the page out of the file.

Let us now turn to our personal relationships.

Why do you seek to join with another in a significant relationship?

Well I think that the most fundamental reason, especially early on in life, is the obvious benefits of procreation. It is true that having a significant other that is invested in you and the shared treasure of a child creates safety and purpose for both. Each has what the other needs to create and nurture that child. The other benefit is that you have learned from your past history that you are much safer and more likely to survive if you are not alone.

Especially in our romantic relationships however, the Ego is out to *get*.

It defines a lack or a need within you that it seeks out another to provide. Therefore, in relationships where you choose the other person you will always want the other to 'complete you'. You may look for 'your other half' or the 'Yin to your Yang'.

A problem soon arises though. Because knowing you have defined the other as having what you want yet don't have, you have unconsciously elevated their importance. Subsequently, you will also unconsciously know that what you are offering is of less value than what you are giving. Consequently, you will start to feel guilty about taking more. An imbalance is then created for both parties.

However, this is fine if you both value what you are giving and getting in exactly the same way and to exactly the same degree. But if you value time but the other party values things like money for example, there will be problems. My ex-husband thought that providing a good lifestyle was important whereas I valued family time and attention; hence why we are divorced. Although we were both giving and asking to receive what we valued, there was a difference in how we defined the worth.

When we met I worked full time and actually earned as much as he did and we were both offering something of equal value. When I had my son and gave up work, my husband may have unconsciously felt like he was giving more than he was receiving. This was because he valued money over attention. There is no judgement about this. I am just using this as an example of how different people value different things. Unconsciously, I knew that on the money issue I was receiving more than I was now giving and so felt guilty on a deeper level.

It was love at first sight when we met and we spent every minute that we could together. The value that we put on time spent together was equal at that point. However, as our son came along and my son demanded most of my attention there was obviously less for my husband. So when I valued our family Sundays together but he felt pressure to work, I started to feel that I was losing. He valued a high standard of living and so to make up the loss in our income, he began to work on Sundays. He would have known that he was now giving less than he received regarding time and attention and so would also feel unconscious guilt.

The other problem we need to understand in terms of being in a relationship is that as you give you receive. As you will see in the chapter on giving and receiving, this becomes a real sticking point. Annoyed and frustrated that he wasn't prioritising spending time together, I gave less and less and valued what I was receiving less and less. Of course, he did the same because this is part of the Law of Giving and Receiving as you will see later.

By thinking about what you are *bringing to* the relationship instead of being unconsciously focussed on what you *need from* the other person can make a huge difference. In this way, if you value what you give, you will value what you receive. Even if the two things that are given and receive look very different remember it is only you that can determine worth. Someone who was a little more materialistic than I would have thought he was the perfect husband. It really is completely subjective as everything has a neutral worth.

When you need something, what you are really saying is that you lack something. If you feel physically weak as a woman for example, you may seek a strong man physically. If you believe that you are unorganised and unable to manage your affairs, you may seek someone that will take control of everything. If you feel poor you may seek a richer partner to support you. However, you must understand that these relationships are in reality co-dependencies. True Love is whole and thus doesn't ask or need anything from anyone else. Loving to 'get' is the Ego's 'poor man' version of God's

Love.

By ever judging yourself as lacking or in need of what another has, you have given them worth that is above your own. Therefore, you will always feel of lower value in the relationship. This then leads to guilt as you perceive yourself as taking something of more value than you are giving. Offering something that you perceive as low value (yourself) you can only receive love perceived as low value back. This will only leave you feeling unfulfilled. When you do not value what you are receiving you will end up not wanting it and become increasingly unhappy. We will see more about this in the chapter on giving and receiving.

The other significant reason why you join together is to learn about and heal yourselves. In our significant relationships, the 'honeymoon' period occurs because you are blinded by lust and so do not see who you are really dating. They, like you, are promoting a 'best' version of themselves. Both parties are far more conscious in the early days of what they are presenting to the other in thought, word and deed. You want to lure the other in and make them love you. Then once the commitment (in whatever form that takes) has been made you can relax into your 'real' self. You will feel safe to expose your bad habits and perhaps more negative traits. Now, if those traits are close enough to your partner's to be tolerable, the relationship may have its ups and downs but will succeed. If those traits are completely unacceptable then it will not.

It is important to realise that you have attracted that partner for a reason. That reason is, that they will have what you need to learn, or to overcome and vice versa. So if you have victimhood running you will attract a perpetrator so that you now have an opportunity to overcome that. Remember from the earlier chapter on how the mind programmes you, the child from the domestic violence household for example, will feel unconsciously at 'home' with a matching scenario in their relationship. You may often marry a substitute for your mother or father so that you may have another opportunity to resolve issues in that relationship, through this one.

Transactional Analysis is a system of looking at how we operate and understand ourselves, developed by Eric Berne. It describes the Parent, Child and Adult triad of Ego states. Basically you move around these states in your life and this reflects through your relationships. If you were Mary's daughter for example, you are likely to go into the Child state and Mary will be in the Parent state when you are together. This will manifest whether you are seventy and Mary is ninety. You will always be the child to the parent and vice versa. However, because this is a hierarchical relationship, conflict will arise. As two adults, you should both be equal and dealing with each other as equal adults.

We can see this most clearly with someone whose mother has

Alzheimer's disease, for example. Let us call the mother June and the daughter who is now the part time carer, Tracey.

June had always ordered very expensive, special beauty products from the internet but was now incapable of using a computer and doing this for herself. She asked her daughter Tracey to continue ordering for her but Tracey was shocked at the prices. She considered this a waste of money and refused to order the items. June still believes that 'she is fine' and cannot comprehend why Tracey will not do this for her. People who have any kind of dementia usually retain a good long term memory.

The real issue is that June still thinks of herself as mother and person in authority over Tracey, whereas Tracey sees the roles reversed. Tracey now sees herself as the person in authority over June, as her guardian and carer. This confusion of hierarchy and status is a favourite trick of the Ego and is the real problem here. June is in her normal Parent state and interacts with Tracey as if she is the Child state. Unfortunately, Tracey is interacting with June as if she *is* the parent and thus unconsciously expects June to become submissive as a child would.

As both are unaware of this confusion of hierarchy, communication becomes troublesome. Whenever there is a confusion of hierarchy in any relationship there can be no peace.

Now firstly there is the wider moral issue about respecting the rights of people with dementia. June had the money and it was something that was important to her. It was not going to hurt her or anyone else to continue to use the products. Tracey obviously believed she was protecting her mum but also was valuing being right over being happy. However, she must realise that it was not really a battle worth fighting especially as it was causing so many arguments. Tracey needed to realise that part of the problem was that June expected her child to do as she instructed, because that was what had always happened in the past. That was the only programming June had. Therefore, if Tracey wanted to be happy she needed to update her files. It is true that Tracey had to look after June physically but mentally she was June's equal; she was now an adult.

Therefore, Tracey needed to re-label/redefine June as 'friend' when interacting with her. This is a hugely successful strategy that I have found works every time when having issues with any other adults that you are in a significant relationship with. A significant relationship is anyone who has a specific label apart from their given name. Examples include Mother, Father, Brother, Sister, Teacher, Boss etc. We will discuss significant romantic relationships further on in this chapter.

So by redefining June with a less emotionally charged label such as 'Friend', there will be two shifts in the relationship. Firstly, Tracey will not activate and open the whole file of 'Mother' with all of the past negative stories and expectations included. This is vitally important in this case because June is definitely not the same person as she used to be because of the dementia. Although June will always be her mother and Tracey will always love her, as such June is no longer able to function in the 'Mother' role. Consequently, the old file is completely irrelevant.

By creating a new file as 'Friend' what you will find is that the file itself is very different because you will have vastly differing expectations of your friends than you would do of your mother. You will often say things to family members that you would never dream of saying to a friend or colleague. You also may treat family members in ways that you would not dare do to anyone else. Morally, that should not happen but *'familiarity breeds contempt'* as they say.

Ideally, everyone should experience the best of you at all times.

What this means in practice is that Tracey must be ready and primed whenever she is in her mother's presence to treat her as she would an equal adult. It is unlikely that if one of her friends asked her to order a product from the internet and had the money to pay that Tracey would refuse to do so. She certainly would not dismiss them or dictate which products they could or could not use. So why should she do this to June who is essentially just another adult requesting help?

If Tracey practices this technique, what she will find is that after a while she will not be reacting to her mother's requests in the same negative way. This is because there is now no old file; no held resentments or emotional buttons to be pressed. Consequently, there are no expectations of how a mother (or perceived child) should behave or be treated. As long as it is safe to do so Tracey should honour all of her mother's wants and wishes. This will transform not only how Tracey thinks about June but also how June reacts to Tracey. Treat someone with love and respect and that is all that you can receive back. June will now feel equal, listened to and in control of at least this aspect of her life. She will thus view Tracey as a 'good girl' if you like, which pleases her and reinforces the good stuff in her file of 'Daughter'.

For Tracey, she will now see a friend which again will relieve a lot of the physical and mental pressure that she felt in her role of 'carer'. She could also let go some of the psychological pressure that she places on herself of always having to be a good daughter. Paradoxically, by being a good friend she becomes a good daughter and how good she feels about herself and her mum will increase greatly. Peace will return to the relationship. So the first shift that occurs for you by re-labelling any relationship in your life is a release of old emotional baggage and expectations of responsibility. You now have a clean slate; both you and other.

The second shift comes with the realisation that you have a secret checklist for everyone with a label in your life. That means everyone, with whom you are in any kind of significant relationship.

Part of your file contains what I think of as your checklist of attributes and qualities that form a definition of said person and role. It is important to note that each person's checklist will contain some generally accepted characteristics and some that come from your personal experience and programming. You should also be aware that said checklist will always includes expectations from day one of your meeting unless you have ever updated the file. It is important to remember that no information is ever lost or destroyed by the unconscious because every experience and data gleaned from it is valuable. You would have to make a conscious decision and take action to update a file.

This checklist is then projected onto the other person and the brain will continually look to check that the other person is fulfilling the criteria of their given role. If a person performs the actions from your list you will love them and if not you are most likely to withdraw your love.

For example, Tracey's checklist for 'Mother' may include:

- Loves me unconditionally.
- Always there for me.
- Feeds, dresses and comforts me.
- Always has my best interests at heart.

All the way through to later additions such as:
- Baby-sits for my children.
- Lends me money if I need it.

This makes it very clear I think that Tracey's expectations about what she unconsciously believes her mother should provide, especially as an adult, needs updating. These are simply her perceptions and not intrinsic truths which is why everyone's checklist is different. The fact that everybody's checklist for 'Mother' is different shows that this is never how it *has* to be. These are just beliefs. Tracey will have no idea that she still has all these expectations until they are challenged or appear to be unmet. Tracey has never examined her own file on 'Mother'.

Some of Tracey's frustrations may come from the fact that although she is now in the 'Mother' role physically, unconsciously she is still in the 'Child' state. She will thus be resentful that June is not meeting any of the items on her checklist for 'Mother'. This is then strongly reinforced, as Tracey in her role of parent to June is not performing to her own definition of what a mother does. To love unconditionally includes respecting that person's wants and wishes. The result is both confusion and guilt for Tracey.

You can see from this example that it is vitally important to continually look at and update who and what you are labelling. It is also vital to look closely at the definitions and expectations that you have on your checklist.

Then you must regularly update it, especially if you are performing in that role also!

As an adult you are a strong, independent and hopefully, a responsible being. Animals for example, will send their young off once they are able to fend for themselves. The adult animal wouldn't then expect their parents to be around all their lives to fend trouble off or even to feed them. Why then should you?

That's not to say that you cannot ask for help or to give and receive love and support, if and when it is needed. It is more about not acting like you are still a dependant child or less than any other adult simply because you are not aware that you are still playing the hierarchy/labelling game.

You need not change your level of love for your family but you should aim to bring friends and everyone else up to the same level of love and respect. In some ways no-one should be more special than anyone else. This is the only place that peace exists.

Let's now look at how the mechanism of attack and defensiveness that can be seen in this example.

June's file on 'Daughter' may include 'doing as I tell you to do'. So when Tracey fails to comply with her request to purchase the products, this love relationship soon turns to a negative relationship. June begins to get angry, resentful and appears not to like her daughter any more. They have now fallen into an attack relationship. It's key to notice here that it is really her daughter's behaviour that she is rallying against not Tracey per say. June is really projecting her own frustration at not being able to get her own needs met. So the real cause of her anguish is her own powerlessness but she is projecting it onto Tracey as the problem. Again it is vitally important to be able to separate ourselves from our feelings or behaviours and catch the confusion of cause and effect. However, in this case due to her dementia this may not be possible for June.

June starts to remonstrate with Tracey and Tracey will react and likely fall into the attack spiral, otherwise known as an argument. When someone attacks you many things are going on unconsciously. As we have already said, you can only be attacked if you define it as an attack. Therefore, all attack is in your head in so far as it is your perception. Everything in life is neutral. The meaning of an event comes from your definition of the event. When you define something as an attack and then react, you have made the attack real. So let us take the example of June and Tracey again to make this very important concept clear. I will also note the vibrational/hierarchical relationship going on.

June innocently requests that Tracey orders her products for her. Tracey innocently explains that she will not, because (in her opinion), they are too expensive. Note that both feel that they are acting reasonably at the beginning and thus are innocently pursuing what they believe is right for them.

June, for the multitude of reasons already discussed, feels this is unjust. She now feels disempowered and hence feels weak and vulnerable or 'attacked'. She now starts to rant at Tracey. Tracey will either become defensive or attack back. Even leaving the room can be a defensive move. Once the attack has begun it can only lead to an emotionally negative outcome, no matter what the physical outcome. This is exactly what Tracey experienced and had begun to suffer from. She could not let the issue go because she felt that her mother's resentment entered every aspect of their relationship after that. You should note that the refusal that caused resentment would now be recorded and thus activated on every subsequent opening of June's file of 'Daughter'; every time they met going forward.

June is projecting blame for her own powerlessness on to Tracey and Tracey is projecting her own powerlessness onto June. Both are now attacking the other because they perceive the other as attacking them. Tracey unconsciously knows that she is playing out her own projection that her mother always criticises her and she can't do anything right.

There is also the confusion of cause and effect at play here. Tracey believes that June is the cause of the problem whilst June believes that Tracey is the problem. If Tracey could reverse that belief and reclaim her projection she would be returning cause to the same place effect lies and the two will cancel each other out. In fact, there has been no attack effectively if Tracey doesn't make it real by reacting as if there has.

There is always another way. There is always choice.

If either June or Tracey decide not to hear the other's words as attack the cycle ends there. If one of them manages to turn the other cheek, spot the spiral starting and not take what's happening personally, a new outcome is possible. In this case, because June may not be capable of a different way of thinking due to her dementia, the responsibility falls on Tracey. This will happen in all cases though, because remember *you* must be the solution. You will wait a long time for others to change. When you define something as attack and then react, you have become the attacker.

Tracey must see that she is at risk of falling into the attack spiral and choose not to hear June's rant at her as personal. A good tip here is to not use personal pronouns such as 'you' or 'my' when arguing. Personal pronouns such as these are often said or heard as accusatory. Instead of saying *"The problem with you is..."* you could say *"The problem as I understand it is..."*

By hearing what June says objectively as her opinion or even just letting it go in one ear and out the other, Tracey can change the state of each interaction. Tracey may feel she is right but is this a battle worth fighting? Her intention is a loving one to protect her mother and so her rant may be justified. However, the truth is that this is only causing disharmony, is not really important and so is not worth defending. Tracey would be better off just buying the cosmetics so that her mother could be happy. Is the cost of the disharmony worth the gain of winning the argument? Her mother is not attacking her; June is just trying to get her cosmetics. Nothing else is really going on other than Tracey's old files opening and as previously discussed, there is a confusion of communication and roles.

Peace and harmonious relationships can only exist where both parties are equal in all ways. But sometimes not falling into the attack spiral can be difficult especially if others do not understand or agree with your decisions.

Your relationships are obviously very special to you. When you label anything as special, as or more significant than something else you set it apart as different and on a separate level to everything else around it. This judgement creates the hierarchical states that cause you conflict because that judgement causes rejection of everything that it is not.

If you judge one race, religion or even skill-set as better than another it will cause unconscious bias against the others that have been rejected, which colours all of your proceeding thoughts and actions.

Hierarchical levels are damaging in all ways and for reasons that you have probably never thought about.

You are taught in the scriptures not to judge lest you be judged. What that actually means is that to judge something or someone, reinforces that things can be different and on separates levels. To judge is to evaluate.

When you judge *for* something; you judge *against* the rest. Rejection of anyone else creates a low vibrational state within you because you are one and equal. When you judge *against* something or someone you positively accept the rest thus isolating and 'endangering' the negatively judged person or thing.

So whatever you are judging and thus rejecting in another, moves you away from the Spirit's unifying thought system into the separatist viewpoint of the Ego. If you are the one judged negatively then the idea of being judged as unlovable, disliked or no longer an asset makes you vulnerable to attack. Therefore, by judging anything you are already creating an element of competition or conflict in that things are better or worse, bigger or smaller etc.

Any judgement will reinforce your current world-view and is only really at its base, a statement of your preference. The truth is that judgement is always personal to the person forming that judgement.

Judgment is simply opinion!

All events are neutral until we assign them meaning. The state of the glass is whatever you judge it to be. If you judge it to be in one state, half empty, the other possible state arises too - half full. Who would be right to say it is half full or half empty? Often there is no right or wrong and sometimes there is just yes to both possibilities! It doesn't have to be this *or* that. Often there is no truth.

Therefore, to judge often creates meaningless and arbitrary differences and always involves rejection of everything that isn't your preference. If you judge you can also expect to be judged, which again sets up the possibility of rejection coming your way too.

If you can refrain from judgement and see everyone as equal then, the term 'special' becomes a meaningless term. Spirit sees no hierarchy or difference and that is why it is a more loving and accepting thought system. I am working on seeing everyone as equal. (And it is a work in progress!) Therefore, I aim not to consider anyone more special than anyone else. I am working on the idea that there is no differentiation between family, friends and colleagues. Here then, there would be no-one rejected by a definition of 'special' for one group or person. By removing all of the arbitrary labels and files on people, I aim to be able to treat others equally and receive equal treatment from others too.

This next example will highlight why these hierarchies or special relationships should be unwanted.

One of my many friends was going through a difficult period in his life and slipping down the vibrational scale into depression. I offered him the most valuable thing that I have and the most important thing that he needed at that point which was my skill as a therapist. Obviously I had no intention of charging him but knew that I could do more for him in that capacity than just sitting with him having a cup of tea and listening to his troubles. This is what he wanted under the guise of support.

I always teach that you cannot help someone sitting in the bottom of a well by going down and joining them there. This is basic Law of Attraction. You will drop your vibration down to where they are and now you are both suffering. You are of more help by staying on top and offering your hand down to pull them up. In reality that means *not* joining in supporting their problems but directing them towards the solutions. This is the most loving thing to do even though they may want to wallow a while in their misery.

Unfortunately there are many people who have become addicted to misery and complaining as a successful strategy for obtaining gains, such as love, attention and support.

Anyway back to my example. Now this friend rejected my offer several times and so I decided that he wasn't ready and just left the offer on the table for the future. He was also being secretive about what the details of his struggles were and so I assumed that he didn't really want me that involved and left it for him to contact me when he was ready.

However, later he sent an angry email saying that he felt I had let him down and not been there for him. One of his complaints was that I did not go to his house and see him. I had never been to his house before and so it never occurred to me to invite myself over now. I had offered him best help that I could give him (which is my knowledge) but at my house.

I noticed from this email that he was setting us up in a special relationship that was obviously a lot more 'special' to him than me. I had no clue that he had such high expectations of me because I had no access to his checklist of 'Friend'. My checklist of 'Friend' was obviously completely different because in times of trouble I usually get myself out of it. If I do need someone to offload to, I go to my sisters rather than offloading onto friends. Therefore the idea that *friends should be readily available for emotional support in the home environment of that person* was alien to me. Please be aware that there is no checklist better than or more right than any another but do remember each checklist is personal to you only. Therefore there is no negative judgement of him or me here.

Now, I myself have been depressed and I just wanted to be left alone so again, wanting people around all the time just doesn't compute with me. What I did understand however, was the sense of powerlessness involved. Whenever you feel powerless you will try to unconsciously regain power wherever it feels safe to do so. In essence you lash out at those you know will be ok in the end with it. I lashed out against my family for ridiculous things. He knew full well on a deeper level that I would not hold a grudge or let it affect me and so felt safe to do so to me.

However, because I was just learning all about the attack spiral stuff I did not attack back or even feel the need to defend myself.

I emailed back as neutrally as I could and explained that I saw there was miscommunication here, that my offer was still open and that I still loved him. He chose to just ignore everything I sent after that, which is his right to do. I continue to treat him as I have always done sending regards for birthdays and Christmas because I see no attack here and so no apology or forgiveness is necessary on either part. I am, even though I miss him, at peace.

However, by choosing to hold on to his anger he is causing his own suffering (or not? I do not know). I do know that the Ego loves to feel that it has been unfairly treated and gains an insidious power from this fact. Think how many times you may tell others how unfair and unjustly you have been treated by friends, family, the government etc.

I have however, had to keep reminding myself that I had acted as a good friend to him within my framework of 'Friend' and that I had offered him exactly what he needed to help him with his depression. At the end of the day that was all that I had to give of any value to him. I knew that I was doing the right thing whether he saw that or not. This was a difficult lesson and I had to continually remember and argue with my Ego that I don't have to be loveable to survive. I know that one day when he looks back from the light that he will see this.

I hope that this example really shows how we can create or free ourselves from the eternal cycle of attack and defence that we are often so oblivious to in our relationships. I also hope that you can see the need to explore how your definition of a special relationship and the resulting checklist can also cause your suffering.

Before we end this subject though, it is important to recognise that you can be in a special relationship with things. The most obvious object that demonstrates this is money. You project on to money all kinds of meaning and power that a little bit of paper clearly, doesn't really have.

You can be in a significant love or significant hate relationship with it depending on how closely it is matching the criteria from your checklist about it. That checklist will have been developed from your programming and experiences about it throughout your life. For many years unbeknownst to me I was living my mother's life around money. Due to early programming, my file and checklist used to contain things like: there is never enough, I need to have a certain amount put away for emergencies etc. Thankfully once I had looked at my issues I had the opportunity to update my beliefs about money and wealth. My relationship with money is now one of abundance and peace since I updated my files.

I was amazed to find myself in a special relationship with the tennis club. It was listening to my language that gave me away. In the last chapter I explained about the new fencing and even wrote: *"We had just paid for new fencing"*. This gives it away that on some deep level I feel that I have personally paid out for this fencing and so it was special to me. Both the club and the fence are me, as they come from my mind. I was projecting all of this deeper meaning about; it is my 'special' fence!

Really the most significant relationship I am in is with myself not only as the environment, but also as 'another' personality that I project out. This is due to the split mind as we discussed earlier in the book. I have a whole file on what I think about 'small-self' me and another on myself as 'Spirit'. My checklist includes my beliefs about myself, what I believe others think about each side of me and I of them. The file entries of whom and what I am in different scenarios defines my beliefs and behaviours. I may be confident teaching and then appear to be a completely different personality somewhere else; I may be a social wallflower for example. If I am projecting out these differences it can only be because inside me I feel like these are actually different characters. This is definitely my experience of life anyway.

It becomes difficult to really know and understand our true self when we seem to be such conflicting things. How can you be shy and confident? By appeasing the quandary with *"You are just different in different scenarios"* just adds to the Ego's idea that you are separate and conflicting personalities inside. If you explore *why* you are confident in one area and less in another, you will uncover the real answer. This is not about you or the environment but really about the level of fear that you have in each scenario. I have knowledge and am in control when I teach and thus feel safe and secure. In a social situation I may have no knowledge of everyone there, what they are capable of or if they will like me. As I believe that I cannot control the situation completely I feel fear. But if I never actually ask that question and fully answer it, I will continue to enhance the two different files as separate ideas about me.

Therefore, peace can only come to your life when you have equalised all parts of you so that one is not rejected in favour of the other. You are a whole person with a whole mind and thus all things that 'seem' to be parts are equally valid and none more special than any other.

So it is very important to review your files about yourself because who, what and where you define yourself to be, is all others can see. That is only where they *can* find you. If as a therapist I set my skill and personal value low I will set my prices low. Clients can only see and find me there because that is where I have put *myself*. Who would know the truth more than I? The answer is no-one and so the client would not question the truth of that. If I place a high value on myself and my work (because as a therapist really you are selling yourself) I will set my prices high. It is nothing to do with greed but your price tariff is a symbol of your value of yourself.

If money was not an issue, would you book a therapist who charges £20 phr or £70 phr? Take a moment to reflect on why that is. What assumptions are you making or subtext are you reading into it by simply the symbol of the price tag alone?

I define this value by looking back at my training, my experience and my successes but unconsciously my fear level too. You are all doing this all of the time and then adjusting your expectations of how you expect people to treat you. If you define yourself as being unworthy then that is where you have invited people to meet you. Indeed that is where they will find you waiting expectantly. Not necessarily because you are unworthy but because you believe you are and thus it must play out on the screen of your life.

The Spirit's view on all relationships is that they should involve two people who are already whole, love themselves and therefore do not need anything from anyone else. As an expression of All That Is and created from the same 'material' you lack nothing. After all, who wants a needy friend or partner?

The Spirit knows that if you would look behind the small-self that the Ego wants you to believe you are, you will see that you already have within you everything that is valuable.

Peace of mind is an internal state that then gets projected outwards. If you can fill your own glass with self love and acceptance instead of asking someone else to do it, you are safe, secure and empowered. Your glass will always be full. Someone else will fill it for you but if they do you are always at risk of them leaving and taking back their portion. They may also remove what you have given them. But this is a game that we agree to play.

In truth, no-one can take anything away from you or even make you feel less. You may be sad and feel the need to grieve for a period of time if that person leaves but after a while you should turn towards the solution which is reclaiming the whole self. If you are whole and have no needs then you can only attract a partner who is whole. Like attracts like! What a fantastically giving and sharing relationship that would be.

The question to ask then is; would you want to be in a relationship with you? Also, if you can't or do not love yourself, how can you expect anyone else to do so?

Focussing on what you love about a person and what gifts they bring to you can change your cycle of thoughts and lift your vibration. If you are on radio station Love, then appreciation and gratitude is all that you will see, hear and attract. Focus on all the negatives and because of the Law of Attraction, that is all that you can receive more of. The exercise at the end of this chapter is a simple but powerful one to achieve this.

Anyone that interacts with you in a relationship of any kind can be your enemy or your greatest spiritual teacher. You cannot fall into the attack spiral if you define them as offering you knowledge because a teacher by definition imparts knowledge and does not seek to attack.

It is your choice how you are going to define and thus experience every person in your life.

Your story - your choice!

Defining everyone as a teacher offering you an opportunity to learn something, to face something about yourself or to have an opportunity to practice a new behaviour, will always have a positive outcome despite the circumstances.

It is those old outdated programmes, definitions and checklists that are causing most of your upsets in life. People change everyday, hopefully for the better, but unless you update your files you can only see and react to them as you always have in the past. As most old files are things that we need to hang onto to keep us from repeating the same mistakes or to guard against emotional pain they are often negative. That's why you may see a more negative world. If you make your happiness dependant on external things then you will always be a victim to their potential loss or removal. That includes people too.

So it is important to practice Love without attachment.

Love asks nothing of the other but shares all.

At the end of the day, your relationships are a microcosm of your relationship with God. Therefore, they should reflect the Spirit's all inclusive Love and not the Ego's love to get.

Buddha said *"Go inside and know thyself"*. So go inside and update the old to create a more Spiritual version of yourself to be in your relationships with. It is really important to be continuously self reflective and update your checklists and definitions of yourself, other people and things.

All of our relationships with other people and the world around us can become peaceful and enriching if we stay awake and in our right-mind. This can save us from pointless battles for the need to be right. It can also help us to weigh up the cost verses gain of any such disagreements. The Spirit's quiet voice will always be there if you care to listen, guiding you to see when you are falling into an Ego's traps.

If you want to see positive things and people all round you then you need to edit those files and to shred everything that is no longer relevant or not serving you.

You are no longer a defenceless baby or child. You are independent, strong and sensible adult therefore you don't need most of the rubbish that you have been holding onto. Enter into all relationships with all people, anew and afresh every day.

Be as little children, see as little children, and do so without judgement or history. Do not hold grudges that will lure you into attack spirals - instead hold to the best of everyone. Everyone is your reflection anyway so growling at a mirror is a waste of time and energy.

Smile, and your loved one smiles back.

In that way, you can both be at peace and you will have changed the world by changing your mind.

How powerful does that make you?

Quick Summary

1. You only ever see your past. All files remain as they were when they were created unless you consciously update them.

2. You have a checklist of physical, mental and behavioural attributes in those files, which you look for in order to verify recognition of a particular person or thing. You see your expectations of them.

3. If you judge, which is to evaluate, anyone or anything as more special than someone or something else you inevitably reject all others. Thus to judge is low vibration.

4. The Ego's reason to be in relationships is to always get something that you think that you lack or need. The Spirit uses all relationships to help heal the issues buried in your unconscious in order to make you whole again.

5. To heal all relationships, it is important to update or delete your old files. Only then can you see everyone anew and through the innocent eyes of a child.

6. When everyone is equal and one; peace exists.

Updating the Files Exercise

1. Take a significant person in your life that you have given a special label to such as mother, father or husband.

2. Write down:

- How you would recognise them.
- What attributes a (mother for example) should they objectively have.
- What personal attributes *they* do and don't have.
- What you think of them.
- What you think that they think of you.
- Any significant events that have happened between you.
- Which traits you expect them to exhibit when you see them.

3. Explore how these expectations get projected onto that person and how that affects each of your meetings.

4. Redefine this person as equal friend and see how that would have changed your interactions at your last meeting.

5. Prepare for your next meeting and resolve to treat them the same as you would a good friend. Let two equal adults meet in future.

6. Explore your criteria, checklist and events stored in their file and see what needs looking at with adults eyes. Forgive, redefine and update your checklists.

7. Write down all of the positive traits of this person. Read and add five more things to your list every day.

Chapter 10

The Gift of Giving

"You set a value on what you receive and price it by what you give."
A Course in Miracles.

Why would someone get upset if somebody they gave a gift to, or let out of the junction in their car, didn't say those magic words: 'thank you'?

It is because very few of us understand the incredibly complicated relationship of giving and receiving.

The Ego has successfully confused and manipulated the way you perhaps understand and use the relationship of giving and receiving. Just like the confusion of cause and effect, the Ego layers so many unconscious meanings onto the relationship of giving and receiving. So much so, that it now can be used as an attack mechanism. It can be used to attack the self or another party.

Let's explore this first with physical objects.

The Ego likes us to think that when you give a physical gift of, say perfume, that you have 'lost' something from your possession. You have paid a price. So you lose the money that you paid for the perfume and your friend (who we will call Jenny) receives or has gained something. So when Jenny says 'thank you' you will feel subconsciously that you have been compensated. You have gained Jenny's love and appreciation of you as the giver and that is your reward. The relationship now feels balanced and peaceful. If Jenny fails to say thank you, then you fail to receive compensation and so you may feel that you have lost something valuable and the relationship is out of balance. The Ego will tell you that this is unfair or unjust and so will want to attack her for being rude and will seek to gain some power back. All behaviour is instigated by need. As the Ego enters all relationships in order to get something, it feels outraged that it has lost something as valuable as power and so needs to act in order to restore control.

When you buy a gift, you are really buying for yourself, unless of course the recipient has indicated something very specific that they want. You will buy something that you think that the other will like and that can only be decided by what you feel about the gift or if you would like to receive it. So to some degree you are giving away something that *you* value. This is also why the level of hurt is increased if the other party is not sufficiently grateful; it's a judgement on your taste.

The other problem is that there appears to be levels of gratitude. If you have spent a lot of time, effort and expense on Jenny's gift, you will feel more aggrieved if she fails to be grateful than if you had just quickly bought flowers from the petrol station. If she opens the perfume that you searched everywhere for and paid £100 for but merely throws it aside, you would be deeply hurt. The Ego will define this as an attack and so you want to start attacking her. You may even consider not bothering to buy her a present in the future. Unconsciously, you have allowed Jenny's reaction to define the worth of your relationship based on the value of the gift. This is only the worth that you have assigned to it, remember? She may be completely unaware of this; she may have been rushing or even embarrassed about receiving gifts. The point is that you do not know and it is irrelevant anyway because you have not given the gift with unconditional love.

As the quote from the start of the chapter states: *"You set a value on what you receive and price it by what you give."* In this scenario, you received a low value response to a high value gift. You are subsequently creating your own suffering only because you have not given freely and without expectation of return, even if that is only a 'thank you'. The gift has really become an offering with conditions attached; that is not a gift!

However, you must remember that this is your projection and that you must separate Jenny from this behaviour in order to be at peace.

If you had extended your gift freely, you would have still received a return, albeit in the form of a rise in your own vibration. It is a sharing of Love, which if you remember from previous chapters is whole and so asks for nothing in return. The act of knowing that you have something of worth to give *is* the gift that you receive back. It was you who concocted a story about the gift's worth in the first place. If you had not made it a measure of both of you and the friendship, then no attack could have been perceived and you would not now be suffering.

It is also interesting to know that the gift is a measure of you in this relationship also. You will only buy the gift to the value that you feel you can afford to lose. If you are in a vibration of lack and fear, you will perhaps spend £10 and when you are in a vibration of abundance you may splash out on £20!

The Ego may also tell you that the gift is a measure of how much the giver loves you. If you are in the place of poverty financially and can only afford a £10 gift, Jenny may see the poor quality present as a measure of what you think about her or how much you care about her. If she gave you a £20 present on your birthday she may feel especially aggrieved that you don't care about her as much as she does you. Thus, the Ego highlights the imbalance and Jenny feels that she has lost something more valuable than she gained. Therefore, the gift that should have been given freely and extended through love has now become a measure of yourself, Jenny and your relationship!

Let us go back to an example from the chapter before with the friend that felt that I had let him down. I thought that I was offering him something incredibly valuable (my knowledge) and in some ways he dismissed it. If we look at that through this statement: *"You set a value on what you receive and price it by what you give"*, then I received rejection when I had offered my treasure. From his point of view he did not value the gift as I did, because tea and sympathy was what he valued more. When you look at what happened from this point of view, it becomes easier to see that there is just a difference of opinion on what is the worth of the gift and thus it makes it far easier to forgive.

The relationship of giving and receiving is further complicated by the fact that some people who are unable to show physical love believe that they can compensate for this by buying affection. In this way, money is seen as being of equal value to time and attention. Because of this perceived equality, the giving of physical gifts can be used to replace love.

It is important to recognise that if the receiver sees money of equal value, all will be fine. If an absent father spoils the child with every toy that they want, the child will learn that this is how love works and values material things as symbolic of love. If as an adult, this person's partner does not have the same value of materiality, then the supplication of material goods will not bring peace to the relationship as they have less value to the giver. The valuing of different *forms* will cause an imbalance in the relationship.

It is true then, that what is returned in place of gifts doesn't have to be like for like but does have to be of equal value to both parties. So it is value that is the key word here. What you value becomes your treasure and you will want to protect your treasure because you value it so highly. The Ego likes you to believe that your treasure can be taken from you and so you must guard against loss at all times. This puts you in a continuous state of fear even if you appear to be performing a positive act of giving.

Therefore, notice how much of the positive or negative judgements are created by what both parties think about the gift. It's not the gift of perfume or therapy that matters, it is the value that you are both projecting on to it that defines if you will suffer or be in joy around the gift.

You may have heard of the phrase *'It is the thought that counts'*. This is vitally important to grasp because what it infers is that no matter how either party judges worth, it is the intention to share a Loving act between two parties that is the gift. The actual physical gift is just the *symbol* of the act of Love. The right-minded thinking of Spirit is that if this is a thought-based reality then there can be no-*thing* of value to lose. Here lies your escape from the Ego's trick.

A thought can only be shared and will still remain in your mind even if you shared the thought with anyone else.

Another escape from the way that the Ego distorts this relationship is to understand that giving and receiving are one act, that nothing can ever be lost and that levels of value are inherently meaningless and ultimately subjective perceptions.

The perfume that you bought Jenny may cost £100 in a high-end shop but let us say that you bought the exact same item from a market for £30. Is the value of the gift £30 or £100? The answer will be completely subjective in that it will be £30 for you but to Jenny it will be a gift worth £100. Like all levels of anything, price is a somewhat meaningless mechanism of worth. By defining anything as something that's 'wanted' you are rejecting, or defining all 'others' as of less worth to you and thus unwanted.

If you say that you prefer tall men, then how tall is tall? You may stand at a mighty 5 ft 3 inches so anything over that is in reality tall. Your idea may be that 6ft is tall and thus fulfils your preference of tall men. But as we can see it is just an arbitrary, meaningless decision. However, by defining tall as 6ft you have unconsciously rejected anyone under this height as unwanted, or of less worth (to you). In this scenario, it is only going to affect you.

However, when as whole societies we make a judgement that this skill, quality or trait is more valuable than another, we reject or demean what is not that. If as a society we value academic skills over manual skills then what message are we giving to those who are blessed with an ability to make or repair things? They are unconsciously thought of as less valuable and paid less than their academic peers. But this is still an arbitrary and meaningless judgement and has no validity outside of that particular thought system. If you were on a desert island which person would you want with you: the professor of philosophy or the fisherman?

Thus, your judgements become the projection of value onto particular things. This is actually the setting of a price. The price is really just an evaluation of worth and relevant only to the person that makes it.

Judgements of bigger or smaller, higher or lower, more or less valuable are irrelevant in the One. These are aspects only meaningful in a duality where opposites and differences are possible. This is why levels are meaningful to the Ego but the thought system of Spirit sees no differences between you or things. A gift is a gift irrespective of what it is because what defines it as a gift is the original intention to give. But the thought system of the Ego uses our continued belief in arbitrary systems of measurement to reinforce a feeling of separation, competition and division to trap us into degrees of suffering.

Now let us look at this in another way.

You have seen the perfume that you want to buy Jenny in the market and you barter hard with the trader and manage to get the perfume for £20. *"Whoo-hoo,"* you think, *"What a bargain!"* You feel that you have won or gained. On the other hand though, this means that the trader has lost. Now, in your right-mind you will know that you cannot win because you are all One and his loss will be felt by you somewhere. Perhaps it will be guilt that you know that you have 'cheated' the trader. His loss and suffering becomes your own. It also reminds you that you could be cheated too at some point.

A student told me about a documentary she had seen where a man bartered hard with a local trader in Morocco (I think) who was obviously quite poor. In reality, it was only a small amount of money to the Western reporter but a lot of money to the trader. Seeing the sadness on the face of the Moroccan man, the reporter felt very guilty and ended up paying the full price *and more* money to the trader. In the end, the reporter had made a statement that his happiness (and health because they are intrinsically linked) were of more value than money. He had also made the statement that the trader's happiness was more important than money. Because he had given more to the Moroccan who was very grateful at this unexpected act of generosity, he had gained much more than that few Dirhams could ever buy.

Remember that what you give is a judgement of you and what you perceive that you have to give. Therefore, the reporter had shown not only that he was Loving and caring but also that he was rich enough to do that.

He got to appreciate himself and his own abundance. What a gift!

What the reporter really gained from this, was that he had now overcome the Ego's wrong-minded thoughts of separation, competition and loss. The reporter had balanced the relationship of giving and receiving because he saw that their actions were inextricably linked. The symbol of goods and money were irrelevant. The transaction was really of energy and Love. If the reporter sees himself as separate from the trader, then it is the merchant against him. If he thinks that he can lose anything, he will be equating the money that he hands over and with the value of the goods that he receives.

The Ego says that in order to be happy the reporter needs to see that his gain is greater than his loss. Usually, if he thought that he had given less and received more, he would feel like a winner but in reality he gained more by giving more. The most precious things are those that money cannot buy.

Remember, the rule is that *"You set a value on what you receive and price it by what you give"*.

Let us say that you have bought the perfume for yourself and paid £20 and so that is its worth to you. If you had paid £100 for the perfume you may keep it for special occasions only. A perfume that you bought for £20 you may wear every day because it seems less special and thus less valuable. This is ridiculous as the perfume is neutral. It is the same bottle of perfume. But because you have paid for perfume worth £20 then that is all that you can receive. Therefore, you want it less because you value it less.

This relationship is very clearly demonstrated with physical objects but becomes even more difficult to unravel when it is used with nonmaterial concepts like love or work.

When I was grappling with these concepts I was working in a part time job that I hated. I was very frustrated as it was low paid but highly stressful. I did not want to be there. The cost of doing it was high in relation to the benefits that I received from it. In fact, I didn't recognise any benefits because the wages would go into the bank by transfer and straight out in bills. Therefore, I was not consciously seeing any reward. However, as I begun to connect what I was giving and receiving back in return, I could see how the aforementioned law was in operation.

I was receiving a low wage and did not think the job was particularly important as compared to my therapy work or teaching. *"You set a value on what you receive and price it by what you give"*, therefore, initially I saw that all I was receiving from this job was stress and so this was obviously not of value to me. I value highly my qualities such as conscientiousness and sense of responsibility. So in my perception, I was giving high value for low return. Or I you could say that I was working hard and paying a high price.

When I realised this I decided to spend time every day re-evaluating this relationship. After work I would connect the gratitude that I felt for the money that I had earned today and focussed on why I needed this little job as my safety net. If you are in potential danger of falling, a safety net is a very valuable thing to have!

So I began to recognise and value what I was receiving from it rather than what I was paying out in terms of unhappiness. By doing this, the Law of Attraction now focuses me on the higher vibration of gratitude for my gain rather than the suffering and loss that I could only see before. I then started to feel happier generally, and more grateful for the job. I began to enjoy the work more. By putting 100% of positive energy in I received 100% of positive energy back because giving and receiving are the same. As you give, you receive because it is two sides of one coin and therefore indivisible.

It is true also that I wasn't motivated to go the extra mile as I do in my therapies etc. So let us say I was giving 20% of value to this as opposed to my other work. What then is the only thing that I can receive back? 20% of positive value of course!

I also spent time looking at my bank statements and connecting the receipt of my wages with the bills it allowed me to pay. In this way, instead of feeling that I was working for nothing, I could now see cost versus gain. I began to see the monthly direct debit to the energy company in direct correlation to my lovely warm house. In this way it was not just another bill I was paying out but something that seemed a pittance when I realised how much I valued the central heating when it was cold! Also, because paying my bills is very important for my happiness, health and security, I begun to appreciate the high value of my wages with the price I paid by the relatively small amount of time given to the company. Thus, both the relationship of giving and receiving and cost versus gain became equalised and balanced.

Now it is important to recognise also that only by looking at what I was giving that I realised what I actually had. I realised how much of a conscientious, reliable and hard-working worker I was. I saw how lucky I was to have a job with perfect hours, being local and with nice people. I got to see how rich I was because all my bills were paid and I was secure and safe. If I hadn't looked at those statements I would never have received this gift.

The gift that just keeps giving is the Spirit's ability to take a negative creation of the Ego and to turn it around. The power returned to me when I learned how to correct my vision; how I defined the situation. In other words, the problem was in my head. The problem as you will be realising I hope, is always how we are defining something. Both giving and receiving are neutral.

Whether there is loss or gain, suffering or joy only comes from your thoughts about a thing; your story. Changing my story and the eventual comprehension of these concepts allowed me to be the master of this creation. The Ego's insistence that you must get something more from the situation that you put in was the belief that was causing the issue. When I rebalanced the relationship my suffering disappeared.

Let us now look back at my love relationship. At the beginning of our marriage, we both put in 100% of time and effort because we valued our time and attention over anything else. Once I had become a mum and not working, the relationship balance changed as my husband became the sole bread-winner. He then had to work longer and more days a week to provide for the needs of the family.

I thus felt like I was being rejected or abandoned because I was not receiving the attention that *I* judged and valued as a measure of his love. Hence, I began to feel grumpy and less receptive to him. This is the acid of resentment building and I was then seeking an opportunity to attack and punish because I feel that I had *lost* attention in comparison to what I used to have. So assessing what I was receiving as low value I will only give the same back. The belief he is inattentive makes me unwilling to be attentive to him. This begins a terrible attack spiral where one withdraws more and more which causes the other to do the same.

If I could have focussed on how hard he was working to provide for his family and that he needs *more* love and attention when he is home, this situation would have been remedied. I would have been setting a higher value on what he was doing and thus value what I was receiving more. I would have also gained in being happier as my vibrational state rose. This would have rebalanced perceived loss versus gain. It would have also allowed Law of Attraction to work positively as I moved to a higher or more positive vibration. By giving out a more loving vibe I would have it returned with increased appreciation from my husband. Therefore, it becomes a win-win situation.

The Ego however, may have goaded me with: *"Well I'm not doing more for him when he is never here, prefers his work over me and doesn't love me any more…"* Remember that thoughts are increased by sharing. So by buying into that story I could have only received that vibration back. The Ego however, says there is a price to pay for everything and by giving, you lose. The price here would have been loss of perceived power, as to give in is weakness in the Ego's eyes. It believes that if you appear weak then you will be taken advantage of and suffer. But even Jesus in the Bible states that *"The meek shall inherit the earth".*

By changing my thinking and my attitude towards him those positive thoughts, which become actions, are increased and return back to me. Somebody has to break the state in this relationship or both end up losing. In the end, only the Ego won because it had surreptitiously reinforced fear, lack and loss as we split up.

So it is clearly wrong thinking to believe that being the first to break the state and give in first, makes you weak. It actually ensures that the natural laws of giving and receiving work as they should do. Spirit-minded thinking reinforces that you are not in competition or against each other. It reinforces that you cannot lose when you give something positive and that the positive vibration elicited by sharing and extending a gift ensures your personal reward is received. You cannot lose by giving unconditionally.

It is interesting to see in this example the projection of blame onto each other. The Ego teaches that when you have projected blame onto another person or thing, then you are free of it. It insists that when you have given something away it is no longer in your possession. It reinforces this everyday with the material world. If I hand you my pen, it is no longer in my hand. The pen is clearly in yours and mine is empty. I have suffered a loss.

However, as we have already said everything is thought and thus I cannot give anything away truly. When I projected the cause of my suffering onto my husband, I truly felt that I was free of any blame. I failed to recognise that I was withdrawing my love and attention because he hadn't earned it. When I was annoyed with my husband for working on a Sunday and sulked when he got home I had withdrawn my love and attention. I was also withdrawing love and attention when I put the baby first (which I had to do). But that doesn't necessarily limit how much love I could have shown my husband. I am 'to blame' or really as responsible as him. Therefore, I was making a scapegoat out of him believing I was innocent because my blame was being projected out and away. This then created an attack spiral followed by guilt and self punishment.

Appreciation of each other and correlating what we both gave and received is key here. My projection shows what I was feeling and thinking via my external environment so that I could have then chosen to react to it, either positively or negatively. Turning my focus onto what I could do to help my husband would have been more positive. It would have moved the situation and my attention away from there being a problem and onto finding a solution. This could have been anything from getting a small job myself to just allowing him to rest when he came home.

That is why in the Bible there is so much focus on the importance of how we can serve our Brothers. The Ego will say *'To serve will cost in time and effort'* or in other words, you will lose. But actually, by asking what you can do for another gives you a chance to share your gifts so that you may both gain.

In truth, you can only know what you have already received by giving it away. You not only see what you have but what you are, by what you give away. By seeing our gifts and talents out there in the hands or mind of another, you can see exactly what gifts and talents you do have and come to know who you really are. Only by writing this book do I appreciate how much I really know. All that I know has been given to me by my experiences, formal and informal teachers, books, and even the tennis club! In fact, everything and everyone that you ever come into contact with gives you something. When you interact with anyone you are both giving or sharing what you are. Therefore, you are teaching and learning all of the time.

If I did not write it down, all of this knowledge just sits in my mind, dormant. Only when I write or teach do I see in real terms how much I have to offer and now I can appreciate and gain from it. If you are a student and you get to articulate what you have learned in order to help another, you share your knowledge, thereby strengthening it. Thus by giving anything away you receive and it 'appreciates' or increases for you.

Despite what the Ego tells you, you must give first in order to receive.

By giving away anything in the material world you get to appreciate that you have it to give. You may not know how rich you are until you give your riches away.

If a family member needed to borrow £1000 for life-saving medical treatment and you manage to scrape it together you may not have appreciated that you were £1000 rich. Now you have realised that you are rich, the Law of Attraction dictates that your positive focus onto how much you do have, must in fact bring more to you, even though you gave it away. Also the joy that you will receive by having saved that family member's life will bring you much more health and happiness than the money could have. This would also raise your personal happiness level. This is of course, as long as you do not let the Ego define giving as loss.

The most important area to be conscious of regarding the relationship of giving and receiving is that of money. The Ego will try to drive home hard that you can see that you have lost £1000 and link it to survivability. Lots of us have such strong programming of fear and scarcity around money that we must be extra vigilant with the Ego in this regard. Because the Ego links our safety, security and survival with money, it is a very difficult area in which to honour this reversed thinking. It is however, essential that you do.

One of the ways that helped me was to heed Bashar's definition of abundance, which is *"Having what you need to have, when you need to have it"*.

I am sure that you don't feel the need to hoard oxygen in case you suddenly run out. You know that as long as you have enough for the next breath you are abundant. You trust that there is an abundance of oxygen for all and so there will be oxygen available whenever you need it because that is the programme on your computer. You don't take any more than you need. There doesn't have to be an emergency store around you. Oxygen is more important to your survivability than money, so why do you hoard only the latter? The answer is because you have a programme about lack and scarcity of money but run a programme of trust in the abundance of air.

Money is simply a concept in reality, just like oxygen is. So there is no real difference. As long as you have the exact money that you need in the moment that you need it then you are abundant. A penny more is surplus and unnecessary. An extra penny earlier or later again is useless.

Concepts exist only in your head. The problem is that the Ego has given us the idea that money is a god and that it presides over us with fear. Therefore, we hoard it, worry about it, protect it and take more than our share. Particularly with money, if you value it highly you will be prepared to pay a high price to get it. This is why some of the worst acts anyone ever does, are often linked in some way to money. Lots of wars have been fought over money, whether that be symbolised by oil, land or power. For most of us money is high value treasure. This is very negative from the point of view of how Law of Attraction works because it is totally focussed on lack and fear which is low vibration.

If you could develop trust that every time you need a certain amount and that the exact same amount will be available for you, your fear would soon be unnecessary. Again, it comes down to whether you really believe that you are creating your reality or not.

Because the Ego believes that levels are meaningful you may feel that it is far easier to attract and manifest £10 as opposed to £1,000,000. Really these two amounts are just ideas. All ideas are simply that; just ideas. In a dream, is it harder to attract £10 or £1,000,000? In a dream you may say it's the same. This is a thought-based reality and therefore, if you could untangle any negative programming around money then attracting either amount is inherently the same.

Your beliefs and fears or programming around money simply create arbitrary levels of difficulty. In other words, you are telling yourself how difficult it is based on your past programming or experiences. So how can you work around that until you have cleared any negative programming? Attracting small amounts, as and when you need them will make manifestation seem more possible and under your control. Having what you need when you need to have it seems to be much more achievable than asking for £1,000,000. Also, it is interesting to realise that most people would invest or save a lot of that money which says two important things: 1. That you did not need that amount and 2. That you fear the supply is going to stop or dwindle. Jesus recommends to his disciples to give everything away. Then, paradoxically they will attract true abundance of having what they need, when they need to have it without worry! By giving everything, you show that you trust in the Eternal supply and then you are in the pure vibration of abundance.

You never actually need a penny more than what it is you need to pay in this minute, now. Therefore, if you can keep focussed on the fact that you have no lack or need, you too can become abundant in every way. That puts you, ironically, on Radio Millionaire where you could attract £1,000,000 if you so desired. The only way to receive a £1,000,000 is to feel like a £1,000,000 literally! *'Money goes to money after all!'*

Thus, being able to appreciate that you have no lack at all, means that you are much more likely to give and be generous to others. By giving more, you reinforce how much you do have and you become even more appreciative. The recipients shower you with gratitude which makes you feel even greater. Your high vibration then attracts more things to feel grateful for and the cycle repeats into infinity. Everybody wins and everybody gains. Appreciation breeds appreciation.

So what is the difference between gratitude and appreciation then? We have already said that every word has a specific vibration.

Think about the word 'gratitude' and notice how it feels.

Think about the word 'appreciation' and see how that feels.

Most people feel that appreciation feels a little better and therefore higher on the vibrational scale. The importance of language is paramount because each word opens a different file. You have different words for different effects but you will tend to use your own personal and often limited set of vocabulary. It is only if I asked you to verbalise and articulate the difference between these to words that you may ever think about the difference.

The difference for me when I really thought about it was that I use gratitude when equating it with the general concept of 'thanks'. It is the thought of thanks for something given *to me*. We say after all 'thank *you*'. Appreciation for me is more 'permanent', or a term of longer lasting thanks. I must already have the thing in my possession and taken full ownership of it and thus is truly mine to appreciate. For me it is more linked to Love, and perhaps best understood when used with art or nature.

Appreciation, for me, is also for those things and acts that are above and beyond the expected. I notice that usually it is more heart-felt term and I use it with 'really'; *"I really appreciate that"*. Therefore, for me, I could say it is more of a feeling of Love. Gratitude is more for the physical things but I 'appreciate' the more non-physical acts.

My go to word then is grateful but really the more powerful of the two is appreciation. To appreciate is to grow. Your money appreciates in a bank for example, because of interest. Thus, what I appreciate will grow and attract more to it. I definitely need to be conscious and appreciate more, rather than just be grateful. Therefore, I would benefit more from using the words of appreciation rather than thanks.

It is a similar situation with giving or sharing.

How does it feel to give as opposed to share?

For most people, sharing seems better or a higher vibration, probably because giving implies that you 'lose' the item. In truth, as we have already discussed you can only share so why not redefine everything that you 'give' as sharing. In this way you will honour the true nature of the relationship of giving and receiving in that you are included in the giving when you share and therefore cannot lose?

How does 'getting' feel as opposed to 'receiving'? Most people say receiving feels better. Therefore, to redefine what you 'got' in life into what you have 'received', again raises the value of what you have gotten.

We have already discussed that the language that you use and how you define everything will colour the result of what you perceive and how you experience it. Tell a positive story and you must experience the event or gift that way. In fact, it would be even better if we were unable to judge the worth of any-*thing* and any-*one*. If everything was a gift then you could appreciate and grow from, and with, everything. This is how the Spirit counteracts the ideas of the Ego; by turning everything into a gift of knowledge or healing.

A really interesting question to consider is: are you able to receive?

Most of us are well conditioned into the ease of giving but not so in the ability to receive. The relationship of giving and receiving must be balanced. Therefore, not to be able to receive is almost as damaging as not being able to give.

Why should you feel uncomfortable receiving? There can only be one reason and that is the wrong-mindedness of the Ego. It will tell you that you are selfish, greedy or worse - that you are unworthy. We have already discussed that you are made from Love and nothing can change that no matter what it seems like in this illusion. Therefore, how can you ever be unworthy? However, if you play the game of being unwilling to receive, then you have the choice and free will to play that game. But it is important to own that choice or you close off the opportunities to receive, should you change your mind.

Everybody can and should allow themselves to receive any, and every, gift with a high level of appreciation. Why? It is because if you do not honour my gift and receive it as such, then I do not receive the opportunity of giving and thus growing. You are denying me the opportunity to share my Love with you. Therefore, to receive is actually to indirectly give a gift back to the other.

So do not worry about receiving. It is impossible to take, as no-one can take a thought. You could steal my symbol, such as money but you cannot affect my thoughts unless I allow you to.

It is more selfish and arrogant to pretend that you cannot receive. The Law of Giving and Receiving is part of God's Will for you; which is for you to have everything and share or extend that forward to others. In this way, abundance is continually flowing seamlessly throughout creation.

If you stop that flow by hoarding resources you have stopped the natural flow of abundance for all of us. This delights the Ego but as one begins hoarding, others fear that there is less for them and begin to copy thus reducing the flow even further for everyone. Hoarding is a fear based act.

Therefore, if we all act with our Spirit-mindedness of giving being equal to receiving, the wrong-mindedness of lack, scarcity and fear can be overcome.

How different would you feel if you only emitted positivity and Love? How much more would you value the Love you received in return? What would the world look like if giving and sharing was freely practiced without any expectation of return?

This would be to give unconditionally.

If you give without any expectation of return then you have truly given and expressed how Loving you are. That is unconditional Love. Love without expectation of return. Loving and giving unconditionally is an act of who you are and not what you do. To be able to give knowing that you will only gain and cannot lose would be life changing. To be able to receive gladly and know that you are giving the most incredible gift back *by receiving* would change the world almost overnight!

To be able to redefine everything into an opportunity to give or share the best of you is God's Will, and if honoured we would all share in God's abundance which is that of Love, Light and appreciation.

You were born abundant. It is the natural state of mind and thus should be projected on to the screen of your life.

Project this Truth and you will see what you are.

Quick Summary

1. "You set a value on what you receive and price it by what you give." A Course in Miracles.

2. If you do not value what you are receiving then you will not give anything of value in return. If you value what you give then you will receive the corresponding value back.

3. Everything is neutral. You are the only one that can determine the value of anything.

4. You not only set a value on what you receive but you equate this with the value of the giver *and* receiver.

5. The Ego gives to get and if you do not receive something of equal worth back, or more, then it will reinforce your loss. Spirit teaches that to give is to receive. They are two sides of one coin. If you give without expectation of return then you cannot lose.

6. You see who you are, not what you have when you give something away. If you are unable to receive you stop the natural flow of abundance to all.

Seeing the Mechanism in Action Exercise

1. Take a current or recent event that involves the relationship of giving and receiving. I suggest you do this once with something simple like a gift given or received and then with a relationship like a marriage, work or friendship. You may want to explore one that is happy for you and one that is troublesome. It does not matter which one is which.

2. Identify what you are giving and/or receiving and what the other is giving and/or receiving.

3. "You set a value on what you receive and price it by what you give." Explore the following:

- What you are valuing and how you are pricing it in this scenario?
- What the other is valuing and how they are pricing it in this scenario?
- Is the giving and receiving balanced and if not why?
- What do you treasure?
- What does the other treasure?

4. If you are the giver, consider how the situation will change if you gave without expectation of any return.

5. If you are the receiver and are happy, recognise the gift of giving that you gave to the other. If you are unhappy with what you received, start to focus on the gift or interaction with that person who was giving of themselves in Love.

6. Use the ABC exercise to change the outcome wherever and whenever you can.

1. An immediate **A**ction to take to improve the current problem in reality.

2. A new positive **B**ehaviour to begin to develop (in life).

3. **C**hoose a new positive belief (affirmation) about yourself to use with the band exercise.

Chapter 11

The Ego Loves Sin

"If you want to live in absolute hell, believe that you are responsible for what other people feel." Marshall Rosenberg

The sociology teacher from my old secondary school had an amazing effect on my life.

When I was in her class, the Falklands war was on and the first twenty pages of the most popular newspaper at the time was all propaganda. It was mostly about how the war was going for the UK and the few remaining back pages were full of the political news that would normally be on the front page. She deftly showed us how the press and newspapers manipulate world events according to their own business and political agendas. She also showed us how it is important to recognise that not only what news we receive is subject to the editors' biases, but also that that bias will go on to go on to affect our knowledge and understanding of the world. She also made a powerful point about what is *not* being reported but still going on around us.

This class affected me deeply for the rest of my life. It made me very aware of how I, as 'man on the street', know only what the 'hierarchy' wants me to know and that I need to be wary, even of that.

She also showed us how organised religion is really about social control. Again, this had a profound effect on me.

Now before I go on I want to reiterate that I separate God from the organised religions that purport to serve in His name. (I use 'His' simply to denote that God is personalized here and known as the Father in so far as, God created (or birthed) you but you cannot create (or birth) God. This will be explained in greater detail in the later chapter Father and Son).

Firstly, I am just speaking for myself here as I know that all religions offer valuable support and comfort for individuals and followers.

Religion, for me, is no longer synonymous with God. God for me now is All That Is; not human, but energy. God is the energy of Love. However, God for me growing up was hijacked and personalised (or I might say demonised) by the Ego for its own uses.

The more I thought about it the more I felt that religion had not only become a tool for social control but was extremely divisive.

The Churches, Synagogues and other religious institutes are at the mercy of being commandeered by individuals and their Ego's for their own gain (such as with the editing of the Bible etc).

Growing up, my parents held no real religious views of any sort. God or religion was just never discussed and was never an issue.

It was however, the done thing to go to Sunday school and so I dutifully complied. Sunday school affected me much more deeply then I ever realised because of the direct programming occurring at a young age. God was portrayed as being a man on a cloud with the ability to judge and display great wrath. Being a sinner and the idea of being cast into Hell, lay dormant within my unconscious mind well into adulthood. It was only when I became a student of A Course in Miracles that I realised that I needed to update the old files about what God actually was. I had been programmed to believe in (and fear) God. I also had, unbeknownst to me, been programmed to unconsciously live the Ten Commandments through my parent's codes and values. This was later reinforced throughout mainstream school. In the 1960s and 70s, we were still saying prayers, singing hymns and having religious studies lessons everyday.

Therefore, I have had to accept that I am much more 'religious' than I realised. The same is likely to be true for you (depending on where you grew up obviously) because to escape the programming of a whole culture is nigh on impossible. The effect religion has on you may have just become background and well disguised. The majority of our laws here in the UK, for example, were made hundreds of years ago when the Church was more powerful than the government.

The whole structure of society and the legal system are fundamentally based on the Ten Commandments. These were given to Moses on Mount Sinai and can be found in Exodus in the Old Testament.

The Commandments enshrined in our laws are essentially that you shall not lie, steal, cheat, kill or commit adultery. You must honour thy parents, which is really all your elders including anyone in a position of authority over you. It is a sin to even just covet your neighbour's wife or goods because in the eyes of God this is just the same as actually doing it. Because everything is in your mind and there is no 'out there' as such; to think of stealing your neighbour's wife has the same effect on your vibration as doing it.

If you commit any of these 'crimes' which you know unconsciously are actually sins; guilt and punishment will follow. Do the crime and you will do the time as they say. There is seemingly no escape from this.

Think about what you were taught as a child. Most of you as children were taught the difference between right and wrong. The morals and values of your parents were taught to you consciously and indirectly programmed into the unconscious. This was not just by their words but also taught by both their positive or negative actions and reactions. Any misdemeanour, whether intentional or not, would illicit a consequence or punishment of some kind for the child. Here you are also being programmed with the idea that cause and effect is inescapable.

Because the 'crime' appears to be something that you did externally (e.g. bite your brother), a consequence will follow. This could range from having your wrist slapped, be reprimanded, removed to the naughty step or even bitten back. All this is being done with the apparently loving intent from the parent who dutifully parents the way that they were programmed to do by their parents. And so it goes on until someone learns better or, culturally, the programme is changed.

This is what has happened with smacking in the UK. As I was growing up smacking was the norm and thought of as a loving thing to do because you were supposedly teaching discipline and boundaries. Today it is totally unacceptable and recently, unlawful too.

As with all things, the event itself is neutral. However, as the attitudes of the times change, there is a new definition of what is and what is not acceptable behaviour. Breaking the law is a sin and so if you even lightly smack your child now you will feel unconsciously like a sinner. You will feel really bad about yourself and guilty, whereas for my generation you would feel like a responsible parent!

This is very interesting because it shows that there is no real truth about what is right or wrong. Therefore, this must also be relevant to sin. The Commandments were scribed and given by God quite late on in Mankind's development - 1,300 BC according to scholars. Modern man as Homo Sapien has only been around for 200,000 years.

Are we thus to assume that before 1,300 BC there was no sin? Are we to assume that no-one lied, cheated or killed before this date and there was no need for the Commandments?

As this is unlikely, the only logical conclusion then is that these things only became *defined* as a sin with the arrival of the Commandments. If we can see the Commandments, then in the same light as the law changing on smacking we can understand that these were new *guidelines* for social cohesion. Therefore, to not follow them may be an error and there may be social consequences but it would not be a sin. The importance of how you define this is crucial to understand, as will become clear throughout this chapter.

God gave everyone free will. Any Commandment that absolutely must be followed can only nullify your free will which doesn't make any sense. To see them as guidelines for a civilised, loving society *does* make sense. Furthermore, God as Love cannot judge as we will see in the chapter called 'Father and Son'.

Let us return to our smacking parent.

If the parent has little patience, a lack of parenting skills or is stressed themselves, then the level of punishment administered and received by the child will be different in every case. Thus, the degree to which the child becomes programmed with fear of making a mistake is directly correlated with the parent's emotional and vibrational state when the child was young. Also the idea that the child gets programmed with grows into an unshakable belief that a mistake *will be* punished. This then can only become the default state of mind and physiology, because physiology follows thought.

As you grow up your parents are the gods of your world. To offend them is the same as offending God. Therefore to break their rules is the microcosm of breaking God's rules, which allegedly is a sin.

Therefore, you may have been continually made to feel guilty for your mistakes and so moving forward you will link guilt directly to punishment. But in order to experience guilt you (or somebody else) must have defined your mistake as a sin. Mistakes get corrected but a sin needs to be paid for. Punishment is the price that you pay for a sin. On top of that, you may start to believe that your parents, who are supposed to be the two people in the entire world that loves you unconditionally, like God, actually don't love or like you. This belief directly links into fear that you won't survive. Fear of death then, if you make a mistake, starts to become your perceived reality. This sets up a continuous feeling of fear and turns on the Freeze, Fight or Flight system constantly in the background.

How many of you, I wonder, have picked up the programming that *'If these people cannot even love me, I must be really bad, very wrong and totally unworthy of life?'* If however, you were lucky enough to have at least one loving parent, loving grandparents or siblings, you may been able to counteract this belief to some degree.

But through my experiences with my clients and my own life, I believe that this scenario is what actually sets us up for a lifetime of negative feelings of self worth. It becomes the root from which the weeds of our life keep growing. Consequently, you must keep pleasing those who have any authority over you and ensure that you do not make any mistake, lest you be punished. The fear is heightened even in adulthood because it is linked unconsciously, to an old file of survivability. Until you go back and update those types of files, you will always be denying your mistakes and projecting them onto or blaming others.

One of the most important files to update is that a mistake is a mistake and despite what the Ego wants to say, sin is impossible as God does not judge. It is also vital to programme yourself with:

'Guilt serves no purpose anyway!'

Your feeling of guilt does not change the experience for you or them.

Now it is vitally important to realise, that if you believe in yourself as a body, that you must believe that you came from your parents. Your parents came from their parents and so on and so on back to the very first parents, let us say. The DNA that exists and is stored in every single cell, goes forward into the next generation via the egg and the sperm.

No information is ever lost by the 'system' as it may be evolutionarily vital, either now or in the future. Let me call this ancestral programming. The majority of civilised nations have been run for hundreds or thousands of years by the 'religious' institutions. That can either be voluntarily or by having it enforced upon you like the Spanish Conquistadors did to the South Americans, for example.

Most religions at their heart are very similar in that Love, Oneness and respect for others and life itself are the foundations from which all the rituals and deviations arise.

Therefore, no matter where you live now in the world, most of you have ancestral programming within your DNA about religious rule and dogma. This is in some ways more powerful than current programming because it has been repeated more often. These ideas then are more deeply ingrained in the unconscious than your own programming from this life or your personal experiences of today. If you believe that you have lived many times before then you may have explored through regression or had direct experiences of ancestral programming. Consequently, your understanding of this subject will be even more personal and relevant.

The file of God as the Father is going to be stored deep in the archives of your unconscious mind having an effect, but not necessarily known or recognised within the conscious awareness of who you are today.

Our parents represent authority and control, especially fathers as most societies are patriarchal. My mum's mantra was: *'Wait until your father gets home'*. At this point, you knew that the punishment was going to be much more painful than even she could dish out.

As your father is the unconscious symbol for the Father (God), I was being programmed with: *'Wait until the day of judgement, then you will really suffer - much more than Mother Earth could mete out'*. This is why I say that you are much more religious and influenced by a belief in a punishing God than you may realise. Because I was taught God was a man sitting on a cloud, it also set up in me that I should now fear all male authority figures more than female authority figures, although both will seek to punish me.

If my parents symbolically represent God then the fact that I have deeply disrespected my parents becomes what I will unconsciously project onto God.

I may subconsciously ask then: *"If God cannot even love me who can?"*

"I will" says the Ego.

The Ego then becomes your pseudo protector and god. Of course the Ego loves and will continue to strengthen this unconscious belief because it is the ultimate tool to keep you in fear.

Not only have you now got to fear death but also the threat of severe punishment heading your way afterwards by the most powerful being in the Universe. The threat of Hell is softened by the slight possibility of going to Heaven. But you can only get to Heaven whilst living in a world of fear, control and limitation if you can somehow manage to overcome those, and be only Love. As fear, control and limitation are opposite traits to those of Love it seems to be almost impossible to achieve being loving for any significant amount of time whilst being under the influence of the Ego.

Some people have achieved it obviously, like the Buddha and Jesus etc but if we are honest most of you seem to think that you are not loving enough, not altruistic enough and that your negative acts outweigh the positive. Most of you will have lied, cheated or had coveting thoughts at some point and therefore must unconsciously believe that you are a sinner.

Heaven then becomes a carrot that you can never reach but the striving for it keeps you motivated in the grasping and striving that the Ego relishes. The perceived state of *'not being there yet'* reinforces your need to keep striving for the unachievable goal.

Therefore, striving to reach Heaven surreptitiously makes our life Hell, thereby trapping us in fear and reinforcing that we are not there yet. If you are not in Heaven then you must be in Hell or 'No Man's Land', otherwise known as our dream world. If Heaven is the highest vibration of Love, with any shred of fear or doubt within you, you will never be able to be in Heaven. If you have tuned your radio dial to Radio Fear on 54.3 htz then you simply cannot hear or experience Radio Love on 98.9htz. It is pure physics. That's why Jesus says Heaven isn't a place but a state of mind or being. Heaven is being pure Love and *nothing* else.

So it is not God that is keeping you away from 'Heaven'. You keep yourself away by your attraction to the Ego, judgement and fear. I believe that the final judgement is the last time that you truly side with the Ego. Then you are Love and free.

It's the same here on Earth.

You cannot be in a state of Love in its real form and fear at the same time. You can create the experience of love (small 'l' love). But, as we have seen in the chapter on relationships: for the Ego, love is linked to having your needs met. Consequently, the Ego can hijack our relationships for its own purposes. Thus, there is really a covert focus on lack and scarcity in your relationships and this has nothing to do with Love as a state of being; that which you actually are. If you are made of Love how can you be lacking in anything, especially Love?

So it becomes obvious that all of the tricks and confusion that the Ego uses to keep you under its fearful control, and that it sells as gains to keep you safe and away from Judgement day, are just ploys. By keeping you focussed in a vibration of fear it can ensure you never reach Heaven.

Fear is a low vibration and Heaven is the highest (Love), therefore the Ego will never reach it! Thus its dread of being left alone and abandoned makes it comes up with an ingenious plan to keep the door to Heaven hidden. It imprisons you with a belief that not only are you a sinner but also that you will never feel strong enough and thus able, to find Heaven on your own. And with the unchangeable belief its master trick, the Ego also suggests that if you try to get to Heaven and fail, you will feel so much worse. For then you will really know that you are now stuck eternally here, helpless and hopeless in the relentless cycle of life and death. The last, little seed of hope is now gone forever. We know from all the depression research that the vibration of helplessness and hopelessness is the lowest that anyone can feel and if not remedied will often lead to suicide simply because there is now nowhere else to turn. Therefore the Ego says *'Don't look, stay here and at least you will always have doubt to cling to'* and so we dutifully follow the carrot like the asses that we seem to be. The Ego loads our backs with more lack, scarcity and fear to keep us dutifully following that carrot.

Death isn't even an escape route if you believe that you will live another life afterwards. If you believe the lights go out and you cease to exist, what do you gain from that? You may have escaped the current pain but won't have the pleasure of knowing it has ended. Therefore, the act of death becomes pointless as a means of escape.

Suicide is deemed a terrible sin because the Ego doesn't want you taking back control and seemingly usurping its power and destroying its temple. So the sin of suicide becomes yet another tool to fear or another stick to beat you with. Suicide appears to be the ultimate act of free will and taking back control. However, it is ultimately an unnecessary act because no-one and no-thing can ever overcome your free will. You can never be in a prison unless you agree to play that game. If you believe anything can overcome your free will then you have succumbed to the lies of the Ego.

The Final Judgement that the Bible and the Ego holds over us like the Sword of Damocles, appears to nullify the truth of free will. But *appears*, is actually he pertinent word here. The Ego has set itself up as the protective, caring parent who has offered you shelter from the prospective wrath of God. As your pseudo parent, it is actually promoting itself to be the pseudo god of your world.

Thus you make a decision that appears to be of your own free will to not even try to make it to Heaven, but to stay safe with the pseudo god that 'truly' loves you.

The Ego even ties you into this with the story of your birth into a physical body. The Ego insists that birth, due to cause and effect, will be followed by death. In order to achieve this, it distorts the truth that you are an Eternal being who is dreaming of this world. But as you will see in the next chapter, even that is a concept or a belief. After all, your strongest root belief from which everything else grows, is that you were born into a physical body and that at some point this will be violated or breakdown and die.

To ensure your complete obedience throughout life, the Ego tells you stories about how sin is very different from making an error. It reinforces that every mistake you make is a sin and not simply an error made from a lack of knowledge, power or strength to make a different decision. The Ego heavily promotes the story that a sin is an offence to God because it breaks His rules: The Commandments.

Sin is very different from making a mistake because sin appears to have a deliberate intention about it. Therefore, if you categorise mistakes, even unconsciously as sin, you have now admitted that you have offended God. The Ego increases your fear of retribution by using time against you. By teaching that sin is firmly set in the past, there can be no recovery from it. From there guilt is inevitable in the pre-sent, and so is punishment in the future, which again seems unchangeable. The only possibility of redemption appears to be to beg for God's forgiveness, mercy and to offer some form of reparation. Any of these simply reinforces the fact that you have sinned in the first place thereby making the sin real!

But as we have discussed previously, God never exacts any punishment.

God cannot judge. However, the fear of the possibility of punishment causes its own problems. As we have already said, fear and guilt are low vibration. Therefore due to LOA, once in a state of fear and guilt, punishment (or things going wrong) will occur but this has nothing to do with God. If you programme into the computer of your brain *"I have sinned"* and you believe that punishment will follow, what is the only thing that the computer can display on the screen of your life?

Because of your expectation, punishment must follow.

But be clear – this is self-punishment due to programming and not because you have sinned. A mistake can always be corrected.

It is important to realise that if you are the one that has been sinned against, then you will drive for the other party's punishment, as retribution. However, when you want payment or vengeance, you must already be defining that you have suffered loss and so you are the one causing your own suffering! If you allow the other to have simply made a mistake then no retribution will be required and you will not suffer the pain of loss.

By its very nature, a mistake feels less serious and has the essence of no malintention about it. You may apologise for a mistake and it is more likely to be accepted than if you had sinned against another.

A mistake then becomes easier to overlook or forgive for both parties. This is exactly why the Ego wants to categorise your mistakes as sin so that it can then raise the inevitable spectre of guilt and punishment.

The outcome of a mistake or sin will look the same. If there has been a 'murder', the police will have to determine the intent. Was it deliberate (sin) or an accident (mistake)? Who would really know the answer in truth except the person that committed the act?

Even if it looks like an act of premeditated murder, the assailant may believe in that moment they were doing a loving thing.

Q: How would you classify a 'mercy' killing in order to put someone out of extreme pain, with the consent of the 'victim'?

Is this a sin or a mistake?

In the UK, this is against the law and so technically is murder. It is also a sin as one of the Commandments is *Thou shalt not kill*. How does that sit with you?

Let us say that you are the one that smothered your mother and now you are languishing for ten years in jail. Also now you regret the decision because new advances in medicine could have saved her. Would you reflect that you had sinned or made a mistake? Obviously the strong minded may always know that they made the right decision and be prepared to pay the price. They may be able to say to themselves that *'I was doing the best that I could with the knowledge and information that I had at that time'* and remain at peace. The point is that only you can define whether it is a sin or mistake. I believe that most of us would suffer extreme guilt for this act even if the person has consented. Not because you have sinned per say. However, the Ego would use that deeply ingrained programming to ensure that you unconsciously fear that you have sinned. The irony is that the Ego itself is punishing you here and it will not let you release the guilt. Thus, you end up continually punishing yourself.

The Ego has then successfully trapped you into a no-win situation and you have to make a choice about who will punish you! Put like that it seems obvious which one to pick does it not? What is worse –the wrath of God or the self punishment through the Ego?

When he was very young, my son broke an expensive ornament playing football indoors. He was so fearful of my wrath that he sent himself to bed before I even got to see the broken ornament. Remember that I am god of his world. He had already figured out that punishing himself is likely to be a better option than waiting for me to do it.

It is helpful to remember that guilt is simply feedback.

It serves no purpose to hold on to it.

Guilt doesn't change what has happened. Guilt doesn't help either the other party or you. It doesn't improve the situation in anyway. Guilt is supposed to show you that you made a mistake which you need to correct or learn from and absolutely nothing else.

Guilt is simply part of the emotional feedback system. It is like any other negative emotion, in that it tells you to reflect on your action and assess if it is going to get you to 'Happisville'. It is important to make that assessment and then take action to correct it; *the mistake and not the sin*. Guilt is only present if unconsciously you have categorised the event as a sin.

If you can catch the Ego in its attempts to make you feel guilty over every tiny little thing and redefine them all as mistakes, you become able to escape the heavy shackles of guilt. You then become free to simply correct the mistake, apologise or make amends and then move on.

Happy, healthy people do not commit crime, which is to sin as crimes usually break one of the Commandments. Apart from the truly insane, most people that commit 'crime' or even serious mistakes do so because they have not had good teachers and have bad programming. In that moment when the crime is committed there may be extreme loss of control or powerlessness. A premeditated crime generally shows that person is lacking in knowledge, money or hope. A crime is a desperate act. It reinforces that person's belief that they are alone, separate and less than others. That is why gangs thrive on being a pseudo family for the disenchanted and powerless. These people need your compassion and an opportunity to learn that they are loved and part of a family of some kind. Remember, there but for the grace of God goes all of you because any of you could have been born into that person's shoes!

To the Ego, even if you upset someone with your words it is a sin and it will ensure that you feel guilty. You can be made to feel guilty for the most irrelevant thing that you choose *not* to do.

For example, I feel guilty if I do not go to play tennis on a Sunday morning. Why should this be? With free will I can choose to go or not and that decision would only affect me. But the Ego throws up guilt that I am not giving my body the exercise it needs. The Ego wants me to believe that the body is vulnerable remember, so surreptitiously it begins stalking me ultimately with death again. It suggests unconsciously: not going equals no exercise; no exercise equals bad health; bad health equals illness and death. Then it will follow through that I am letting others down. Remember if I am not reliable then I am not likable, lovable or an asset to them. If I need help, I will be on my own, they will not come to my aid and I will die. Death stalks me again! You can transfer this thinking onto many situations, including not wanting to go to that social occasion, not wanting to go to care for someone that you think you should or any other decision that you want to make that isn't in the interests of the Ego.

That is why it is so key to be awake and alert to exactly what you are thinking and why, and then own the decision.

It was only that I took time to delve into the guilt that I could see how the Ego was tricking me. Of course I will not die if I miss tennis for one day - that's insane! The master magician is presenting my issue as laziness but really it is something completely disguised and hidden; my survivability!

The Ego relies on our unwillingness or inability (through lack of knowledge), to look deeper and question its authority.

I cannot tell you how many times I explain to my clients and students that their problem is simply that they do not own their decisions.

For example, I had a lady who was suffering because she felt that she could not tell her husband's best friend to move out of their house as it would upset her husband. Their marriage was already rocky and she was afraid that he would actually choose the best friend over her. I explained to her that it was not that she couldn't say anything but that she wouldn't.

She has a mouth and can formulate sentences, so objectively she could say it. What she is actually doing, is choosing not to say anything because she did not want the perceived consequences of speaking up. Note here that I say perceived consequences because no-one could actually know what would happen. The point is that she is making a choice based on the biggest motivator which is, that it is best not to risk it as that will keep her safe. Now this perceived 'positive' choice is in fact the very thing that is bringing her unhappiness.

How can that be if the choice is supposed to be positive?

Well it is because she has made a choice from fear and then does not own it. The 'positive' choice for safety is not really a positive choice because it is being made from fear. It is not made with a sense of freedom but of avoiding pain. The subject of the choice is unconsciously focussed on pain.

Paradoxically then, making what seems to be the positive choice only increases her pain.

The Ego wraps you up in chaotic thinking like this exactly so it can keep fear relevant, and you focussed on it, completely unbeknownst to you.

If she could own the decision with a good heart and genuinely accept that she has 'invited' the friend to stay because it saves her marriage (which is actually what she has chosen on a deeper level) then she can be at peace. She has brought the cause back where it belongs - into her mind and thus this nullifies the effect. It all looks the same on the outside in that the friend is still there but she will feel empowered in the situation and not like a victim to it. It will also nullify the attack spiral that she has fallen into with the friend and her husband, as she projects blame on to them for her own unhappiness and disempowerment.

The problem is not the friend or the husband.

The problem is (as it always is when we blame another person or thing) is that she is allowing these people and/or the event to affect her. I can save you a lot of time and searching for the answer to your problems because it is always the same.

Whenever you point the finger of blame you are allowing the other person or thing to dictate your thinking and thus feeling.

But is it always your choice what you think and feel.

Therefore, if you reclaim your projections then nothing has happened out there to feel guilty about.

The Ego was also using guilt by threatening her with the guilt that she would suffer by chucking this friend out because he had nowhere else to go. This was to keep her away from making the right-minded decision to be assertive and honour her own wishes. She is not responsible for this other adult. Any adult is responsible for themselves but would be greatly assisted by Spirit to discover their own resiliency and skills. By analysing the reality of this guilt, and bringing new evidence or new thought to it such as the aforementioned principle she could overcome this. She could then own her decision to speak up without guilt.

We have previously discussed the idea of the scapegoat. This idea is fundamentally wrapped up with the idea of sin and guilt.

Let us say for example, that you feel guilty because you have been lying to your partner over a past affair. Then a friend lies to you and you feel disappointed, aggrieved and disgusted. You resolve never to speak to them again. In reality you are now facing your own 'sin' of lying that has been projected out onto the screen of your life. Therefore, it is reminding you of how terrible you are or have behaved and how your partner would feel if they discovered your lies.

Guilt becomes overwhelming and so you drive the friend away, not because they have lied but because you cannot face your own guilty face in the mirror of your friend. Remember the Priest drives the goat out of town so that the villagers do not have to face their own guilt everyday.

As we have said, guilt requires punishment and if there is no-one there to punish you, you will unconsciously punish yourself.

This may take the form of continuously beating yourself up, creating illness or loss somewhere else in your life. You may even call this Karma but a price must be paid, the Ego insists. You will also notice the reversal of cause and effect in that you are blaming your friend for lying to you but the cause is really your own guilt in the mirror. You will also see how your guilt leads you into an attack spiral because you want to drive the guilt away.

This leads us onto another important point about blaming and attacking others. As a society we seem increasingly addicted to 24 hour news and reality shows about judging others. These shows are popular because if you can see other things, people and events that are 'worse' than you, then you get to feel less guilty about your own sins. As guilt builds up in you and your life, you will need to project it out and disown it in more and more varied ways.

All media is just as much as *your screen* as your local environment. You are the dream creator remember and so you cannot cherry pick things that you will take responsibility for.

So if you are addicted to, or enjoy watching and judging others on the screen then it is actually yourself that you are judging. You have projected it out and away so that you do not have to face yourself.

It is important to notice how it seems that everyone is seeking to be a victim of something now. It seems as if offence can be taken from the mildest of things by someone, somewhere. Victimhood is never a gain on any level and so you must be aware that you do/should not lay blame and guilt at anyone else's door either.

The compensation culture has definitely not helped this drive.

So let us bring this all together now.

God will not join you in judgement, fear or guilt. God is whole (Holy), unchanging, Eternal and Love. Truth is unchangeable and whole. It does not have parts and anomalies.

Truth is not open to perception.

Sin is perceptual because what constitutes a sin depends on where you live and in what time period.

It depends on the cultural beliefs and decisions. It also depends on what the true intentions of you as the 'sinner' was at the time. Therefore there is no sin, only mistakes. In this way you can free yourself from a belief about sin and from the pain of guilt.

Punishment does not have to follow guilt.

This is only true of the Ego's thought system.

But, the only means of escape from this insidious threat of punishment is to redefine guilt only as feedback. Create a new file about guilt; re-label sin as a mistake and then you will not open the big file that includes all your past misdemeanors.

If the file is not opened then it cannot be used to influence you.

If you see all negative emotion only as feedback, you are free to look at your action and correct it if necessary. You must learn to unravel guilt much like fear by facing up to its arguments and bringing other 'evidence' to light.

You must own your mistakes and your decisions. If you can understand and own your decisions then it is possible to amend them, thereby returning cause to its rightful place which is in your mind.

Doing this, you will remember, nullifies both cause and effect and therefore nothing of significance has happened. After all, a sin is only a sin once you have defined it to be so or accepted that definition from another.

You are not a sinner. You can make mistakes but the mistake is not you. A mistake is a thing; a noun; behaviour or an event that is separate from you. You must always separate yourself from your behaviour and you must also give this gift to others. You are the Light *behind* this persona. You are the dreamer that is dreaming that you have done some action that you are now defining as wrong. The action is not you and the dreamer (like you) is separate from their actions.

Guilt is very personal. Guilt covers your light because you did this to yourself and it is actually you that metes out the punishment and suffers the pain. Guilt is a decision that seems inevitable if you are not prepared to look deeply past the lies of the Ego. It feels inseparable from you. But this is an illusion set up by the Ego to keep you tied to it. Guilt is felt in the body which you believe is you. But none of that is true. This is why it is important to understand that you are not the body.

This is a thought–based, holographic experience and guilt serves no purpose in anyway shape or form.

You are made from Love and expressed as Light. No act, distortion or trick can ever touch that.

Light is all God can see.

It remains forever pristine and forever out of the reach of the Ego, no matter what you think you may have done!

Quick Summary

1. To sin is to break one of God's laws. Sin leads to guilt which leads to punishment.

2. Sin is impossible however, because God gave you free will. Sin is also impossible because God does not judge. It is also impossible because what constitutes a sin changes with time, culture and location.

3. However, sin is perceptual and only becomes so, once you or another has defined it to be so. All sin should therefore be reclassified as a mistake and corrected. Do this for yourself and others.

4. When you do not want to own your decision you will project it onto a scapegoat and seek to drive it away so that you do not have to deal with your own guilt.

5. Guilt serves no purpose and is only feedback suggesting what you did was not in yours or another's best interest, or that you are not owning your decisions.

6. Separate your Spirit self from the behaviour. It is the action that is wrong, not the person. There is no-one judging or punishing you except you. All attack is upon and suffered by, the self.

Reclassifying Sin Exercise

Select a current or recent event in your life where you feel or felt guilty about something. When there is any guilt know that this can only be because you have unconsciously or consciously defined it as a sin. For the example, I will use the story from earlier of the woman who wanted her husband's friend to leave the house.

1. What is it that you feel guilty about?

E.g. I want to ask my husband's friend to leave but he has nowhere to go.

2. Why is this a sin and is this guilt serving you or anyone else?

E.g. Because you should treat others as you would want to be treated. My husband wants him to stay and I should honour his wishes. I am being selfish I suppose. Also he has nowhere else to go. But me feeling guilty isn't doing anything constructive to help the situation.

3. How is this guilt covering up that a decision that you want to make but will not make?
E.g. I can't tell him. No it is actually that I won't tell him because I do not want to suffer the arguments. I am a little worried that my husband may choose him over me which means I will lose everything.

4. Now see if this is really a sin with a negative intention or a mistaken attempt to do something else?

E.g. No, it is a mistake showing me that I need to either be assertive and discuss it with both of them in a kind, loving way or say nothing. I have made a decision to let him stay so I could honour that decision with a good heart.

5. So who or what really is the cause of this problem and what sin have they committed?

E.g. I am, and there is no sin here.

6. Can you see any reason to hang on to this problem or to continue punishing yourself?

E.g. No

7. Use the ABC to move away from the problem and resolve the issue.

1. An immediate **A**ction to take to improve the current problem in reality. Talk to my husband and the lodger

2. A new positive **B**ehaviour to begin to develop. Work on developing my assertiveness and owning my decisions.

3. **C**hoose a new positive belief (affirmation) about yourself to use with the band exercise. "I am in control of my thoughts and I am in control of my behaviour."

Chapter 12

Forgiveness

"The weak can never forgive. Forgiveness is an attribute of the strong."
Mahatma Gandhi

To forgive is one of the hardest things to do. *'Sorry seems to be the hardest word'* as the Elton John song tells us. This is not because it is difficult to say sorry and forget everything that just happened. It is difficult because the Ego needs you to hold onto grudges; to never forget and certainly never allow any other person win over you.

Victims after all are the ones who must forgive, not the perpetrators. Victims are weak and vulnerable by their very definition – or so the Ego will tell you. But Jesus in Matthew 5:5 said *"The meek shall inherit the Earth"*. That seems to be an insane idea doesn't it? We all know that it's survival of the fittest; being meek and mild gets you eaten in this dog eat dog world doesn't it? The key to understanding this statement fully is to really understand what forgiveness really is.

A Course in Miracles purports that forgiveness is not a concept known of in Heaven. As Heaven is about Oneness, equality and unity there is no attack or conflict. Then, what can there be to forgive? Therefore, forgiveness is only required in a duality, such as our physical world. You only need forgiveness if you believe that you have committed a sin.

As I have just explained, there is no sin in Heaven as there is no-one to judge it as sin or even to anyone to sin against. Only physical bodies can attack.

Forgiveness then is only required when you or someone else has defined a behaviour, conflict or attack as a sin.

As we have already discussed, these qualities only come in to being if you believe in the idea of separation and division. One cannot attack, as there is nothing else to be in conflict with. One cannot attack itself unless it has in some way formed division within itself and split, essentially becoming 'two' parts.

Forgiveness became a necessary facet of life after the formation of the split brain. As we have discussed, there is the Ego thought system and the Spirit thought system; the split mind. The brain which is essentially whole has developed ever increasing compartmentalisation to cope with the ever growing complexity in your life. The Ego, as we have seen, has taken more control of your life at the expense of the Spiritual brain.

This has also taken away your innocence.

As you have lost more and more connection with the right-minded thinking of the Spirit, the Ego has convinced you that you are something very different to what you actually are. It has, over time, created a small-self persona that exists because it has created a seemingly physical body to exist within. Because you now believe this is what you are, you must now be wary of other bodies that are different and separate from you.

By developing the beliefs that scarcity exists and bodies are vulnerable, the Ego directs you to compete for resources. It stalks you with the threat of death at every turn. This ensures that there is always fear, which in turn elicits either aggressive or victim-like behaviour.

As both of these qualities are actually weakening to the Spiritual you, a conflict of interest begins internally that is projected out externally.

Spirit cannot be aggressive and sees no scarcity because it understands that the body is not real and that this is just a thought-based reality or dream. There is no limitation on consciousness as consciousness is all there is, just as there are no limitations on creativity in your dreams. Therefore, the Spiritual right-minded thought system is operating with completely different criteria and a completely different world view.

The Spirit's world view says nothing of importance is happening and the reality is that you are the dreamer and not this dream character. With this worldview, there is no 'body' to be harmed and thus nothing and no-one can threaten you. There is no other 'real' person out there, only your projections.

Subsequently, there is nothing real and thus worth fighting for and consequently peace and harmony should reign. When you awaken from your dream at night you feel exactly the same way. No matter who did what to whom in the dream you do not hold a grudge or seek to punish them in the waking world.

Unfortunately, the Ego knows that peace and harmony begets whole-mindedness and its own perceived death. Therefore, it will fight tooth and nail to keep you away from that mindset. That is why its own thought system is fear-based and totally focussed on ensuring its own survival. It needs victims and the act of forgiveness, to do this.

So perhaps the first thing that we must forgive is the Ego itself. It has been laden down with so many jobs to do that it is cracking under the stress. Who gave it these jobs? Well you did, when the mind was whole. Thus, you must show it love and compassion. You must return to whole-mindedness by unravelling exactly what it is doing, relieving some of its duties and correcting your errors. You must reclaim all blame, as this is what you have projected on to the Ego and fully accept that it is not out to get you. It has faulty programming overlaying the pristine quality of Whole Mindedness. We will go into this much more in the chapter on whole life living.

This book has endeavoured to allow you to understand the Ego: the way it works, the consequences of that operating system and how to over come it. I think that it is easier to forgive on the Ego level of our everyday lives when we can understand how and why something has happened. So let us look at how we can deal with forgiveness on the Ego level of reality.

Forgiveness is only required *after* you have defined that an attack of some kind has taken place. The Ego's story is that the cause of the attack is outside of you and comes from another body, be that from words, from a physical action or an object.

When you blame another person, object or situation for anything, you have defined yourself as having been attacked.

This has made *you* the victim. As a victim you have now lost 'power' to the other and had its will imposed upon you.

In order to recover some of that power, the Ego suggests that you can attack back, whether that is internally or externally; aggressively or passively. You may physically or verbally retaliate.

You can fight back internally by imagining what you would like to do to them or attacking them verbally in your mind.

Remember though, that thinking has the same effect as doing. This only leads to resentment. To think about something is the same as doing it except that you don't get to release the emotional energy. Emotions are energy in motion and thus need to be moved. If they are kept suppressed within the body they will create blocks and cause dis-ease. They become acidic and start to eat away at the body.

They also eat away at the mind because you are still harbouring the thought, whether that may be consciously or not. As we have previously discussed, defence is the same as attack because it is still fear-based and has reinforced the reality of the attack.

By making the attack real you have just confirmed that you are not in the right-minded thinking of the Spirit. Spirit can see no attack and thus no reason to forgive anything because it knows only Oneness and the unreality of the dream. Thinking that any response is necessary to an attack is a confirmation you are not identifying with yourself as Spirit. Paradoxically then, by actually choosing to forgive someone one, you have mistakenly made the attack real for both of you. This is why in the Bible Jesus teaches you to *'turn the other cheek'* and to recognise that nothing of importance has happened.

To turn the other cheek does not mean that you allow others to abuse you but it does mean that you do not accept that strike as an attack. How can you strike me if I do not have a body? If you strike me and I know that it is just in a dream do I need to respond? A dream says there is nothing happening here and nothing took place.

Notice that this is very different from forgiving the person *after* the act. Again, forgiveness makes the attack real. Seeing no behaviour as an attack creates peace for both. Remember that that person's behaviour is not the cause of your suffering. Your suffering is caused by your definition of the behaviour. You must be able to differentiate between the person and their behaviour when they are not in their right-mind.

I am sure that as you read this, the Ego will be throwing up all kinds of arguments about why this is a crazy way of behaving in the world and how it will get you walked over if not killed. But stop and look at its arguments. Are they all not dependent on its beliefs about scarcity and pain, mistrust of others or even death of the body, ultimately? But how can that be true in your dream unless you choose to make it so?

As we know, the Ego likes to play the hierarchy game, as I call it.

I can demonstrate this better to you if you physically play along and place your hands on the varying levels as you read. (The following scenario will contain arbitrary numbers just for the purposes of this analogy but represent the vibrational scale, with 100 being pure Love and 0 being total fear/powerlessness.)

Let us say that Paul and Jack are on a happy vibration of 50, usually. Therefore, at 50, both hands sit side by side; level and equal, let's say at heart height. Paul has called out Jack on his selfish behaviour and Jack feels deeply hurt. Our attacker, Paul, appears to be 'over' his victim Jack (so place your right hand (Paul) above the left (Jack) with a 6 inch gap). Let us say that Paul is at the 90 mark as he feels energised by his righteous win and Jack is now at the 20 mark of victimhood.

Now if Paul apologises for his misdemeanour, he is recognising Jack's importance as equal to his own. (Bring the right hand representing Paul, down to the same position as Jack's at 20). The interesting thing is that Paul, by apologising, has made the attack real and dropped down to Jack's low vibration. You may have assumed that apologising would keep him higher up the scale. But Paul drops to a low vibration because he and Jack have both acknowledged that Paul has 'sinned'. Now he must feel guilt and unconsciously be fearful of the inevitable punishment.

If Jack accepts his apology, he will feel better and a wrong has been righted and his vibration will rise. (Raise the right hand of Jack to 40). But again by accepting the apology, Jack will have a momentary boost but has also reinforced that the attack was real and has therefore has only served to reinforce his own wrong-minded thinking. (Drop the left hand back down to 20). Please remember that when we see this hierarchical relationship anywhere in our life we reinforce its reality.

The Ego and your general understanding of forgiveness would suggest that the act of offering and accepting apologies would leave both parties back at their ideal vibrations. Let us say that is at the 50 mark. But as we can see both are now at 20. A pseudo peace can be found here but this is more akin to a truce. Both have suffered and that suffering cannot end until both have truly wiped it from their files.

Paul's guilt must elicit some punishment. Also, his 'sin' has been recorded not only in his file on Jack but also on the file he has about himself. The file on Jack in relation to himself will open every time that he now sees Jack. Therefore, the incident will always be in the background and unconsciously affect their meeting. You could say that Paul will always be waiting for Jack's punishment to arise.

What do you do in an argument but bring up the past hurts that are on your file about that person's past treatment of you?

Jack's hurt has been recorded in his own file, together with his file on Paul which will open every time that he now sees Paul. Jack will now be unconsciously looking to punish Paul or expecting him to criticise him again.

Therefore, although it seems that they can forgive and forget, forgetting for either party is not possible while the incident is still on file.

That is why you often find it so difficult to move on after an incident.

Now place your hands palms down, side by side at 50. This is the only place that peace resides.

Here the two beings are back at equal status again. This is where they started and the only place that true forgiveness exists; back here where nothing has actually happened and both parties are innocent. If Jack did not allow Paul's original criticism to affect him or did not define it as an attack, he would have remained at 50. Interestingly enough so would have Paul because he would not have received any Ego boost by trying to make himself right and Jack wrong! If Jack had just heard Paul's words as simply an observation or merely as Paul's opinion then neither person's files would have this negative stuff in them and thus could not affect their futures. Going forward, nothing would have actually happened and again, both of them remained in a state of innocence.

That is why Jesus advised to turn the other cheek, because then a perceived attack cannot hurt either parties' pre-sent or future. And that is also why the meek shall inherit the Earth; only the strong can do this.

It is important to note that sometimes Jack will attack or feel that he is stronger or even more 'right' than Paul (left hand now above the right) because this hierarchy is never static. They will 'swing' between these positions, as they try to define who they really are in each situation.

You can see by now hopefully that the unravelling of the Ego's power is totally dependant on you loosening your grip on the world and the body being real. True forgiveness is absolutely dependant on acceptance, to at least some degree, that this premise is true. Otherwise you fall into the trap of a pseudo-forgiveness that says: *'I decide whether I forgive you or not'*. What the Ego is normally saying is: *"I will not punish you this time and I will (or will not) forget"*. You think that you can forgive and forget but most people practice pseudo-forgiveness without forgetting.

Remember a thought never leaves the mind of the thinker. Thus, a thought that person 'x' attacked or has wronged you can never be truly forgotten. Once seen and experienced as attack it is always an attack, unless you consciously overwrite the memory file.

Therefore, the only escape from attack spirals is to never see or think of yourself as being attacked or wronged. But just as importantly, never being an attacker yourself. In that way, the thought never enters your head. Consequently, there is nothing to forgive or be forgiven for as nothing happened, either internally or externally.

I have heard many people insist that they have forgiven but they never want to see that person again. That is not forgiveness. That is suppression or denial. Clearly the event is still on file and affecting them but they can't face it and so 'scapegoat' the person away. If you cannot be in the same space with that person without total neutrality, then you evidently still believe the person attacked you. You still believe that something real happened. Or I could say that you still believe the dream is real.

You have made that person a scapegoat and cannot bear to look at them anymore. Every time that you do, you are faced with the unconscious knowledge of what you have done and your own guilt. Or you are faced with your own suffering and fear. Consequently, if you drive them away or avoid them you do not have to face any of that.

The guilt that you actually have, is in truth the guilt for projecting on to them and making them the cause of your own choice to suffer. Perhaps it is yourself here that needs to be forgiven and the behaviour forgotten once learned from.

You have only truly forgiven if there is no memory of the incident and therefore you have a clean file about that person whenever you see them.

Forgiveness is the Ego's appeasement ploy in the dream world because it says *"Ok, I'll play this game."* It will play the forgiveness game because it knows very well that if you have reacted with a need to forgive, it means that you have totally accepted the attack was real. The only difference is that now you have become attacked again by the Ego itself but you don't even realise it. The Ego has just reinforced how generous and kind-hearted you are by forgiving. In reality, it has just secretly kept you in the world where attack is possible, you are a victim and forgiveness is still necessary. *"You have forgiven this time, but do not worry, there will be many more attacks to have to forgive",* it whispers.

So you may ask the next obvious question that arises and which is, *'Do I need to apologise for my wrong doings, as if I do, have I not acknowledged my attack was real?"* Well by even asking the question you have made the attack real and so then you must play the Ego's game of forgiveness as best you can.

Let us say that you have judged your attack behaviour as an error instead of a sin but you still feel bad about yourself. The normal practice is to offer a correction. This could be an actual action to correct or improve the situation, or it may be a verbal action to rectify your mistake.

In some ways, this is the acknowledgement that there is an action to take rather than a price to pay for a mistake but it does not have to be seen as punishment. If you offer a rectification, then you must do so with a good heart. You must be able to separate the self from the action so that it is not you that you are 'apologising' for but the mistaken thought, word or deed.

If you have felt bad or guilty then in some ways it is too late because that feeling is the recognition of your attack; it is feedback. Once you have attacked, whether that be consciously or unconsciously, the only way to rebalance is to correct and that may take the form of an apology. Although the ideal is obviously to keep awake so that you do not attack at all, once you have done so it is at least better to rebalance the energies by apologising than doing nothing at all.

If you do this via the Ego, it may feel painful to admit your mistake. The Ego may try to convince you that you are bad, stupid or now weak in the eyes of the other party. It may see that you are asking for mercy from the other. This reinforces again that they are the strongest party and you are now vulnerable to their decision or counter-attack. This isn't forgiveness. This has now become the Ego's game of pseudo-forgiveness and has now become an act of self-defence. In order not to be punished by the other party, who you have now defined as stronger than you, you must accept self-punishment disguised as guilt as your defence.

If the other party does not accept your apology or correction, then it may appear as this is an attack back. It may seem to you (and them) that they are reclaiming power or making you pay. But as we have already discussed at length, all attack is actually attack against the self. They have to feel aggrieved enough *not* to forgive. But they will feel that first and longest, even if they think that they are hurting you.

You will return to the beginning of the attack spiral where you now have a choice to also be aggrieved because they will not accept your apology *or* you could choose to *not* let it affect you. It is the thought or intention that counts after all. In this way you can halt the attack process, for yourself at least. This is not so that you can get 'one up on' them as the Ego will want to define it but because you have chosen not to suffer. You have extended your positive energy freely and that is all you can do. You will have still received the benefit of the rise in vibration as you extended that apology to the other. If you offer your gift of an apology without expectation of return or outcome, then the work is complete. You must understand that it has been received on a deeper level anyway because we are of One mind.

Any act of giving is the same. If shared freely without any expectation, then the gift is truly a gift. Forgiveness given only begrudgingly or to keep the peace is not forgiveness for either party.

If your corrections or appeasements are accepted by the other party then a rebalance has occurred and both are free, as long as the act of forgiveness is also done with integrity. You have or can delete the incident from your files and the attack spiral has ceased. You could now return to the pre-attack state. Now both are innocent.

Let us now consider the wider subject of forgiveness from God for your perceived sins.

As we have already discussed, by both your personal programming and cultural laws, you are heavily entangled in a belief in sin. The Ego loves you to believe that you are a sinner. When you innocently act because you didn't know any better, lacked skill or information *it is a mistake* and not a sin. Sin is always followed by punishment. If punishment is not delivered by God or another person, you will punish yourself. Usually an act of self punishment is lot harsher than anyone else would mete out and the suffering lasts a lot longer. But you can forgive yourself for all your past sins as these have only ever been mistakes. Nothing has ever happened that you need to be punished for. Better still, forget all of your mistakes going forward and see no other sins or sinners. Then you can forgive yourself for what you have not and did not do.

Even better than that, know that it is a dream and in reality nothing ever happened and there is nothing to forgive anyway. If you hit me or I hit you in a dream neither would not hold a grudge in the real world.

In truth God cannot 'see' anything other than Love and Truth.

To recognise anything of a lower vibration would drop Him into that vibration and He would cease to be Love/God. As you know sin is a perceptive judgement and so sin cannot be a Truth.

Therefore, sin cannot be recognised by God, because He did not create it. There is a difference between things that are created which are original and unique, as opposed to things that are made from existing 'materials'.

God created All That Is in the beginning. By definition, All That Is, is all inclusive and unchanging. We then, can only make things out of existing ingredients and materials within All That Is. Therefore, creation is only of

God. Sin and guilt are negative, low vibration actions and emotions *made* by the Ego and thus cannot have been created by a God that is only the high vibration of Love. The idea of sin, guilt and forgiveness must be man-made!

God only sees what He created. If God cannot see our sins then how can He punish or forgive them?

However, because we believe in them, He offers the only thing that he knows - which is Love. His method of 'forgiveness' is to know nothing real has happened and there is nothing to forgive.

This is exactly what you can do by reclaiming your projections. By taking the other person out of the equation and knowing that an attack has not occurred, then no forgiveness is necessary.

If you find this difficult to do at first, then do it because *you* want to be happy. Remember that nothing is a problem unless you define it as so. An attack or a sense of being wronged can only occur when the victim has defined it so.

No cause; no effect. No attack; no forgiveness required.

Remember that it is you who is creating your suffering when you choose to see an attack. It is you who will suffer if you attack back. You will suffer from the guilt and/or the resentment.

Gandhi's quote at the beginning of the chapter is key. You are not weak, or letting anyone off the hook by forgiving. Forgiveness is an attribute of the strong and strong-minded. Forgiveness is an attribute of someone who truly understands the relationship of giving *as* receiving. It is an attribute of someone who sees with vision rather than the blinkered eyes of the Ego. Therefore, forgiveness is the healing remedy for both. It is good to weigh up the cost to you in terms of health and happiness versus the perceived gain of a moment's righteous jubilation. Fully understand that it is your vibration that will be swinging uncontrollably if you play the hierarchical power game.

Forgiveness heals and clears out the mental and physical residue of hate and fear. It is you that feels the hate or hurt – only you! It is your body and your mind that will be eaten away by the poison of guilt or resentment. But it is your mind and body that will be saved by the gift of Love.

Everyone is your 'Brother' in that they come from the same source as you. You were, and so remain, innocent and so do they. You need every one of them to reach the vibration of Pure Love because the puzzle can only be completed with them at peace with you. If you define them or their acts as attack then neither can be at peace, nor can you reclaim your innocence.

You can only get to Heaven with them at your side and that can only happen if you are both at peace.

Quick Summary

1. 'All That Is' is Whole and One and therefore there are no parts to be in conflict or attack. God, which is Truth and Love, cannot recognise attack and so forgiveness is unknown in Heaven. Consequently, sin, guilt and forgiveness are man-made concepts.

2. Forgiveness is only required when you believe that you or someone else has attacked or sinned against you.

3. To ask for forgiveness is not required following a mistake. There are only mistakes which may or may not need correction. Sin does not exist unless you allow the Ego to define it as such.

4. If you choose not to see anything as sin or attack then there is nothing to forgive. No event has happened and therefore nothing is recorded in your file to affect the future.

5. If you forgive the other you may think that you become 'higher' than the other. In fact, you drop to their level as you have still recognised an attack took place!

6. True peace can only be found when both parties are in agreement that nothing is happening, or by turning the other cheek.

Forgiveness Exercise

Think of a current or recent scenario either where you have not forgiven fully or you have forgiven but the relationship is not perfect. We will take an example from the relationship chapter. Tracey is angry with her mum (June) for not listening and not appreciating all she does for her.

1. Notice what you are projecting onto the other or blaming them for. Reclaim that projection by reversing cause and effect.

E.g. I (Tracey) blamed mum for shouting at me and accusing me of bossing her around. Really, I allowed her to affect me because I should have stayed calm, especially in light of her dementia.

2. Now forgive the other for what they did not do.

E.g. Mum (June) was only expressing her frustration about not being able to do these things for herself. I would feel the same in her position. I caused this by not helping her just as she asked therefore she is innocent and so there is nothing to forgive.

3. Take action in the world to apologise and then correct your mistake. Forgive yourself as there was no conscious malintention on your part.

4. Now play out the scenario as if you never took offence in the first place. How would the situation have played out if you saw no attack?

E.g. If mum shouted and I allowed it to flow over me instead of reacting and defending myself, we could have had a calm conversation about it. I would have responded differently, had a chance to explain my concerns and we could have made a considered decision together.

5. Use the ABC exercise to change the outcome wherever and whenever you can.

1. An immediate **A**ction to take to improve the current problem in reality. Apologise and order the cosmetics

2. A new positive **B**ehaviour to begin to develop in life. I will always respect mum's wishes as I would if she was well.

3. **C**hoose a new positive belief (affirmation) about yourself to use with the band exercise. "Only I can affect me."

Chapter 13

The Illusion of Time

"When a man sits with a pretty girl for an hour it seems like a minute. But let him sit on a hot stove for a minute and it's longer than any hour." Albert Einstein

To not see attack means that you must remain consciously aware and in the moment. You must be mindful.

Mindfulness has become something of a buzzword lately. Mindfulness is all about becoming consciously aware in the present moment and conscious of how and what you are feeling. It advocates staying in the now, being with any emotion (energy in motion) in neutrality, until it passes. So in some ways, Mindfulness is really teaching you to *be* rather than do. It is advising you to look inward and away from the illusion.

It leads you gently away from the duality of the external world into the stillness and unchanging safety of the internal Oneness. This is where you experience the now. The now is something very different from the present. The present is the pre-sent experience. Now is a location in space that only you fill and is not an aspect of time. Please think about that for a moment.

The only thing that you can be sure of in life is that things will change because life is energy and is generated by your thoughts in motion. Change is the only constant.

Time is dependent on process, or change and motion.

Therefore, this world cannot be a creation of God which is perpetually in a state of static completion and Oneness. All That Is, by definition is complete. There can be nothing outside of it, missing or anything that can be added to it. It is Eternal, and thus changes - and with it, time - are impossible. It follows then that time must be, made by man.

Before clocks, time was really a measurement of the movement of celestial bodies: the sun, moon and stars. The earliest clocks were sundials and thought to date back to around 3500 BC. In some ways then it is a measurement of the movement of light. As you are Light, time then is a measurement of your consciousness. Therefore, the question arises as to whether things move in the external world or is it your consciousness moving *through* a vision of the external world, which itself remains static. An analogy would be; reality is akin to a bike (the physical you) moving past a mural as opposed to there being a static bike (Consciousness) in front of a moving mural.

It could be argued that traditional clocks actually measure the space between the markings of the minutes on its face.

Albert Einstein said that time and space are one indivisible thing and *"Time is relative and flexible."* (Like his earlier quote about the pretty girl above). A Course in Miracles has suggested that you think of things that are in your now, as space and things that are not in the space or further away as time. I guess this is because it would appear to take me time to get to you (to move through the space). I find this so interesting, especially as I believe that your Universe only goes as far as you can see, hear, smell, taste and touch in each now moment.

At this point, it may help to imagine a film strip with lots of individuated frames. When the film is run through the projector you will experience it as a time continuum but each frame is really an individual, static scene in itself.

Each frame is still; no movement in time or space.

Each frame is complete and all that is. A Universe within itself.

Each and every frame then is analogous to a now moment filled by you and whatever your senses are recording in that frame. As there is no time or distance in the individualised, single frame called the now moment, then time becomes irrelevant or more properly put, ceases to exist. Time as a continuum only appears when the film is running through a projector.

Your brain is the projector that makes millions of now moments seem like a continuous experience in space-time.

Taken together, time and space would equal 100% of time-space as one whole. If something is here and now one could say that it takes up 100% of time-space or that it is taking no time (0%) to travel to you and is filling up 100% of space.

Now, I realise that this is very difficult to grasp. The only reason that you need to be aware of this is because it perfectly supports the Law of Attraction which states that what you think about the most will manifest quickest. If you give 90% of your attention (which is *time* spent) to your manifestation, it has only 10% of space to travel through in order to manifest. That means that it appears quicker. Simply put, the more you focus time by thinking about something, then the quicker that it will manifest in your space. If you were only to give your wish 10% of your time and attention it would take longer to manifest in space (90%). Therefore, the less attention that you give to something the slower or less likely it will be to manifest.

How much time to do waste worrying and how much more quicker is it likely to manifest?

More interestingly, Einstein stated that *"The dividing line between past, present and the future is an illusion"*. In some ways, *your* perception becomes the dividing line as things are in the past, present or future *for you*.

Take the New Year for example. It occurs at a different time across the globe. New Year chimes ringing in London at 12pm GMT are in the now for me. But when the bells chime for New Year in London at 12pm GMT, for Australia, New Year is already in the past. Their celebrations are over. However, for my cousin in Australia, New Year chimes ringing at 12pm Australian time, is in his now for him but the welcoming of New Year in London is yet to happen to me and so is in his future. So New Year is not an aspect of time but is relative to whatever space you are in. You are the measure of New Year for you!

Now if all that has confused you please do not worry. All that I want to do is to loosen your grip on time being a set thing with three separate phases that appear to be a Law of the Universe that is unchangeable.

As we have previously discussed, the Ego is obsessed with the past and the future. The Ego wants to keep you moving, doing and away from the now where your only power is.

It has introduced the idea of the present, (or the pre-sent) to disguise the now. It does this in order to make you believe that the past is responsible for whatever is happening in the 'pre-sent' time. In reality nothing happens in the present because the present appears as an aspect of time when really time as you may have been taught to think about it doesn't really exist. In short the Ego wants you to simply watch the film rush past and not to stop to examine the individuated frames. If you did this you would be able to start cutting scenes out, move them around thereby changing the nature of the film in the past, present and future! That is why your true power is in the now moment of awareness, which you have to physically stop to catch and make a new choice.

Therefore, the Ego *has* to make you believe that the past is the cause of the present which makes the present an effect (or pre-sent). We have already learned that an effect cannot be changed. The Ego also wants you to believe that the future is a result of - or an effect of - the past or pre-sent and thus cannot be affected by you in the now. This is because if you really believed that you could create a reliable outcome in the future then you would become cause. A cause is creative and so this is where the real power lies. This is then clearly dangerous to the Ego. The Ego wants you to believe that the external world is the only cause and you then can only be affected by it. In this way, your power is seemingly removed from you. This keeps you a victim, unstable and in fear. You are trained to believe that the future is a result of your past and is therefore inevitable. So the future becomes an effect, and again only a cause can be changed, not an effect.

Consequently, you anticipate an ever repeating future based on your beliefs about what has happened in the unalterable past. Again, as fear is always about an imagined or unwanted future event, it appears as if fear is unchangeable because it looks like the cause is in the past or pre-sent. This is completely nonsensical if linear time doesn't exist.

I know that this is confusing and complex stuff but that is exactly the idea. The Ego doesn't want you to unravel and understand this because then you become a powerful creator, instead of a slave to time. Therefore, it really is worth investing attention to get these concepts clear in your mind.

Until you accept that you can (and do) assign meaning *after* an event has taken place, you will only see meaningless events that appear chaotic and unpredictable. They also appear to be in the past, to have happened *to you* and are now unchangeable. Remember we have already discussed how you are only ever able to see the past. This is not only because of the mechanism of recognition and data matching that the brain does but it is also because of the *time that it has taken* your senses to have sent the collected data to the brain. Therefore, the event is already over. The film has moved on.

You, in your whole or right-minded state are the Eternal consciousness and thus the only real moment is now, in 'space'. Nothing real exists outside of the now because it is, and you are, all that exists (All That Is). So, if time in itself is created by the the illusory movement of your own consciousness, then how can you use that to your advantage?

We have already seen that the Ego loves the idea of sin because it says that sin is an act of the past which is unchangeable. You experience the pain of the guilt always in the pre-sent and you will pay the price by means of punishment in the future. However, if you can let go of time and accept that there is only what is in this space now, (which is only your current thoughts), then the past need not affect the now or the perceived future.

The now is the choice-point.

The now is where you can see what looks like a past event differently. You can only overwrite 'past' files and programming in the moment of now. Therefore, it is important to grasp that emotion, (or energy in motion), is the way that we re-access any thought in a meaningful way.

The energy or e-motion can only be 'in motion' now and you can only think about something now because you would be using the conscious mind which only knows the now. However, the content of the thought can be *about* the past or future. You can also imagine an emotion about the future but that is still a thought occurring now. Therefore, it is important to differentiate between the form of something and the content. These are two different concepts completely and again the Ego loves to confuse them.

This is akin to knowing that the intention, which is the content, is separate from the act itself which would be the form.

As we have already said, it is vital to be able to separate the person's intention which is content, from their behaviour which is form. In this way, you can see much more easily that the behaviour may have been negative but the intention was positive which makes forgiveness much easier.

Let us say that you are feeling guilty because you had an affair five years ago. This is clearly being defined as a sin because you are still holding onto the guilt and punishing yourself five years on. The event appears to be in the past but like looking at an old photo, you are really experiencing it now. Therefore, for all intents and purposes, the event is happening now because the conscious mind and the body only knows the now. You will feel very real emotion in the now. You can only be guilty now!

Earlier in the book we discussed how the conscious mind only processes what you can see, hear, smell, taste, touch, feel and think in this current moment. You are looking at the photo or thinking about the affair with the conscious mind. Therefore, it can only interpret that this is occurring now and instructs the body to produce the matching emotional state within the body. The body is hardware and has no idea that this event is a memory from five years ago. It may not even know that concepts called past or future exist.

However, because the Ego would have you believe that it is in the past, it will make it appear that it is unchangeable. But can you prove this event that you are supposedly remembering ever actually happened? What happens if you suddenly get amnesia for example? Is it not true that the event would cease to exist for you?

As a Hypnotherapist I spend much of my time overwriting people's past memories so that the effects of a trauma or phobia are eased or erased. In fact, as a Hypnotherapist I must always be very careful not to implant false memories into the client's mind. (Just to reassure you however, each of us has a Reticular Activating System which is like your personal policeman. This is always alert and guards against a therapist implanting anything that goes against your beliefs and values.)

However, the fact that someone can help you to overwrite your past, demonstrates that creating memories that are not strictly yours is possible. You have probably had this done already. Have you ever experienced your family or friends recalling a party or something but you have a differing memory or even no memory of the event at all? But the more they say *"Yes you remember, and this happened..."* the more you begin to create a new story and you will say *"Well vaguely..."* or *"Now you say that, it is coming back to me now..."* You are adjusting your memory to fit their suggestion. They just changed your history. History is *his*-story.

There is no solid past. The past only exists in your head - now. The past is your story about time because it does not exist in the space now. So although you think that you are remembering, you may really be creating a story that fits what you want to feel or think about yourself or others now.

In some ways then you may actually be creating a back-story to make sense of what you are creating now. When you wake up in the morning you need to create a story about getting into bed last night that explains how you got there. In this way, you can make sense of your life because you have put together a logical, chronological story. It is still only a concept though. There is absolutely no proof that you are not doing that every minute of every day.

If you did not individualise 'time' as separate frames of 'now' then you could not have an experience of life, as everything would happen all at once.

You might imagine this as a book. The whole book exists now as all that is. But to experience the content in a meaningful way you must sequentially read the book page by page. Each page would be analogous to a separate time-frame. You could read page 18 then page 99 because they exist as separate pages. The story would make no sense to you but it is possible to do. This is how quantum physicists think that existence is truly made up of: individual moments they call 'quanta'. If you read up to page 50 of a book and then jumped to the end, in order to make sense of that ending you would have to fill in the middle yourself, as such. Again, this would only be conjecture and assumption but you could make a story that fit.

So the Ego creates and continually reinforces the idea of time being real and a separate thing from space. It does the same with the future. Future as a physical thing does not exist. The future is again only a concept or vessel into which you pour your wants and wishes that are not in the space in front of you now. Whenever you get to the future you will experience it as now. So the future only exists in your head! Tomorrow can never be reached because when you arrive it is now today! Tomorrow has outrun you again.

In order to make sense of and order your thoughts you will define your experiences as the past, present and future. Time then, in and of itself, is just a mechanism to make our thoughts coherent. Space then becomes the scenery onto which I can project those thoughts and experience them as meaningful.

Ideas such as cause and effect support the mechanism of time and space because they are only possible within a frame-work of time and space. That is why reclaiming your projections from the external space in which they appear to exist brings cause and effect to the now. Only in the now, can you remove the cause. By removing cause, effects cease to exist in the space of now.

If the aforementioned person could reframe the affair, the sin ceases to be a sin, because what looked like the past has changed in the now. Thus, neither guilt nor punishment can follow in the future if there is not a cause in the now. All that has changed is that the definition of what you thought 'happened' feels different in the now. In the same way, if that person suddenly developed amnesia, the affair ceases to ever exist for that person. Guilt and punishment cease to be relevant because you need a negative story to cause guilt. Therefore the absence of thought in the now has changed the past, and consequently, the future!

If you do not develop a full understanding of time and how the Ego uses it, you will forever create the same future based on an ever-repeating pattern of the past. Your life will be pre-sent.

Your files are written as you go along. If the same file opens every time you think about a certain person or thing, then you can only add more of the same to what is already in there. A belief is merely information or thoughts practiced so often that it now appears that there is no other way of thinking. So it is so crucial to notice that you, as the Ego are only ever seeing the past. You are opening the same old outdated files and then wondering why nothing ever improves. If you stand and look out of the same window everyday you can only see the same view. If you want a different view then you need to move to a new window.

You have to continuously update and amend your files.

An even better way to use time to nullify the Ego is to be as little children. Jesus in Matthew 18:3 says, *"Unless you change and become like little children you will never enter the kingdom of Heaven"*. How do little children behave? They are free because they live in the moment of now. They have no concept of time, past, present or future.

Their wants and wishes only revolve around the now. They do not comprehend scarcity, limitation or understand why they should not have exactly what they want right now. They know there is only now and so to tell them to wait an hour is a meaningless concept to them.

They see the world anew and fresh every day. They do not hold grudges nor have large files on who they think you are, what you have done or any thoughts about who or what they are. Their files have not been formed yet. They can be in a rage with you one moment and love you unconditionally the next because their past doesn't yet affect the now or future.

Sadly they learn that as they grow and try to make the world meaningful.

Children allow you to be who you are without judgement. It is only adults that fill their heads with right and wrongs, do's and don'ts, the enslavement to time and must do's. They are born innocent, just as we all were. If you were born innocent and sin does not exist other than as a man-made concept then you must still be innocent. You may deny it, hide it, forget or suppress it but it cannot change the fact that the essence of You is innocence. The body may appear to grow and age, wither and die but the innocence that you really are can never be touched.

If we as adults could remember, live and be more like the children then many of our issues would disappear overnight.

To enter Heaven we must be free of time, limitation, separation and judgement. All of these imprison us because they form barriers to the seeing and being of our true nature, which is Love and Light. But these things are merely mechanisms and products of the belief in a physical universe of matter.

The past and consequential future is not unchangeable because the mind from which they originate can be changed.

In a dream, time is meaningless and you jump from scene to scene; from time frame to time frame. There is no beginning or formulated end to a dream.

Shouldn't that tell you something about what you think of as reality, if you have understood any of the ideas just presented?

Herein lays your path to freedom, not only from time but also from the crazy Ego dream of fear, guilt and punishment.

Quick Summary

1. Time and space is one indivisible thing. You are the measure of time and time is measured *from* you. The now is not an aspect of time but of space.

2. Past, present (pre-sent) and the future are only concepts created from the moment of now.

3. The Ego wants you to *only* believe that time **and** space are separate things. It teaches that these are real and out of your control because you are then subject to them and not them, to you.

4. Now is all that exists and so this is the only place that changes can be made. Now is the only cause; past and future are effects. An effect cannot be changed but a cause can.

5. Have the mindset of a child who lives for the now and for whom time is meaningless and who is thus, constriction free.

Chapter 14

Case Study Revisited

Let us now revisit the case study that I presented in chapter 5, of a real life incident that happened to me recently. I will briefly recap and then highlight the other elements that we have discussed in the intervening chapters so that we can bring all the learning together.

I was going for a short, silent retreat in Spain.

I was travelling alone and so had my earphones on shutting out the bustle of the world and was fully immersed in an inspirational download. I was in my own world and everything was flowing beautifully. I was clearly in my right-mind, had a high vibration and was aligned in joy with Spirit.

In some ways, I was not under the influence of time because I knew I had plenty. I was simply in the now. Consequently, the flow of my actions was being dictated by events such as the calling of the flight for boarding rather than me checking the clock. There were no queues at check in or passport control. I had a peaceful breakfast that ended just in time to get easily to the gate. It appeared as if everything was one big, boundless event. One ripple gently caused the next to flow as a natural consequence of the last. The small-self 'I' was not present. I was not aware of being a body but merely being part of the flow. I had no old files open about airport chaos, cancellations or trouble. My mind was clear of old programmes and so no negative experiences were being manifested at that point.

Then, out of the blue something changed.

'Out of the blue' suggests that all of a sudden it can all go wrong and for some reason that is out of your control. In truth, you have slipped back into Ego-minded thinking. The Ego doesn't want you to think that you are a creator of everything or else it fears its own demise. It will activate the *'all good things come to an end'* or *'it is too good to be true'* programme that most of us have, as its trump card.

The plane almost took off but as the engines began to roar we suddenly had to return to the terminal as a member of the crew was taken ill. This caused an hours delay. When I got to the villa where I was going to stay, lots of things were not working. My efforts to sort the things out were very stressful. I ended the day tired, cold and fed up, wondering what on earth happened to my bliss.

The next morning, once rested and back in the flow of my right-mind, I begun to self-reflect. When I traced my steps backwards, I could pinpoint the exact thoughts that changed everything.

At the airport was that there was an exact moment when my energy changed. Because this is my Universe, everything around me had to change (on my screen). I actually felt that drop in my vibration but did not catch the thought. The moment of change was when I started seeing people who appeared to be separate and in competition with me.

My attention was drawn to a mass of people waiting at the front of the gate. The Ego immediately turns to my attention to the presence of other people, competition and the story that their agenda could negatively affect my life.

The Ego had projected onto these other passengers the following story: I was only travelling with hand luggage as most people do with budget flights. This causes a rush to get on the plane first to ensure that you can fit your case into the overhead locker where you are seated. My Ego suggests to me that this brings out the selfishness in people (and me unconsciously) because there is never enough locker space. Or at least that is my Ego's perception. This is clearly the projection of what I think and do, projected onto other passengers who have now become my 'scape-goats'. If only they would not be so selfish there wouldn't be a problem, obviously!

Now, I knew none of these other people and had no objective evidence at that point, that any of these passengers had an agenda that would affect me. I had made a huge generalisation that everyone is selfish. This was my Ego's cleverly cloaked story or projection, designed to bring about a fear-based vibration.

Nothing had actually happened in reality and yet the 'suffering' had already begun.

The Ego was able to concoct this event because of a seemingly past experience. I had to put my case in a locker far behind me on my last flight which meant I had to wait to get off the plane last in order to retrieve it. It caused no problem really because I caught everyone up at passport control. But the Ego convinced me this was a problem. By doing this, it can then successfully make me believe its story by using the past as evidence. The Ego has taken a negative past experience which now seems unchangeable and projected a negative outcome from it, into the future. This resulted in fear and negativity arising into the present (pre-sent). From there, the body has to generate reactions and emotions which match the instructions from the mind. Fear arises from these thoughts and so the symptoms of low level anxiety must now be produced by the body. The body is simply hardware, remember.

The Ego had reminded me that I am vulnerable to the competing wants of other passengers. It had surreptitiously led me into fear; hence the drop in vibration.

But as we have discovered, past, present and future are created from the now and so there is no reason why anything that has happened 'previously' should repeat. However, because I had never updated my file from the last trip I now have an active file opened on budget airlines, selfish passengers and lack of locker space.

Therefore, this is my responsibility and I am the cause and everything else is simply an effect of my rogue thoughts about locker space. A belief occurring now, that appeared to be of a past experience was used to destroy my peace by projecting that the future would be the same. As we now know, the past and future do not exist but the belief in it was used by the Ego to pull me abruptly out of my right-mind. The Ego makes it appear as if the cause of my potential suffering would be a shortage of locker space. However, the real cause is also my belief that the future will be the same as the past. Let us call this Trick 1.

Trick 2 is that I had started identifying myself as a body (Ego/wrong-mindedness) instead of part of the flow, (Spirit/right-mindedness), as I had when everything was going well. If I had held to my perfect Oneness, the flow into a locker space above my head would have had to manifest perfectly. Perfect flow means *everything* becomes perfect, or it could not exist within a perfect flow.

Trick 3: Because of the Ego's belief in loss it will fight to protect what it believes are its goods and territory. Fear had arisen over the potential (not even real yet) lack of locker space. The Ego, projecting stories about other people being out to deprive me of something, had now thrown lack and scarcity into the mix. It is when we feel that we will lose out by another's action that we behave badly.

Trick 4: The Ego has now launched me into the attack spiral with my fellow passengers from which I must now defend myself or attack back.

As I see them start to move and cluster around the gate doors I say to myself *"I better get up and queue or I won't get a space."* So I do that; ridiculously defending my little space in the queue. I start vigilantly protecting it from those darned hoverers who, in my insane mind, were conspiring to push in front of me.

Trick 5: The Ego makes it personal. They were out to get *my* space! I am acting as if the locker space is mine; valuable and absolutely crucial to my happiness. There is no locker with my name on it. As I write this, it seems so silly but I and all the others in fear were all doing the same! What would

I do if they did jump the queue? I must attack and tell them the queue starts behind me or something just as unpleasant and unnecessary. If I had been in my right-mind I would know that none of this mattered. The plane would not leave without my bag. A space would be found somewhere. All that pain and suffering for nothing. I could have also caused pain and suffering to others if I had gone into full attack mode. Annoyingly, if I had just even been awake enough to spot that I was in danger of falling into the attack spiral I could have stopped it there. I would not have attracted the other negativity through the day caused by the drop of vibration that started to snowball from there.

The Ego had led me to believe that these 'others' and a lack of locker space was the cause of my suffering (effect). Really it was my old belief programme from the last trip that was the cause. Bringing cause and effect back to myself I could have updated the file there and then the cause would have been nullified. If I had updated or deleted the file before travelling, there could not have been any effect, especially one of potential suffering. Consequently, I could not fall into any attack or defence position because there simply would not have been a story about lockers in the first place. The Ego had successfully projected this crazy story about other passengers that surreptitiously led me into fear of attack and a defensive position.

Trick 6: In truth, these were simply the projections of *my* fear that I would not get a space. I had programmed into the computer the scarcity of locker space and so this became the visible evidence on the screen of my life, of my programmes running. I got exactly what I expected.

Trick 7: The Ego's other favourite thing to enslave me with is the perceived lack of time, the spectre of which was now haunting me again. What would it really matter if I was last off? It is because my Ego mind believes that time is precious, and that it can be used to enslave me. Precious time wasted by potentially getting off the plane last again, raised fear and then put me into a negative vibrational state. What was I really saying? That an extra few minutes on the plane was a loss to my precious holiday time? That's only possible if I am saying that my holiday doesn't begin until I am off that plane. Surely the holiday begins the moment I leave home? Then, incredibly it means that those who get off the plane first have gained more holiday than me and 'won' at my expense. I.e. I've lost.

Can you see how when you question these things, our behaviour can be so stupid sometimes? Can you see how mad the Ego has become, despite its reasoning being seemingly logical and rational?

The interesting thing was not only do I remember feeling the shift in vibration but I also heard the quiet Voice say *'It will all be ok'*. However, I allowed my Ego's fear voice to override this good advice. Neale Donald Walsch said *"The Soul speaks to us in feelings"* and my Spirit didn't let me down (as it never does). Spirit gave me the message which I clearly felt and heard but did not heed.

Wow, what a learning experience this was for me once I had carefully unravelled the Ego's tricks. If I had listened to Spirit when I felt and heard the Ego's warning that I wouldn't get a locker space, my bliss would have continued. There would not have been the downward spiral for the rest of the day.

As I said in the first chapter you never have a single thought and true to form, my crazy mind went on from there, on to stupid strategies about how I should queue up now, not let latecomers get in front of me and on and on and on! It was my responsibility to catch this shift but I failed miserably and paid the price. Those other passengers and what they did or didn't do was irrelevant. It was my wrong-mindedness that was the only cause.

Trick 8: Notice how the crazy strategies were actually put forward as a gain by the Ego? Rushing to get ahead would mean that I gained a locker space, and thus more time and peace of mind.

I would also gain power and a boost in energy because I was quicker and smarter than the other passengers who did not get a space. My holiday would even start quicker than theirs. What a winner!

Sadly the opposite is true. I gained a locker space but lost a day of my precious life to wrong-mindedness which only boosts my Ego's power. I will never get that day again. It's gone forever on to the pile of other days that I've ruined because I didn't catch the Ego's tricks.

"You set a value on what you receive and price it by what you give".

I received low vibration and upset because I had given out only fear and negative judgments about others. As you can see, I certainly got what I paid for! I also suffered emotional pain of guilt over upsetting my sister. In reality, I was treading over other people to get my needs met. So who was the selfish one, me or the other passengers I was accusing of being selfish? This was clearly projection in action.

I paid a heavy price with lost alignment with my Spirit and bliss.

My own condemnation of others, as always, only injured me.

Was it a price worth paying for the gain of a locker and a few measly minutes saved? As always with Egotistical behaviour the cry is a resounding ***no!***

Now the good news is that the Spirit will always take what the Ego has created and reinterpret it into something positive. When I was back in my Spiritual space, it began to show me all that had happened and why. When you offer the experience up to Spirit with a sense of forgiveness for all involved but especially you, any mistakes are corrected and annulled. As nothing in reality has really occurred there is nothing to forgive. In truth, I need only to forgive myself because it was only I that got attacked and suffered.

Although in reality, this was an insignificant incident, this has become a huge learning experience for me and now hopefully for you. If you were to now ask me if this experience, and the day of negative vibration, was a price worth paying then my answer would be a resounding yes!

I physically felt the lift in my vibration when I recognised the point where everything turned. It was palpable. Revelation always has this effect on me and then I know that I have received a very valuable lesson.

Over my holiday in silence, my vibration had risen again to bliss.

I worked to delete the old file on budget airlines.

My opportunity to practice the learning of this lesson came on the return journey with the same airline and bag.

I once again floated in bliss to and through the airport, unaware of others or time. I had decided that I would not rush to get on the plane and so I joined the end of the queue in peace. As we went through the gate we had to catch the buses to the plane and obviously I was last on. As expected, with perfect flow my bus stopped right outside the back steps that I needed for my seat. I was first off and on to the plane. Obviously, I got a locker space above my seat without any problem. I chuckled to myself to see that even though the plane was full, there was strangely locker space left when the plane doors closed. No problem in my mind; no problem externally. No negative programmes running on the computer of my mind; no negative outcome on the screen. The Ego had been proved wrong again.

My flow continued as the only empty seat on the plane was next to me and so I got to spread out and relax. Unbelievably, despite taking off ten minutes late we landed fifteen minutes early due to a strong tailwind. Again there were no queues at passport control and my dad was just arriving as I came out of arrivals. I could not have planned any of it better; perfect flow indeed.

What I want you to really understand is that the Universe works perfectly and miraculously if we can keep out of the Ego mind. Law of Attraction dictates that you will attract to you whatever you think about and thus expect. Your vibration will be set accordingly. You cannot be in flow *and* in fear. They are polar opposites. As you have just seen through this one incident in my life, your choice of thought system will be the cause of your own suffering or bliss.

We are making these choices every minute of every day and that is why self-awareness and self-reflection are so vital for all of us. Take a look at the incidences that happen in your life, large and small, to unravel the Ego's tricks. Get used to spotting them so that you do not fall for them again. Allow the Spirit to reinterpret events into great learning opportunities so that you are always getting the best out of life.

The choice is yours. I can only give you the tools but you must pick them up and fix your house. The responsibility is yours but the power is yours too.

Quick Summary

Trick 1: A belief now, that appeared to be of a past experience was used to destroy my peace by projecting that the future would be the same.

Trick 2: The Ego had me start to see myself as a separated body (Ego-mindedness) instead of part of the perfect flow (Spirit-mindedness).

Trick 3: The Ego convinces me that there is now scarcity and loss and I need to fight to protect what it sees as its goods and territory.

Trick 4: The Ego makes me believe this fear and launches me into the attack spiral with my fellow passengers. Attack is always against the self and only ever injures the self.

Trick 5: The Ego makes it personal and says the environment is me. The passengers are out to get my space! I am acting as if the locker is mine, valuable and absolutely crucial to my happiness.

Trick 6: The Ego had concealed the fact that the initial projections were of my own selfishness and fears.

Trick 7: The Ego hides my enslavement with a perceived lack of time.

Trick 8: The Ego's strategies are put forward as a gain, whilst disguising the true cost, which was suffering.

Offer these things for reinterpretation by the Spirit who will turn it into learning for you.
Also be aware that you will receive an opportunity to practice and correct the behaviour again.

Chapter 15

Father and Son

"God has a thousand names or rather he is nameless." Mahatma Gandhi

This next chapter includes some of the most challenging and hopefully thought provoking concepts so far. Therefore, even if it is far outside of your comfort zone or current beliefs I ask you to simply read it slowly, and consider the logic and rationale of what is presented, objectively.

You will already have developed your own set of beliefs on the subjects presented so all I ask is that you compare, contrast and be open minded to the fact that there is always a different perception possible. I obviously have no proof of what I am about to offer you but it does makes absolute logical sense to me. Most of this is what I have understood and pondered for many years and lessons I have learned from A Course in Miracles and personal revelation.

So although this is simply my interpretation, it has completely helped me to recognise the power that the Ego has over me.

If you unravel the Ego, which is really letting go of your physical reality, you need to have something tangible to replace it with.

If you do not develop a firm basis of surety about 'what comes after' the unravelling of the Ego, you will be too fearful to do it completely. It will feel like you are risking everything for potentially nothing. I don't believe that is true but it will be the Ego's last stand if you like. I cannot stress enough how you really have to get your head around this. In this book I have been proposing that 'replacement' is the Spirit's thought system. What you call it is irrelevant. It is important to know however, that you are giving up nothing for everything; removing darkness to reveal the Light. This is your Spiritual birthright and is in fact simply a return to the glory of what you truly are.

I sincerely apologise for continuing to use mostly Christian references for this section but that is only where my knowledge is. Please adapt the names and labels as best fits your definitions or religious language.

God is referred to as many things but in the Bible and other texts, He is known as: God, Yahweh, YHWH, Father/Abba, and All That Is, to name but a few. When Moses asks for God's name from the burning bush in Exodus 3:14, he is told *"I Am That I Am"*. As I have previously stated I will use He in relation to God, not to humanize it but to denote the one way relationship of the Father creating the Son, as will be discussed later.

As human beings, we need labels and names to try and make sense of the world. So it seems just as important to have some meaningful reference for God. The problem is though that by naming God, we risk humanising 'Him' and He is then made in our image. It is said that God made us in His image, which definitely is not the human physical form, as this is as we have already discussed, self-made by the Ego.

Without an image, things are very difficult to conceptualise. God as energy is difficult to have a relationship with.

As we have discussed, your parents become the micro version of God in your world. As you begin to reconnect with the pure essence of Love that your parents are, it can be very helpful for your reconnection with God as the Father. Your parents are the only tangible thing that you have, on which to 'hang' that Love because as I have said, you need to have a 'vision' of something to make it comprehensible.

If I say look at that Grimhashga over there, your brain will try to make up something that fits the sound of the word. In truth, you won't really have any idea about the reality of what it is. YHWH is meaningless to us. It gives us no information about what God is, what He looks like or how He behaves.

It should be impossible to humanise God I believe because God is not human, physical or even conscious in the same way that we are. *'I Am that I Am'* is circular in nature and so may be intended to show that He is something that exists out of time and space, with no beginning or end and is all inclusive, like 'All That Is'. These different labels are perhaps designed to show that God is omnipresent and thus has no body or form of any kind. A physical body can only exist in a plane of time and space after all.

I think that is why we have Jesus as 'the way to God' because as a man we can imagine His form and thus relate directly to Him.

I prefer to think of God as 'All That Is' because it is clearly defined and includes everything as itself. There can be nothing and no-one outside of it. However, it is true in a physical environment that the whole can express as the parts of itself, like with a jigsaw. A jigsaw begins as a whole board that is then divided into separate pieces. The whole can be cut into many pieces that all look different but in essence are exactly the same; pieces of the whole. Each piece is simply and temporarily, expressing as a part. It is also important to note here that even though each piece is intrinsically equal, the corners may *look* very different and thus 'more special'. This is not true. Every piece is just part of the board and will always be a necessary and equal part of the puzzle.

We could say that every other jigsaw piece is your Brother. As siblings come from the same source, when they meet up together with the parents they become the whole family.

The puzzle cannot be completed if any part is missing.

Therefore, every part has equal value. We are all the jigsaw pieces. We are an expression of God. We have the same source 'material' and thus the same characteristics and creative power as God. Our function is to rejoin all the pieces back into the whole. To become One again. You are God, except in 'order' of relationship and that differentiation is vital to understand here. The only difference is really that God created you and not vice versa, as the Ego would have you believe.

You experience your parents as god of your physical, material world especially when you are very young and dependant on them. God is referred to as the Father because it demonstrates the relationship that God created or birthed you, but you cannot create or birth God. Your parents birthed you but you did not birth your parents. It is a one way road.

Also consider this point for a moment: could you have created yourself? The Ego may have made a small-self persona but where did the Ego come from? Is it not part of the grander You (Spirit/God's Son)? Then, who created that? Whatever you believe, it is undeniable that it cannot be you because things cannot create themselves from nothing…

You are not small-self you; you are God's 'Son'.

The Yin-Yang symbol is one symbol, seemingly expressing two different parts. We can use this as an analogy for God as the One that has two seemingly opposite aspects of the Mother and the Father. Thus, the Mother is one part of the whole 'Parent'.

One seemingly 'presents' as two in a duality. Day and night look like two opposite things but are one time continuum. Where does night begin and day end, for example? Thus, the dualistic version of God would be the Mother *and* the Father, forming the Parent. Remember in the Garden of Eden that Eve is made from one of Adam's ribs.

'Made' is the significant word, rather than 'created'. As we have already discussed, in this world you can make but not create anything new.

A mother gives birth to a baby but the baby cannot give birth to her. It can give birth to its own baby and this represents the 'creative' power that God gave you to go on and make things for yourselves. Because you are made of the same material as God - just as a baby is made of the same material as the parents - you inherit their powers, as you inherited God's. This power is the ability to procreate for yourself. However, you can never make anything outside of 'All That Is' as that is what you are *but* you can imagine or dream that you could. This is what you must be then doing.

As a child you will believe and expect that your parents should provide everything that you need and want. This is what we expect and project onto God. However, He has already 'provided' everything by creating All That Is which is without lack. You can give yourself an imaginary experience of having lack but in truth if you are All That Is, what can be lacking?

Now in the physical world it appears as if the baby is thrust out and away from its mother at birth. It appears as if it has become separate and individualised from its source. But on some level, the child is an idea and thoughts can never leave their source.

I can for example, share with you an idea that I have. I have shared it with you but the thought has not become diminished by the sharing. The idea still remains inside my head as the original idea. Therefore, the child will always be the child in the mind of the parent and in the mind of the child; the parent will always be the parent.

As we saw in the Significant Relationships chapter, this fundamentally affects our relationship statuses for life. The unequivocal truth, or form of this relationship, can never change but the quality or content of it can. Therefore, you as a thought of God can never be apart from his mind; you are never out of his thoughts.

Now if we can at least agree that God is not physical then He must be non-physical and invisible. You cannot see non-physical things in a physical environment. So we could say that He is nebulous energy.

Let us imagine there is only ocean. The ocean here represents God or All That Is. God's Son (You) is akin to a paddling pool (your physical body) with some sea water (Spirit) from the ocean in it. This sea water is seemingly physically separated from the wider ocean by the plastic pool. The pool then is akin to the physical body but the sea water (You/Spirit) is still intrinsically made of the same stuff as the ocean; it is the same sea water. In the same way, God is still within and surrounds your physical body in the form of Spirit today. The body, like the pool, is an arbitrary form of separation. The pool, like the body, is still contained within All That Is, in so far as it can be nowhere else. The pool and its contents still float in the ocean but simply on top of it, instead of submerged within. There actually is nowhere else or anything else that they could be. In the same way, it may appear like you are somewhere else but you are always within All That Is or God.

Therefore, you may be having an *experience* of being separated by the pool or the body, but the truth of what you are, is inside. If the paddling pool were to burst, the sea water would flow back into the Oneness of the ocean and seem to disappear forever (Death). However, the water from the pool has not disappeared. The water has just been a freed from a confined space. In truth, it has just become more difficult to differentiate it from the whole.

You are still One with All That Is but the belief in a body is temporarily withholding you from rejoining the 'mass'. As there is nothing else, all that you could be is God and an Eternal part of All That Is. This is undeniable.

Alongside the natural power to create comes the free will to create *anything* that you choose. That includes a Universe that is dark and fearful if you so choose. God cannot destroy it or forbid you to create whatever you choose as that would completely oppose the Law of Free Will.

Let us imagine that you have put your children in a completely white room with glorious coloured paints, paper and brushes. The only thing that you say to them before leaving is that you have the free will to do anything that you want. How could you then get angry and punish them because they have painted on the walls?

The gift of Free Will is the most loving and trusting act. It is, I believe, the true meaning of unconditional love. God says *'I love and trust you enough to be totally free and I will Love and support you whatever you choose to create'*. Sometimes you may not agree with your children's choices but you respect their right to live their life. You know they have free will and no doubt you still love them anyway. Love is what you are and not what you do.

Therefore, God is incapable of opinion, I believe, on what you do and 'knows' that the essence of who and what you truly are can never be touched or tainted.

When you sleep there are only two ways to wake up from your own nightmare: one is by gradually withdrawing yourself from it and the other is someone or something awakening you. I personally do not believe that God can actually see our dark creations in this world (like the parent cannot see the nightmares of its child). The parent does not enter the child's nightmare but gently soothes and calls him to awaken from outside of it. The Voice of God via the Voice of Spirit does that for you here. God could not enter the nightmare anyway because of Law of Attraction.

God as the ultimate vibration of Radio Unconditional Love at 100htz could not pick up any signals from Radio Fear at the other end of the scale. This is why we must rid ourselves - with the support of the Spirit within us - of all fear that blocks our true self as Light. By doing this, we are moving up the vibrational scale until we ourselves can pick up Radio Unconditional Love. So we really have nothing to fear from our creations here, or from 'His' judgement of them. The parent doesn't judge the child for having a nightmare. The parent recognises that it's a pseudo-experience of a creative mind.

If you believe that you are an Eternal being created by God then you must understand that you have always existed and therefore cannot live and die. We run into a difficult concept here then about time being linear and the belief that you must have been 'birthed' or created at some beginning point.

In a dream, is it not true that you can never remember the beginning and there is never really a conclusive end?

Q: Can you know for sure that you were ever born?

You certainly will not be able to remember it. Your only proof is that other people tell you it is so. As these people are your dream characters, then of course they are going to reinforce the story that you are a real, physical being. Let's imagine that you were able to create another adult human and slot them into a perceived timeline at age 19, for example. You would have to convince them they had been born and had grown up on Earth so that they could live a normal life.

Q: How would you do that?

Would you not plant a few odd memories here and there that would convince them that they were actually 'there' at that time? Would you not create a few characters around them like parents and siblings who would reinforce that reality? Isn't that what you do in your dreams? You are never born nor die in a dream because you as the dreamer could only be *witnessing* the dream character being born or dying. Therefore, whoever is being born cannot be you.

There really is no ultimate proof that you are alive in a solid, physical environment. Your life has many of the same qualities as a dream and yet you unquestioningly accept that your dreams are not 'real'. If you remember my strawberry moment story, you get to choose the most empowering version for yourself. There is no real truth out there. Being born wasn't the beginning for you, because your existence didn't start there. If you were not born then you are not a physical body and so cannot be hurt or die.

Maybe, being born is just the back-story that the Ego creates in order to make sense of the fact that you are conscious *now*.

It is crucial to understand that you cannot believe in yourself as both an Eternal Spirit dreaming of life *and* that you *are* a physical body suffering the apparent cycles of life and death. These are two fundamentally different ideas and diametrically opposed. One is out of time and space and the latter exists firmly tied into it.

So at this point in our journey together, everything circles back to our earlier example, with the choice of taking the red or blue pill in the Matrix. The Matrix, as I have discussed previously is a computer-generated reality programme, which here represents the physical world of the Ego. Every human is 'asleep' in a watery cocoon, wired up to an artificial reality computer system having their senses stimulated. Those people, like you, are not physically in the world that their senses tell them they are. They are oblivious to the wider truth and believe fully that they are living a 'real' life with real experiences. The lead character Neo is told that he cannot exist in both and must take a red or blue pill that will make his choice permanent.

At some point in our development, this is the choice that we all must make. Are you going to believe that you are an Eternal Spirit and that you can wake up and go home to God? This means completely overcoming the Ego by giving up belief that you are a physical body and that death is real. (This is necessary because these are the two foundational beliefs that prevent our escape via Enlightenment.)

Or are you going to continue to believe the opposite? You will have already seen which thought system I am advocating.

So when did your life really begin then?

I haven't been able to find a satisfactory answer for myself. My earliest memory is of my younger sister being born and being shocked about this. In reality then, that is where my consciousness began as far as I know. Therefore, is this the beginning of my dream? This fits with the fact that a dream always starts in the midst of the story. The other very interesting consequence of not being born means that you are not a physical body then. This leads us back to the mind-based or dream world again. Even more interestingly, if you are not a body that was born, how can you die?

I, as a Hypnotherapist, have done many, many Past Life Regressions on people. What I find most interesting is that no-one is ever in the body at the point of death. No-one suffers the pain of that actual moment. They will recount the last few minutes and then be floating outside and looking down at the scene in peace mostly, but sometimes regret. The transition of consciousness is always seamless and sometimes the client goes straight into another life at a certain age. Is this actually because you don't always start a life by being born but merely reinsert yourself into a timeline whenever you want? If it is your dream, then of course this is possible. If you do create a scene of being born or dying, maybe that's because it is just another experience or 'frame' that you want to experience.

I believe that birth and death then are just scene changes in the dream.

Like in a dream, when you are falling for example, you never actually experience hitting the ground. Is this because death is actually an invention of the Ego to control us with fear? The Ego knows full well that you will go on after so called 'death' and so will it. It is an integral part of your thought system and consciousness. Therefore, although it is an inconvenience to the flow of its work, ultimately death serves a powerful purpose for the Ego's gain. As we have seen, it gets to stalk you with that fear.

Is death actually, as I believe, merely a scene change or a dream-within-a-dream? Is it a temporary respite where it appears that you can design your next lifetime of learning? Is death just another thought or change of mind?

The belief that there is always more to learn and that you are not the highest vibration of Love *yet* is the Ego's trick to keep you learning. If you came from the same source material as Pure Love and you are 'All That Is', then you are already complete. You are everything, therefore you already know everything. What else can you learn if you know it all?

Why do you need to keep coming 'back' then? It can only be because either you do not know what the Ego's trick is *or* that you want to return for the drama or fun. Often there may not be a strong enough faith that there is anything else other than the relentless cycle of life and death. Consequently, all that you can do is fall straight back into the cycle.

One morning, after being on an intense weekend course learning the art of astral travelling, I awoke on Monday morning completely disorientated. Although I recognised my surroundings, I felt disassociated from them, as if I wasn't really in them. It's very difficult to articulate but it felt like I had woken up 'dead'. Now I know that sounds crazy but that's exactly how it felt; I was a consciousness in the room but not in the physicality of the room. It is like Patrick Swayze in the film 'Ghost'. He is murdered but doesn't realise it and carries on chasing his assailant.

So what do I do now I thought... and thought and thought? My son was away at University and so I was alone in the house. No dead spirits were coming to collect me like you see in the films so I thought what do I do? I couldn't think of anyone to ask about it so I thought well I better go to work then. But this feeling was still very strong. When I got to work, no-one else was in, which wasn't in itself unusual but it just meant that still I had no contact with the living as such. As I kept looking for a rational explanation all I could find was evidence to the contrary.

Now, on the day before, on my way to the course I had a weird experience on the station. Even though I was standing to the edge of the hoardings, a couple of people walked into to me as if they couldn't see me. Then, a man stood right up close to me, again as if he didn't realise I was there. This struck me as very weird but I didn't really give it that much thought.

On the course, the instructor talked about 'Soul Rescue'.

When someone passes over but doesn't realise it, then some people in their sleep are able to reach them and take them over to the 'spirit world'. I remember asking how you would you convince them they were dead and the teacher said *"Well you may bring them to a course like this"*. OMG! - I laughed so hard as I now thought that *'This is why I was on the course! They are trying to tell me that I am dead!'* I felt like I was going mad but yet was as sane and clear thinking as I had ever been. It was a strange anomaly. Eventually, I rang the college and they said that I should come back or go to the GP. I thought *'There's no way I could tell the GP this!'*

Then I remembered a dream I had had recently after splitting up with a partner. I dreamt of being stabbed through the left shoulder with a lance and it was a particularly vivid dream which is why I remembered it. Was this my real death and not a dream? There was no way of telling. It was like in the Leonardo Di Caprio film 'Inception', where Cobb and his wife are experimenting with lucid dreaming. Eventually his wife loses touch with which is the dream world and which is the real world. Nothing he did could convince her that she was in the dream world and he was in the real one.

Anyway, after a few days the feeling left me and I just carried on doing what I've always done but every now and again I do wonder if I am alive or dead. I often question what is the difference when it is all in your head anyway? If death is a scene change, did I 'die' in this play but just reinserted myself back into the timeline to continue as if nothing had happened? If I had physically 'died' in my sleep no-one would know if I just reinserted myself back in, the next morning. I find this so, so fascinating and totally possible if time, as I said earlier, is not what we think it is.

But is this what the Son of God did as Consciousness first dawned upon it, and then it saw itself as separate from its Father? Did Consciousness awaken to find itself in a strange world and so created a story of being birthed into a location in time and space that it called the body? Did the Consciousness then follow on with a whole story about its own identity and why it was here?

If you awoke from a coma with amnesia what are the first things that you would ask? They would be: Who am I? Where am I? And- How did I get here? Are we just here now endlessly searching for the answer to these questions after our consciousness first awoke?

Did the Consciousness then just continue forward creating stories to fit whatever was caused by its next thought which turned into action? This would have made it a creator and reactor at the same time, causing a split in the mind. Is this not exactly what the Bear cycle is doing now?

It is so interesting to ponder these questions.

Are we all just lost in one eternal thought?

Now I know how mad that waking up dead experience makes me sound and I thought long and hard before putting it in this book. I decided to be honest about it because lots of people have experiences that don't fit with the mainstream view of reality. I know lots of people that see spirits and are not mad, for example. The 'mad' label is one given by the Ego because it doesn't want you sharing these stories or questioning reality.

So let us return to the Ego view of death.

The Ego having taken this life story as far as it can, simply creates a new 'life story' in the Spirit domain before it thrusts you back into another seemingly, physical life. On entering the new life, the Ego induces complete memory loss, breaks all connections with the past personality and their contacts. In this way, the Ego ensures that you will have to relearn everything all over again. This is actually exactly what we have to do by being born as a baby. Isn't that an ingenious way to limit your ability to ever complete the race back Home? The Ego just keeps moving you back to the beginning of the race track so that you can never cross the finish line!

If I bet you £5 that you can't get home to London, how can I ensure that I win? Perhaps I could keep wiping your memory so you have to keep relearning how to travel on the transport system. I could sabotage your progress by misdirecting you. I could prevent you going the quickest route by suggesting there are muggers on that tube line? Any of this sound familiar to you?

Well is this, in some ways what the Ego does?

Has it has created a small-self character and implanted a few memories here and there? Then, like the character in 'The Truman Show', is the Ego then directing and controlling you with a range of fears? Has it has already engineered and embedded these controls so deeply within your psyche that you don't even know what's there?

The Ego also funnels and directs you to where it wants you with pain. What does a hangover tell you, for example? That the body doesn't want you to do this any more and there will be a price to pay if you do! However, this produces a fear that giving up drinking will make you a social pariah within your group and you fear ending up without any friends. However, the fear of being unlovable is the greatest one the Ego uses against you and so you carry on drinking even though it causes you pain. The Ego doesn't want you to be happy - ever!

However, with all of that said, it is important to realise that this is ultimately your dream. Do you choose to stay in the dream and recreate the Ego because… you actually love the drama of it all and love having the opportunity to express your creative abilities?

You often choose to go on the most frightening roller coasters time and time again despite complaining that you are scared. You continue to drive your car even though you are actually risking death every time you do. You keep choosing pain and suffering on a deeply unconscious level. You may know people who are addicted to their misery. Why? The only sane answer is because secretly they love and value it.

Although with your 5% of conscious mind, you may think that you have had enough of the cycle of life, you still continue to choose it. However, unless you believe 100% that you will go on after death then it is very difficult to risk everything for the possibility of nothing in return. Without a concept and structure of what is the alternative to the cycle of life and death, you can only get more of the same; exactly as I did when I thought I was dead! It felt like there was no other option other than to continue with what I knew. You have the gift of Free Will. You may create whatever you choose but often you don't think there is anything else *to choose*.

The Bible says that we are God's precious Son. As I suggested earlier, God loves us so much he gave us the gift of Free Will. He values and loves us and so would never dream of destroying us. Therefore, as we are made of the same stuff and blessed with the same powers, so do we too, love and value our creation(s) - warts and all!

A father gets that label when there is a son, which by its birth now makes him a father. Before that, he is just a man. You will only know this man is a father through knowing that he has a son. Therefore to know the father you must also know the son and vice versa. You are the 'father' to your creations (your son). I can only know you as a 'father' through your creations and you only know yourself as a 'father' through looking *at* your own creations. That is why you will not give up your world; it is your creation or your baby. You only know yourself through it.

Ultimately, the fear that you have, may be that if you give up the world you cannot know yourself as a creator any longer. Thus, you love and value your creations even if they appear negative. This is your Universe and you must be creating it all. If the world were to disappear, you would have to deal with the very real, if hidden, consequence that you would cease to be a Creator (Not cease to exist yourself.)

Or so the Ego would have you believe. The Ego would assure you that you will have thrown this great gift back in the face of God, your Father. You will then feel guilt and expect punishment. Therefore, the Ego can now stalk you with the inevitable threat of God's wrath. And so you keep creating yet denying that which you are; all the time disassociating yourself from your creations.

"Hide out in this physical body and we both get to survive and be punishment free", the Ego whispers! This is like the *'If they can't see you, you will not be able to see them!'* mentality that animals have. However, even though the Ego has set itself up as the pseudo god of your Universe, it, itself, is fearful of being discovered by God. Thus, fearing punishment itself, it must keep you away from enlightenment. If you are isolated and controlled by fear in a vulnerable body then you need a protector, but believe me the Ego isn't it.

The Ego reminds you that *'This world can never hurt you as much as God is going to when he sees what you have thrown away'*. But God isn't a person with that or any kind of mind-set. But the Ego wants you to think you were made in the image of its pseudo god, which does judge and does attack.

I believe that God is merely the energy of Love which forms All That Is. It extends and shares its Light which is part of what you really are. Light is the creative resource with which we extend and share that Love.

Mainstream science purports that the only thing that exists is light. How can you offend that? How can you not be what you are made of? That is an impossible feat. Therefore, if you take the red pill and take the Spirit's path then you are free and can awaken to the Truth. This is the only road that leads to a positively joyous life.

If you should dare to harbour any positive belief in God as a benevolent being, the Ego will immediately attack that idea by pointing to God's unreality. It will point to lack of proof of His existence, to how many people don't believe in him or even use Jesus' death as evidence (completely ignoring the resurrection) to your physicality and vulnerability. The Ego will even point to the fact that God appears to never answer your prayers and appears to have abandoned you completely to this life of ongoing suffering. It asks you: *'Where was God when this happened?'*

Remembering my strawberry moment; it is important to realise that there is no proof either way.

Therefore, believe whichever idea makes you happiest.

God, although He cannot and would not come into the dream, doesn't leave you without help or comfort. You may hear the Voice of Spirit that rests quietly but steadfastly on hand to help as soon as you ask. It cannot do anything else because it is already a part of you. But you must ask for help because any interference with your choices violates the Law of Free Will.

It is the gentle voice of the parent gently whispering to the child to wake up, reminding you that you are safe and at home already.

It is in you for eternity and will reinterpret every scary tale you have created, into a fairytale if you will listen. It is always trying to support you; to teach, to guide and remind you of who you really are. It is incessant in this and will continue to be so until you release the want to keep recreating the dream. To save you is its only function and it can do nothing else.

As I question why I am not performing miracles in this dream of mine even though it feels like I believe it's 100% possible, I hear the Ego whisper: *'Look what happened to Jesus.'*

So the mind is surreptitiously programmed that you really don't want to be able to create and demonstrate miracles or you too will be crucified. In the world today, that would look translate to people ridiculing and attacking you. It may look like people suggesting that you are mad and dangerous, threatening your livelihood, sanity or relationships with family and friends.

I had a direct experience of this recently with a persistent sore throat. The usual questions that I would ask if I develop a throat chakra ailment are: Am I living the life that I really want to live? Am I doing the things that I really want to do? Am I saying the things that I really want to say? This time though I couldn't get to the real answer. Then, one day in class I had a lady who was struggling to accept some of the less mainstream ways of thinking about the body and illness. I realised that I felt that I had to constrain saying what I really knew as the truth. I later realised that my healing could only come when I let go of this fear. If it is not too dramatic to say, I feared being crucified for speaking my truth.

Also because this may not be the mainstream line of thinking, I guess I feared losing my reputation, respect and even livelihood. This was yet another trick of the Ego attempting to demonstrate that I don't fully believe that I create my own reality.

This was also reinforced by a client later in the day, whose fear was of being 'crucified' by her partner for secretly food binging. She had great shame and was doing things in secret. We discussed being able to own who she was and be open and honest about her decisions. If she wanted the chocolate bar then she needed to own the decision to eat it, enjoy it and hear anyone's opinion about that as feedback. The key to overcoming any negative behaviour is to first own your choices. From this, I realised every time I say *"I believe in God but I am not religious"*, I am not fully owning who I am. Every time I deny being religious, I deny who I am. If I deny who I am, then I am trying to be someone else. I am not accepting my truth.

Let us remember the jigsaw analogy; that we are all equal but unique pieces that only fit in one place, as the shape we were created to be. If, then I am not being true to the 'shape' that I am, I will never be where I want to be and fit. I and all those that should fit around me can never be at peace and All That Is can never be All That Is; fully complete like the puzzle. None of us will ever find Oneness or Heaven if even one puzzle piece is out of place.

Knowing all this, I continued to ask myself *'Why do I still continue to create this dream?'* This is the Ego's most well disguised deterrent. If you can achieve enlightenment, can produce miracles and teach others how to do this then you will suffer the same fate as Jesus. At least that is the way my Ego plays it. The only obvious escape from this premise is then to get myself to the place where I really believe that I could deal with the same fate. But the Ego counters with *'How arrogant for you to even compare yourself. Look at all the bad stuff you have done before. You couldn't take all that pain and vilification!'* And so I go dutifully fall back into the safety of the dream again.

However, one day it was revealed to me from the Loving Voice of Spirit that the crucifixion was Jesus' choice in order to teach a powerful lesson about the Resurrection. I don't need to make that choice. Also, with Law of Attraction, the more loving and peaceful you become, the higher your vibration. Therefore, it is an impossibility to attract an experience of being a victim if you are at the other end of the vibrational scale. You would have to consciously choose to lower your vibration as Jesus had to have *chosen* to do in order to have that experience. Therefore, fear of crucifixion must be an Ego trick to keep you away from the end goal of being Love.

Why do I keep dreaming this dream when it feels as if every part of me wants it to end? The only rational answer is because I must value it.

As I said earlier, God values and loves You as his creation and would never dream of destroying you. You would not think of murdering your own children (unless you were insane) and God is not insane. Therefore, as you are made of the same stuff and blessed with the same qualities, you must love and value your creation, warts and all. Perhaps the truth is that you see the ending of the dream as the ultimate death for your 'children'.

However, you or your creations can never cease to exist.

By definition, there cannot be anything that is not a part of All That Is. Stop for a moment and really think about that.

So everything that has ever been created (including you) cannot cease to exist on some level, somewhere for eternity. Otherwise, All That Is would become All That Is, except that 'thing', which is impossible.

Therefore, you can let go of any worry that you or any of your creations can ever cease to exist. They and you can change form but neither they nor you can ever cease to exist. Also, how can God continue to know himself if his Son ceased to exist?

So maybe I keep creating the dream because on some level I understand that it is my child, my responsibility and I have a duty of care to not take its life force away from it. I value all of the experiences and live through it the way that my parents live through me. Maybe like procreation, it ensures that in some way shape or form that I will always go on. The fear otherwise is that if my dream ceases to be, so do I. You will always protect what you value which will be what you treasure most. Your creation, much like your art, is an expression of you. Is your value too linked to your creations to be pried apart?

A Course in Miracles says: *"You set a value on what you receive and price it by what you give."* If you are giving all of your love and attention to this life then there is a high price to pay to lose it. But if you receive a high value return even unconsciously from it, such as God gets to know himself through you, then the Law as stated has been fulfilled.

As I teach in mainstream colleges, I have had to be very constrained in what and how I say things. Therefore, I teach the mainstream psychology of the Ego. This is extremely useful but actually dismisses a whole portion of the deeper teachings and meanings that everyone also needs. Which is why here, I whole heartedly recommend that everyone reads and studies A Course in Miracles. You need to get the whole picture and deeper healing.

As you will see by now I am trying in this book to balance both mainstream views with the deeper relationships of the Ego, Spirit and God. However, in this book, I can only scrape the surface. In my experience, the Course works with you to complete the unravelling of the Ego and produces true healing. Healing comes from a release of fear and that is what appears as you unravel the Ego and get to be in Heaven on Earth.

Or maybe like Dorothy in the Wizard of Oz, you are dreaming that you are in a fantastic land somewhere else. When you have completed your unnecessary journey, will you find that you have always had everything that you thought that you lacked or needed? Maybe you already have the perfect mind, heart and courage.

And finally, maybe you just need to think only of 'Home', to wake up and realise that you never really left.

Quick Summary

1. God is: energy, All That Is, Oneness, out of time and space (Eternal), unknowable except through yourselves and others, Pure Love. 'He' cannot judge and is not in your dream.

2. As a child particularly, your parents are the microcosm of God in that they represent gods of your world. The Ego also claims to represent the god of your small-self 'I'.

4. The Ego is a punishing, judgemental god that projects these qualities onto the real God and possibly your parents too. The real God gave you Free Will and thus judgement of your actions by Him makes no sense.

5. As the sole creator of your Universe, but not of yourself, you love and value all your creations. As this is your treasure you will instinctively want to protect it rather than see it end.

6. You are a unique puzzle piece that despite seeming to be individuated now, you came from and still are part of the One; the original board.

Chapter 16

Whole Life Living- The Integration of the Ego

"We are shaped by our thoughts; we become what we think. When the mind is pure, joy follows like a shadow that never leaves." Buddha.

Let us start to bring everything together now, as the basic premises that have been presented throughout the book are crucial to understand and to live by.

Q: What is the most important thing to a suffocating man?

The answer is air. Money, cars, good looks or any of the things that we are told by the Ego are important; do not matter in that moment.

When that man finally takes a breath, does he connect that breath as a gift of God?

On the physical level, the sun, the rain, air, food, metals, water, fire; all of these things are provided abundantly by source for you. You never have to worry that any of these will run out. Without the greed of man, somewhere in the world these elements will always be freely available. Not only that, but every one of these and indeed everything in existence, brings you service in some way. Every person, seen or unseen brings you service in some way: the firemen, the postman, the delivery drivers, designers and even the government. Even your greatest enemies serve to teach you something.

How blessed are you?

If you believe the world was created for you, or by you as a creator by any name, you should at all times feel very blessed.

But perhaps blessed is not the right word if you know that you are the creator of the world.

If it is your dream and these are your dream characters, this *should* be *exactly* how the world runs.

If you prefer to fight, you have to create oppressors to fight against. If you want to have an experience of choice, you need to create that which you do want and that which you do not, in order to have contrast. You need duality. Therefore, even the things and people that you say that you wouldn't have created, exist for this reason. If you want to play the game of limitation and fear then you must forget or deny that you have made that choice. You must first accept that *you* have put limitations and things that scare you in to the world, especially if you now choose to be free of them.

Why would I choose to play the game of limitation and fear you ask?

In A Course in Miracles it is purports that the dream began when we had a brief, crazy thought that we could be separated from God and then we forgot to laugh about the absurdity of it.

I imagine this as having a thought like *"I wonder what it would be like if there was something other than All That Is (God)?"* This is obviously a mad idea because All That Is, by its very nature is all that is, but a creative mind could day-dream about this possibility. Most may think about the possibility for a moment and then laugh and get on with their day. But what if this idea deeply intrigued and entranced you until you became lost in thought for what seemed like eternity?

The opposite of All That Is, must be All That Is Not (ATIN), or non-existence.

Well you must already exist to be able to think about non-existence and so non-existence for you must be impossible. And technically you cannot explore what doesn't exist. Therefore, ATIN can only be an *idea* or *thought construction* about what the opposite of God is.

Once you have that constructed that crazy thought, your attention or consciousness now becomes fully focused into ATIN because you can only think of one thing at a time. If God is Love and Light, then the opposite, which is Fear and darkness are what you would be exploring.

You are wholly 'there' because at this point you are only Consciousness. Once you have 'gone' into the idea of ATIN, a virtual division between the two 'worlds' or thoughts would be created so automatically, that one part of your mind would not remember its creation. This would be akin to the mind splitting perhaps.

All thought has a frequency. Once lost in thought your vibration drops into something other than Love (which is on some level fear) and consequently you cannot return 'Home'. You will now need someone or something to come from outside of that world, in order to remind you that you were only day-dreaming and have not 'gone' anywhere. Remember the character in 'The Truman Show' only finds out he is on a TV film set when someone from outside comes in and tells him? He has great resistance to the truth for a long time before he starts to open his eyes and sees for himself.

The outside source of salvation for the small-self you, is the part of You as the Son of God that is still at 'Home' in Heaven day-dreaming. Let us call this the Day-dreamer for the purpose of this analogy. Spirit is the voice of the Day-dreamer within the split brain calling you back.

This Spirit is of course the original thought system before you created or developed, the alternative thought system of the Ego.

Even though you may be day-dreaming in the classroom, for example, you are still fully conscious. It is only one part of the mind that has become lost in thought. The other part is still performing its normal functions such as keeping you on the chair until the teacher calls your attention back!

Spirit is still conscious and remains in connection with the Son of God and the Day-dreamer and so sees beyond the dream but the Ego does not and so must guard against this unknown force that it fears. Obviously, here is the triad that makes up the Holy You; The Son of God, Spirit and the Ego. The Ego is the fear based thought system that keeps focussing back to ATIN, not because it is evil but because it simply lacks knowledge. It is the confused and frightened part of you that doesn't know how this happened and how to get Home. In order to make sense of events, the Ego mistakenly starts to believe that rather than getting lost in thought, you have deliberately turned your back on God. You know you did this because it is your day-dream but you do not know how to resolve it. Now you are in such low vibration it is possible to believe the Ego's lies that your Father will be angry and He will be looking for you to punish you. Therefore you create a body to hide in and produce the Ego as your protector god. By disassociating from these acts and denying that God exists, you get to live in some perverse/mad idea of peace and safety.

As long as you hold on to the delusion!

In order to convince you that this reality is the only one, the Ego creates the following mechanisms to limit and control you: the body in time/space, a pseudo-personality, limiting concepts such as life and death, duality and fear, projection and scapegoats, learning & teaching and finally false idols like money and sickness. The Ego also ensures that God in any real form stays out of the picture. You, through the Ego, have created such a convoluted and entangled web of self deceit, that you cannot find your way out on your own. You now believe that the Ego is god of this world and that you are trapped within its laws of time and space. You are this physical body that ages, gets sick and will die.

This is purportedly the end of you forever; oblivion!

Therefore you are from birth being pursued by pain and death. You live in darkness and fear, defending yourself from attack or attacking your own shadow projections. You will try to find a place of refuge and safety by making yourself either: the richest, most powerful, most beautiful, most helpful or least troublesome. The Ego will try to appease you with shiny, glittery jewels, faux happiness, technologies and material goodies. These appear to make you happy or distracted for a tiny amount of time until the shine wears off.

Then suddenly you realise where you are; separated from your Brothers and Father in Heaven. The Ego will then immediately jump in to comfort or distract you with something bigger, better or shinier.

And so sadly, you keep on wanting, running and trying to get.

Once you are tired of running and striving for nothing of any real value you may now at least want to find the light and escape.

Be aware, your punishment will be harsh. The Ego will sabotage any bid for freedom and will then remind you that you tried and failed and so now there is no hope. Any future resistance becomes futile.

You will get depressed and retreat inside. You have now been rendered completely powerless.

However, in the bottom of the well of your depression, there remains just a glimmer of light.

There is the God spark that remains untouched in your heart. In the darkness you can cry out for help. Here is the key, because that cry for help is actually the decision that you are ready to give this up and return Home. The Spirit within has now been chosen - whether you are conscious of that decision or not. Your attention will now be turned towards the alternate reality.

This is exactly what happened to me as I fell into my deep depression many years ago. As the Spirit can only be heard in the silence and stillness, you start to hear a quiet Voice that has a different opinion and method of communication. It speaks in feelings, through books, nature, songs and great teachers. As I started to find my way out of my depression through books and courses, I realised that God was speaking to me through books. I know that it is true but I also understand that it is the Spirit that speaks for God through me and through books. There is an interesting theory that becomes self evident if you believe that you are creating your reality and that is that all books are blank until you open them. You write every book!

The Spirit never shouts and it never attacks, even at the Ego because it has to remain as the vibration of Love or it would become powerless. It will not overcome your God-given Free Will and so you must ask for guidance and then choose to listen to its way of thinking. It speaks only of Love and Forgiveness. It sees no physical body and no suffering. It sees only your choices and it always has a re-interpretation for your faulty thinking. The Spirit is who you are when you are in your whole (Holy) mind. It links you directly back to your Father and the Day-dreamer in Heaven.

Spirit reminds you that you are still an innocent child who is dreaming and thus you cannot sin. He sees you lost in thought only. Your Father sees the innocent child dreaming and continues to Love you unconditionally. No-one can see inside of your dream except you! A mistake in a dream is still just part of a dream that doesn't actually have any real effect.

So if you can identify yourself as that little child and see everyone with no back-story and no agenda, then you become free. Children see everyone as neutral and equal. Other people only give to a child. It has nothing material to offer anyone and so nothing can be taken away from it. A child can only give, share and extend what it is, which is unconditional Love.

An innocent child's love is Love without judgement and nothing to do with the Ego's love to 'get' something. You must be without the burden of faux responsibility just as a child is. It is the parent that holds all of the responsibility for all of the child's needs.

In the same way, God through the Spirit within, wills this for you too if you allow that to be and have trust in it.

The innocent child surrenders willingly to a greater power with full trust and no doubt. The Ego fears this as the truth and an unassailable route of escape. Once you return to the high vibration of Love, the Ego ceases to exist as it is. Like you, it believes itself to be a real and independent entity.

The Ego needs you to believe that you are *not* innocent, and in fact are terribly guilty.

It may thus seek to create a complete story, which is a tissue of lies about how bad and uncaring your parents were. It fills your head with thoughts of victimhood and powerlessness as a child of an uncaring god.

It then becomes impossible to think of yourself as the innocent child of a loving Father.

The Ego collects detailed files on the computer of your brain then plays them out like an endless film from an unknown projector somewhere.

The film rolls on and on because the unseen projector is locked away in a hidden room somewhere that seems unreachable to you.

Trapped in a belief that the unchangeable past is the cause of the present and the future, your continued victimhood and powerlessness is guaranteed to be recreated day in and day out.

Like poor Truman Burbank, you have nothing else to suggest that this is not the truth; that this dark world is not your real home.

Then, for me personally, a book appears called A Course in Miracles that purports to come from a source outside of the dream. Channelled by Helen Schucman, it begins to teach me that the world is not what I think it is. My Ego jumps into action and tries to sabotage my escape with making the book too difficult to read. So by the end of my first reading I am resigned to the fact that I didn't really understand a word of it. Only seven or so years later am I nudged to pick it up again only to find the text much easier to understand. To my shock, I realise that in the interim, I have been taught so many of the themes by other teachers such as Bashar.

Darryl Anka again, is simply accessing and sharing information from an outside source by channelling Bashar. I quickly became addicted to his early teachings which were really all about our psychology and how to overcome it. Those of you who know his work will recognise his deep influence in my thoughts as presented in this book.

Bashar, which means 'Messenger' in Arabic, even admits that he is just a mirror for our Higher Selves. I would simply change this label to Spirit. It is even synchronous how I discovered Bashar. I was at a Law of Attraction event and a guy who was unknown to me, with a very strong aura of peace sat next to me. Despite being a complete stranger, he was very insistent that I write the name of Bashar down. He was extraordinarily firm that this was who I should study. It took me a good few months after returning home to even look at his work. But again, the Spirit will not force me to do anything, so it simply kept nudging away at me until I took action.

The Dalai Lama said *"Pain is inevitable; suffering is optional"*. How long I valued the current life of pain over accepting a gift of help was clearly my decision to make.

Spirit is always appearing in various guises to reinterpret and correct my creations. When I had a baby who only lived for an hour, the pain of the loss was indescribable. But after the grief, anger and self-recriminations had subsided I realised that it had a different meaning. I still remember the name of the beautiful Spirit that manifested as the neo-natal Health Visitor. She sat on my bed a day or two after my son passed away and gave me the poem 'Footprints in the Sand' by Mary Stevenson. The poem affected me deeply and was about how Jesus carries you in times of despair. However, because you only see one set of footprints in the sand, you wrongly assume that he has deserted you in your hour of need.

After years of Atheism, was this Spirit's attempt to reintroduce me to God? In my experience, Messengers turn up just at the right time, with the exact thing that you need. They may be called Soul Mates by some, Guides or Angels by others. It matters not how you define them but it does matter that you recognise their frequency in your life so that you may begin to trust and appreciate their help.

The other gift that I resisted for a long time was meditation. Every self help book I read would mention it. But then why wouldn't they, as I am writing every book in my dream?

It was meditation that eventually developed into a love of silence and reconnection to Spirit, which was exactly what I needed next on my journey towards the Light.

Call it meditation or prayer it does not matter, but my willingness to enter into the timeless, fearless world of silence and meditation reconnected me to the calm inner Voice of Spirit.

I began to see myself as something different. I began to hear that there was a different way of seeing and thus feeling about the world. I begun to hear a different Voice in my head and it became stronger every day. In my work now, I feel that the therapy or teaching comes through me. My Spirit completes the therapy or teaches the class now and they are so much more effective because of it. I have voluntarily surrendered to the only will there is; the Will of God, delivered in this dream by my Spirit.

The Ego fought meditation for years.

'It's too hard' or *'I cannot stop my thoughts'*, became my mantra. It told me that I didn't have time to meditate or even people will think I'm a Hippy!

Notice the Ego plays the survival card again. By defining Hippies as something to be ridiculed by society, it persuades me that if I continue then people will define me as such and ridicule me. I will no longer be lovable, likable or an asset and will not survive should I ever need the help of society! So much sabotage took place but thankfully I was able to overcome it by the continual refocussing of the Spirit.

It would not let the need for meditation go, as it was essential for my awakening.

So every negative the Ego would put forward would be reinterpreted as a positive by the Spirit. At that time, no-one in my close circle of friends and family knew anything about meditation. The Spirit cannily reinterpreted the Ego's need to be special and different into a positive thing which allows me to feel special and different *because* I could meditate. How clever is that? The Spirit didn't attack what the Ego had made and I what was choosing to believe in at that time. The Spirit took over the Ego's wish to be special and granted it in this way, therefore not violating my Free Will in any way. The Ego will even sabotage my attempts at prayer by using it as a mechanism to *get* something.

I would use prayer to ask for something that I felt that I lacked or needed help with. By doing this, the Ego was buying me into the negative beliefs and reinforcing that I believe that I am powerless alone. It told me that I am not the creator of my own reality and that my focus is now away from the All That Is. It continually demonstrated that I am the small-self being that *is* in lack and is in fear. If I am 'All That Is'-how then can there be any lack in me? What is there to ask or pray for then? If you wish to pray let it be so that you reach the same vibration of Love/God and not to increase your fears or reinforce your lack!

This analogy is great for kids.

If you were created from a potato then that is what you are and will always be, even if you have divided yourself up and dressed yourself up as a crisp with a fancy flavouring. You can forget, deny, repress or disassociate yourself from what you are, but you will still always be it. A crisp is made from potato and no matter what flavouring it covers itself in and becomes unified with, it is still potato at its core.

You come from All That Is and so this is what you are. You will always be made from the Love that God is and that is only what you can ever be.

Therefore, you never have to doubt or prove that you are Loving. It is impossible to be anything else.

And so slowly but surely the Ego is being unravelled as Spirit tries to keep your focus on what is happening in the dream. In this way, you can consciously create and correct yourself if you have chosen with your Ego-mind. By teaching yourself the tricks of the Ego, such as the reversal of cause and effect and how the attack spiral works you can, at least most of the time, straighten out your thinking and stop the negative flow.

During my silences, I receive my teaching which I call 'downloads' and 'revelations' which put the puzzle pieces together for me. I will then see this learning in the projections of my world. Clients and students will either be experiencing my issue or want to talk about that subject.

In this way, day by day, I am becoming enlightened, in that my mind and thus my vibration are continually lifting. Tiny step by tiny step I am, as indeed we all are, becoming enlightened. The heavy, old and out-dated files that I carry around and used to add to every day are being cleared out. The outcome is that I live a simpler, quieter life. The treasure that the Ego offers as gains to keep the dream alive, interest me less and less everyday. In truth, I am withdrawing my focus from the world, little by little.

I am not so enamoured by food, by alcohol, in socialising, in proving my worth by collecting friends, either in real life or on social media. I do not look at or listen to news, reality TV or soap operas that reinforce the Ego's themes. I honour and prioritise my sleep because I know that when I am tired (or identifying with the body), the Ego can manipulate my thinking with ease. Tiredness can only happen in a physical body. When I identify with myself as a body, all of the other mechanisms of the Ego get ignited. A body exists in the prison of time-space and is vulnerable to pain and attack.

I am not dictating that anyone else has to do any of these things, as we all have free choice but these are the things that work for me.

As I cannot enter Heaven alone, you, who are ultimately my 'Brothers', must be healed with me. I can only be in the matching vibration of and thus enter into Heaven if I truly see no difference between you and me. We must become of One mind; have the same mind in order to be fully awakened and thus released. There are no parts or differences in Oneness. Thus, all of the ideas and information presented here are the ways that I have managed to put a myriad of resources together to make a fairly consistent and productive theory of what is going on in my world; my dream.

In some ways though, it is all meaningless work. It is impossible to make any sense of something that is itself meaningless, save for the meaning you give it.

However, I am still dreaming and I keep asking why? I have seemingly hit an impasse.

The Course says that learning is not of God because there is nothing to learn when you are All That Is. I am very conscious of how much I love to learn and teach. I know that I have made an idol of these things. They define me and are my treasure. Attack, by trying to take them away from me and I will defend them to the hilt.

The paradox is that valuing knowledge and learning has brought me to the point where I do know that it is a dream, that I am not separate from God and I am a powerful creator - to a point.

Do I keep choosing the dream then because I am not prepared to give up what this treasure trove of learning gives me? And yet until I do, I cannot receive the joy of experiencing this treasure or going Home which is what I've done all this learning for. This is a Catch 22 situation. My Ego tells me that obviously I haven't learned enough *yet* because I am clearly not Home. Yet to be One with God I must accept that there is nothing else to learn. I must just leap off the cliff with faith that God will catch me. This is still work in progress for me and anyone else still here!

Is this the final judgement in my dream? Will the final barriers to Love fall away and Heaven be revealed right here, right now when I make the final judgement that I have learned enough? I feel fear arise because of all the other times that the Ego has said something was true and it turned out to be a lie. And yet on a deeper level I know that this can only be resolved by total faith in and adherence to the Spirit's thought system.

Some years ago, when I had convinced myself that I had cleared all my programming about need and money and could give up my mainstream job, I bit the bullet and did so. It felt so right on every level. But as soon as it had lulled me into a false sense of security and I left the job, the Ego started to pound me with fear. My vibration dropped and I just started attracting one disaster after another. The Spirit came in and eventually made it all ok but the lesson had been learned; the Ego was a trickster and I was a fool. How could I trust my decisions after that?

And so the work of forgiveness begins.

I had to work to forgive those I blamed, to forgive myself and to forgive God for seemingly not stepping in to save me.

As we have already discussed, God didn't step in because He is just watching his Son sleep, offering him comfort through Spirit. He knows nothing can really hurt me. He knows that to come into my dream is unnecessary, even if it were possible. Nothing real is happening here. It may feel very real as it does when you are dreaming but when you awake in the morning you are just as you were when you went to bed. You may not even remember what happened; it was so insignificant. Forgiveness, for any perceived attack or grievance made in the dream is completely unnecessary on awakening. As I awaken here, forgiveness is only necessary when I have defined an act as attack. Ideally, I should never define any action by a dream character as an attack.

But if I have played that game, then to forgive the other for what they did not do (because they are my projection), nullifies the event. Then I can be in the same space as that person with the same Love that I was before the supposed attack.

This is only possible because nothing of any significance has happened. There is no-thing to forget and forgiveness without complete forgetting is impossible anyway.

This is a choice, as everything is. There is always choice, even if it feels like there is none at times. You must consciously understand and own all your choices. You must not let the Ego choose by default what you do not want. Even if you are choosing what feels more negative or what you think that you 'should' do, then peace can only be found by owning and loving that choice. You can choose to see your attacker as your greatest spiritual teacher reflecting back to you your projections. Or you can choose to just let everything flow through you, surrender to creating anything and just let God in.

You must choose to prioritise your happiness and peace over everything else. You must prioritise peace over the Ego's need to be right or feel more powerful that another.

Peace is Light.

Light can be shared without diminishing the source from which it comes. Light is light. It may appear less intense within the dream, but at its source it remains as powerful as it has always been.

The Ego however, simply loves to bring in the darkness by encouraging comparison and competition against others. It is happiest when investing in completely meaningless levels of difference and hierarchy because this separates and divides everything. That's why it loves to label and group things and then to judge them. Divide and conquer is its mantra.

But the truth is that you were made from Love and Light and so you can only be Love and Light. Everyone else is the same because the world is simply a mirror that reflects your own light back to you, just as the mirror in your bathroom does today. That's why you light up every room that you enter. That's why you light up every face that you look at. You simply cannot do anything else. Light lights and Love loves but you can deny, hide or suppress these things.

I awoke one morning after I had written about four chapters of this book with this at the front of my brain:

L-Love
I- (the) 'I'
F- (the) Fall
E- Enlightenment

I realised that really this is the story of the circular nature of our current journey. I believe this is what, on some level, Jesus was referring to in the Bible as the Alpha and the Omega.

There was just Love (God/All That Is) until this was extended and God's Son was created; the 'I'. Then came the Fall and the separation from Heaven occurred. 'I' became *i*: the small-self, a body, living in a seemingly physical world of fear, lack and limitation. The self-created, physical world will appear to exist until we are able to return to our natural state of Love, through ever increasing Enlightenment.

I have also realised that even though I started writing a book that would mainly be classed as psychology, this work is something that I hope will be a guiding light back to a spiritual awakening for others.

This Light may dissipate the darkness of unknowing or confusion. This Light I hope, will dispel the tricks of the Ego and return your creative power to its real source, which is within you.

Remember that Love is what you are, not what you do.

And so as we have revisited all that has gone before, you now have an opportunity to decide whether you wish to take the red pill or the blue pill. Will you choose to go back to the same old way of living or will you begin to unravel your Ego and start to live a positively joyous life?

Quick Summary

1. In Heaven, as the Son of God, you had a crazy thought in which you got lost. You pondered if there could be something other than God.

2. If God is pure Love and Light, then the opposite which is fear and darkness are what you would be exploring. The opposite of All That Is, is All That Is Not, which can only be lack and scarcity.

3. If you are 'All That Is' then in order to explore scarcity and fear you must forget or deny that you have made that choice.

4. Once you became lost in thought, a veil was created and so you forgot where you came from. You now need someone or something to come from outside of your dream in order to lead you back out of it.

5. In order to protect you from fully remembering, your Ego creates the following mechanisms to limit and control you: the body in time/space, a pseudo personality, concepts of life and death, duality and fear, projection and scapegoats, learning and teaching and finally, false idols such as money and sickness.

6. You now believe that the Ego is god of this world and that you are held under its laws of time and space. You are this physical body that ages, gets sick and dies. This is purportedly the end of you forever.

7. If you start to realise where you are, separated from your Brothers and Father in Heaven, the Ego will seek to offer you comfort and riches or distract you with something bigger, better or shinier.

8. There is the God spark that remains untouched in your heart. This is the Spirit which is the Voice for God. It cannot overcome your Free Will and so you must ask for guidance and then choose its thought system. Spirit speaks only of Love and Forgiveness. It sees no physical body and no suffering.

9. The sun, the rain, air, food, metals, water, fire; all of these things are provided naturally at source for you. Every person seen or unseen brings you service in some way. Your greatest friends and foes both serve as your greatest spiritual teachers. Everyone and everything is you.

Chapter 17

Unravelling the Dream

"All truth passes through 3 stages. First it is ridiculed. Second it is violently opposed. Third it is accepted as being self-evident "Albert Einstein

My very earliest memory is the birth of my sister at home when I was two years old.

I know, *and* I find in many of my clients, that the sudden arrival of a sibling causes much more pain and faulty programming than many may realise. This is because your power of being the youngest child suddenly gets usurped by the new arrival and this causes an unexpected shock. The young brain is not mature enough to make real sense of what is happening. Therefore, things that happen out of the blue and loss, become connected and a link is created that gets permanently recorded by the brain.

This perceived loss of love and attention is exacerbated if you are the middle child. Not only will you be pushed aside by the next sibling's arrival but you will never be the 'special' first born or the eternally cherished 'baby' of the family. The Ego loves to remind you that this is unjust and unfair.

My very first memory is of my older sister and I standing by the fridge in the kitchen when my dad brings in my new sister; this 'thing'. I say 'thing' because aged two I didn't really have a clue what a baby or a sister was. I can though still remember the sense of *'Where did this thing come from and why did nobody tell me it was on its way?'* All I knew was that now I was downgraded to sitting next to mum and the 'thing' is now on *my* mum's lap! 'Thing' is now the centre of everyone's world and I am a second thought, or at least this is how my Ego tells the story.

Now, I am sure that my parents had tried to tell me what was on its way but my immature brain could not take it in. Of course a span of time is also meaningless at that age. Many, many years later I recognised a repeating pattern seeded from this incident. Whenever I was with my family, I would

The Ego Unravelled

continuously complain that *'Nobody ever tells me anything'*. The root programme had obviously been set from this experience. Completely oblivious to me, this programme continued to play unchallenged until I spotted it and updated the file a few years ago.

I also developed middle child 'poor me' syndrome and so at some point must have listened to the Ego. The Ego comforted me that if no-one cared about me then it would look after me. *"We will be independent, strong and not let anyone in to hurt us again"* the Ego assured me. The Ego thus became god of my world, usurping the place of God which was of course who my parents had represented in my dream. Now, it seemed that I had not only been let down by God my creator but also the surrogate god's that I had created. No wonder I turned to my only 'friend' who was always there; the beloved Ego.

This early memory then is where for me my conscious life begins. There is no proof that that is not when I was 'born' as such. When I remember my dad who seemed very big and powerful to me at two, bending down showing me the baby, I can still access the negative thought of fear and rejection.

However, I often wonder; is this a very different kind of memory? Is this actually a microcosm of what happened in Heaven?

As I have previously said, I have the image of the Son of God having the idle thought: *"I wonder what it would be like if there was something other than God?"* As I was writing this book, I woke up one morning with the image of God bending down with a baby that clearly was me, in his arms. Was this the point at which God or Spirit tried to remind me of who I really was; still safely sleeping in his arms? But, had I fallen too deep into fear and chose the Ego or small self 'I' instead? Or does this simply represent the choice I am continually making? I find the similarity of the two events very unsettling especially as this image exactly mirrors my real life memory of my father holding my sister.

You will remember that up until the age of about two years a child does not have the ability to differentiate themselves from the people and the environment around them. When I originally made this mistake, did I not realise that I was that baby in God's arms and I could mentally return to God's loving embrace just by choosing to hold my attention there? Is this when I separated and am in fear of God now, because I mistakenly think that I turned my back and chose wrongly?

I know now that until I studied the Course, I was thinking of God as someone whom I have rejected and offended with my sin. A God that I believed sought to punish me for those sins. From there, have I and the Ego concocted the story about a body within which to hide my Spirit in? Does this include a body that I can project blame, sickness and illness on to and then discard? Have I created death so that I can create another body with a relevant story and personality in order to keep myself disguised and hidden from God?

Am I simply creating multiple, consecutive identities through the cycle of life and death to confuse my hunter?

Is this just the product of a vivid imagination, metaphor or truth? How can I ever know for sure?

Well if you think back to my strawberry moment earlier in the book, you may remember its significance. It taught me to believe whatever makes me happiest because there is no real truth out there. So I have made a conscious decision to believe the teachings of A Course in Miracles because it makes absolute sense and has undeniably changed my life for the better in so many ways.

What I have presented here is only *my version* of what I understand that the Course purports happened at the beginning of the dream. The fact that I can find a direct experience of this in my own life, obviously adds weight to its truth *for me*.

The Course goes on to teach us that the only truth is that you are still at Home in Heaven dreaming of this world. You can only have a nightmare when you are asleep after all. God sits gently by your side calling you home. God could not and would reject you because He cannot and would not judge. You just dreamt up a crazy story that it *could be* possible.

The whole story in some ways mirrors the story told in the film The Wizard of Oz.

A young girl called Dorothy runs away from home after an argument. She finds herself separated from her parents (God) when a cyclone hits her house. After being knocked unconscious by some debris, she dreams that she is in another very different Technicolor world. She tries to find her way back, meeting characters who feel that they are missing something and so are 'less than'. These characters all wish that something be different. (These are her own projections). Dorothy fights the evil witch (Her projections of her own fears/Ego) and is helped and guided by the Good Fairy (Right mind/Spirit). Her perceived saviour, the Wizard, eventually turns out to be a fake, using smoke and mirrors (Ego). She eventually discovers that she and her friends (projections) are not lacking anything other than self-belief. The Good Fairy (Spirit) tells her that she knew how to get home (and wake up) all along but she needed to learn that she knew it. She awakens in her own bed at home after never going anywhere because it was just a dream and everyone is very pleased to see her back. (God and your Brothers).

I believe that this is our story too. We have fallen asleep in Heaven. We dream that we have become separated from God. Realising our mistake, we try to return home only to find ourselves in a strange new world. We have become so engrossed in the journey; entranced by the colours, the tastes, the distractions, and the drama. We enjoy battling good and evil. We are tricked by the Ego and guided by the Spirit. We are continuously seeing our own projections and believing that they are other, real people. We believe that we are lacking strong minds, courage and a good heart but of course none of this is true.

The Ego, a master magician, has built itself into a powerful pseudo-god that uses smoke and mirrors, distraction and distortion to rule and threaten. It does this whilst all the time pretending to be our saviour. Once we find our way back home we too will be welcomed just like the return of the Prodigal Son in the Scriptures.

Is this life mirroring art or art mirroring life?

You need to expose the Ego in the same way that Dorothy exposes the tricks of the Wizard. Everything that you need is within you. In your perfection you lack nothing. You are already Home and all you need to do is to awaken. However, the decision to awaken has to be a conscious choice that you make. You must be prepared to give up the dream and everything that you thought was real about yourselves and the world. You must be prepared to completely surrender this identity to the Will of God. This is perhaps the most difficult part because it is a huge act of Faith. You don't really know (only because you may not remember yet) what little you are giving up in comparison to the greatness of what you will receive. The Ego's ideology, that to give is to lose needs to be replaced with the truth; that to give is to share and extend. Giving up nothing to receive everything is an obviously positive choice.

You must remember that you are not the small-self personality that the Ego tries so hard to convince you that you are. You are the Son of God. It is not arrogant or delusional to say that. You are part of the Omnipresence of All That Is therefore it is more arrogant and delusional to believe that you could be the one thing that is outside of it. This is physically impossible anyway. All That Is cannot be anything other than all inclusive.

If one insane thought created this mess surely it takes only one sane thought to reverse it. If the original thought was: *"I wonder what it would be like if there was something other than God?"* then *"I am All That Is"* surely serves to correct the misperception. Your whole Universe is one thought in many forms; that there can be an opposite of God. You now have a choice to believe something different: that there is *only* God.

The Ego has made a pseudo-god in its likeness but in truth God created you in His likeness; Love and Light. You then made an amazing world and as God loves his creations, you must love yours. It feels like to leave everything behind is akin to leaving your kids forever because you made these too. All 'others' that appear to be out there are merely the dream characters that you have created. In the dream you need to Love and honour every one of them as they truly are your greatest teachers. They show you about yourself and where you are on the road. If I don't know where I am I cannot navigate home.

But your real creations are not in the dream. They wait patiently in Heaven for you to awaken. Just as Dorothy awakens at home to find the *real* people who had appeared to be the Scarecrow, the Tin man and the Lion in her dream, waiting to greet her.

And so here we reach the crux of everything.

Is this a dream or not?

For now, perhaps we have to play the small-self game of the Ego but for every time that we catch the inversion of cause and effect; every time we halt our rush to attack or defend; every time we reclaim a projection and every time we forgive others for what they did not do, we have taken another step on the yellow brick road to home. God only sees his perfect child sleeping. He does not see what he is dreaming of. He may notice your squirming and see that the dream has turned into a nightmare and speaks to you to offer comfort in the dream. *"Wake up. It's ok Daddy's here..."*

We have used the terminology of the Spirit's thought system in this book but in reality this may be the Holy Spirit appearing as the Voice of God. Ultimately, He knows the dream cannot hurt you and so He simply awaits your awakening so the fun of the day ahead can begin.

The good fairy in the Wizard of Oz reminds Dorothy that three clicks of the heels and to think of home are all she really needs to get there. But really, there is no-*where* to go to and it takes no-*time* to get there, because there are no such things as time and space in a dream. Thus, in truth you can never have left because everything is in your head. Heaven is a state of being. Consciousness is all that exists and Love is just a thought away.

The Law of Attraction says that what you think about, you will manifest. Think of Heaven and the closer it becomes. Remember 100% of time equals 0% space. Total attention manifests that reality, now!

So think *only* of Love or God all the time. Keep your thoughts away from fear, scarcity and lack and you will be home much sooner than you think.

After all, now you have been shown the Light will you still choose to stay here bound in the darkness?

My destination is Heaven and I shall definitely look forward to seeing you all there, where we will all get to live happily ever after.

But until then let us at least create the dream to be positively joyous.

saecula saeculorum

The idea of eternity ….."Unto the ages of ages."

Bibliography

The Foundation for Inner Peace. (1976). *A Course in Miracles*. USA: New York Viking.

Huxley, A. (1932). *Brave New World*. London: Chatoo and Windus.

Schiffer, F. (1999). *Of Two Minds*. UK: Simon and Schuster.

Bolte, Taylor. J. (2009). *My Stroke of Insight*. London: Hodder Paperbacks.

Filmography

Horizon: The Secret You. Dan Walker. BBC, 2009. Documentary.

The Matrix. Dir. The Wachowski Brothers. Warner Bros Pictures, 1999. Film.

The Dog Whisperer. Caesar Milan. MPH Entertainment Inc, 2004. Series.

The Truman Show. Dir. Peter Weir. Scott Rudin Productions, 1998. Film.

Inception. Dir. Christopher Nolan. Legendary Pictures/Syncopy, 2010. Film.

The Wizard of Oz. Dir. Victor Fleming. Metro-Goldwyn-Mayer, 1939. Film.

Ghost. Dir. Jerry Zucker. Paramount Pictures, 1990. Film.

Downloads/ Websites

Bashar channelled by Darryl Anka   www.bashar.org

Abraham-Hicks   www.abraham-hicks.com

Institute of Heartmath   www.heartmath.org

BBC.com/future/story   www.bbc.com

Science News   www.sciencenews.org

The Ego Unravelled

ABOUT THE AUTHOR

Theresa Borg BA (Hons) DHP DCH GQHP is the founder and director of Positively Joyous Hypnotherapy, Coaching and Meditation, which is based in South East London. She has been a qualified Clinical Hypnotherapist since 2009 and completed her Psychotherapy diploma the following year. She has since built up a successful private practice based largely on word of mouth. Theresa is a Grade 1 'outstanding' teacher of positive psychology, spirituality, Law of Attraction and meditation courses. She is also a Reiki healer and runs private spirituality, health and wellbeing courses throughout the UK.

This is Theresa's second book following the hugely successful **Tour the Core – The Pathway to a Positively Joyous Life.**

Subscribe to her **YouTube channel Positively Joyous** for lots of self-help and coaching videos. Also see the monthly ACIM study group lessons.

Find out more about the book and Theresa's classes and courses at:

www.positivelyjoyous.com

Made in the USA
Lexington, KY
10 May 2018